In Search of a Safe Place

Abused Women and Culturally Sensitive Services

Marginalized in the larger society and in the mainstream women's movement, immigrant women are also outsiders in women's shelters, where racially sensitive and linguistically appropriate counselling is generally unavailable. In this book, Vijay Agnew documents the struggles of Canadian women's centres to provide better services to victims of wife abuse from Asia, Africa, and the Caribbean.

The study looks at every aspect of community-based women's organizations, including their funding, operation, and services. The result is a detailed picture of the problems and challenges they encounter on a daily basis. Agnew uses case studies, reports, and interviews to document the work of these groups and to show how race, class, and gender intersect in the everyday lives of the women who depend on them.

Although the women's movement initiated public discussion of wife abuse, the fight against abuse is now conducted primarily by the state through its allocation of resources. Agnew underscores the tension that often arises between the patriarchal state and feminist-inspired organizations, and the resulting difficulties in bringing about social change.

VIJAY AGNEW is Associate Professor of Social Science at York University. She is the author of *Elite Women in Indian Politics* (1979) and *Resisting Discrimination: Women from Asia, Africa, and the Caribbean and the Women's Movement in Canada* (1996), which was named an outstanding book on the subject of human rights by the Gustavus Myers Center for the Study of Human Rights in North America.

In Search of
a Safe Place

*Abused Women and
Culturally Sensitive Services*

VIJAY AGNEW

UNIVERSITY OF TORONTO PRESS
Toronto Buffalo London

© University of Toronto Press Incorporated 1998
Toronto Buffalo London
Printed in Canada

ISBN 0-8020-4278-3 (cloth)
ISBN 0-8020-8114-2 (paper)

Printed on acid-free paper

Canadian Cataloguing in Publication Data

Agnew, Vijay, 1946–
  In search of a safe place : abused women and culturally sensitive services

  Includes index.
  ISBN 0-8020-4278-3 (bound)   ISBN 0-8020-8114-2 (pbk.)

  1. Abused women – Services for – Canada.   2. Minority women – Canada.
  I. Title.

  HV1448.C3A45 1998   362.82'92'08900971   C97-932586-2

University of Toronto Press acknowledges the financial assistance to its publishing
program of the Canada Council for the Arts and the Ontario Arts Council.

This book has been published with the help of a grant from the Humanities and
Social Sciences Federation of Canada, using funds provided by the Social Sciences
and Humanities Research Council of Canada.

For
Nicole, Tom, and Rita

Contents

Acknowledgments

This book owes a tremendous debt of gratitude to the service providers in the community-based organizations who met with me to share their insights into the trials and tribulations of abused immigrant women from Asia, Africa, and the Caribbean in Canada. The service providers, often immigrants themselves, were proud to be helping women from their own communities, while providing for their own families. The many interviews that I conducted with immigrant women gave me a sense of belonging to a larger community, and I valued the sense of fellowship that it created in me. In subsequent months, when I sat alone in my study trying to find the words to communicate the meaning and significance of the work of the service providers for abused women, I retained the memory of their commitment to their work, and that gave me the psychological and emotional energy to do the writing. I am happy that the book documenting their work is complete, but at the same time I regret the fading of the feeling of community and friendship that the research and writing provided me with immigrant women like myself.

The research for this book was supported by a grant from the Social Sciences and Humanities Research Council of Canada. I would like to thank John Shafer for reading many drafts of this book and for his suggestions. I would also like to thank Virgil Duff and Margaret Williams, both of University of Toronto Press, for guiding the book through its many stages. Thanks are also due to the anonymous reviewers of the book and of the papers that I published on this topic in journals. Colleagues at York University have supported my work by reading drafts of chapters and research proposals. I would like to thank Paul Axelrod, Naomi Black, Judy Hellman, Craig Heron, John Hutcheson, and Carla Lipsig-Mumme. My husband, Tom, has always supported my writing career by never making me feel guilty for spending countless hours in my study absorbed in my work. My daughter, Nicole, was pleased that I was preoccupied with my work and thus less of an over-protective mother. Both Tom and Nicole have sustained me with their faith in my work and have encouraged me to continue writing, and I thank them both. The love and friendship of my sister Rita and my nephew Arjun and of my brother Subash and his wife, Linda, have cheered me on many dull days.

In Search of a Safe Place
Abused Women and Culturally Sensitive Services

Introduction

Research on racism within the women's movement in the 1970s and 1980s has confirmed a widespread belief among racialized women (women who are labelled according to arbitrary racial or ethnic categories like 'black' or 'Oriental') that systemic and everyday racism within the movement (dominated by so-called white middle-class women) tended to marginalize them and issues of concern to them. Even so, some who remained on the fringes of the movement and did not become active participants in it have established community-based organizations through which they struggle against the racism, sexism, and classism experienced by themselves and by other women in their communities.

Many community-based organizations for racial and ethnic groups emerged in the late 1970s and the 1980s. These organizations were and are distinct from organizations established earlier to help members of ethnic and racial groups settle in Canada and adapt to the new country or to provide social and recreational activities for them. The community-based women's organizations that emerged in the late 1970s and the 1980s perform some similar functions, but they also provide feminist-inspired services such as helping abused women escape from the violence in their lives. They also differ from their earlier counterparts in being dependent on governments for financial resources and in providing social services primarily through paid workers.

In the 1970s feminists initiated public debate on wife abuse. They argued that wife abuse was a manifestation of male domination and of women's lack of equality in the larger society. The ideology of the family and the distinction between the private and public spheres perpetuated the oppression of women by protecting the heinous acts of husbands in the home from legislative or social sanctions. Feminist struggles to eradicate wife abuse received support from federal and provincial governments in Canada. The federal government appointed the Canadian Panel on Violence against Women to study the many forms of violence against women and to make recommendations to eradicate it (Canadian Panel 1993). Health and Welfare Canada created the National Clearing House on Violence against Women to coordinate research and educational programs on violence against women. Provincial governments allocated funds to programs within government agencies (e.g., in Ontario, the Ministry of Health, the Ministry of Community and Social Services, and the Ontario Women's Directorate) to initiate projects to inform the public that wife abuse is a crime, to document the need for services for victims of abuse, and to provide services for them. Governments also introduced new legislation to protect victims of wife abuse and to prosecute its perpetrators.

Community-based organizations have been created largely through the initiative of middle-class racialized women who have obtained funding from government agencies to provide social services for abused women in their communities. These funds enable the groups to conduct need-assessment studies, to document the difficulties of racialized women in accessing social and legal services, or to write handbooks and manuals on how to counsel abused racialized women. When community-based groups receive funds, they rent space, hire staff, and begin their work. In the economically buoyant 1980s, government agencies funded a variety of services, but in the mid-1990s services and programs have been curtailed. Since community-based organizations are dependent on government agencies for funds, the services they provide are contingent on the survival of the programs of the agencies.

Many groups have produced numerous need-assessment studies, handbooks, pamphlets, and brochures for government agencies over the years. Community-based groups that receive funds from government agencies are required to produce audited statements of their expenses and to make annual reports on the kinds of programs they have provided. Most of this documentation is unpublished and is available only through the organizations (if they have taken care to preserve the records). What has been published (e.g., reports documenting abuse in immigrant communities) has had limited circulation among members of ethnic and racial groups, and it is not catalogued in libraries or listed in periodical indexes.

Most community-based groups have not devoted much time to documenting their work in providing social services to women from their communities, and there is little public knowledge of the groups organized by racialized women or of the ways in which their struggles against race, class, and gender oppression have shaped the politics of their groups. Roxana Ng (1988) has studied one community-based group which aimed to help women locate jobs, and I have documented the history of a number of others in *Resisting Discrimination* (1996). Other literature on community-based organizations includes Wine and Ristock 1991; Ng, Walker, and Muller 1990; Davies and Shragge 1990; Pal 1993; and James 1996.

What will happen to the records of community-based groups that are compelled to downsize or to close altogether is uncertain, and early indications do not bode well. Even a government agency like the Ontario Women's Directorate has had to close its resource centre.[1] The situation of community-based groups, with few staff and limited funds, is in comparison even more dire.[2] It is unlikely that many of the records of a community-based group will be preserved if it moves to smaller premises or closes altogether. The records are not the property of specific individuals, and staff turnover is high, so that few people will be concerned to preserve them. Records of community-based groups are likely to disappear as restructuring occurs, and they will be lost to future researchers.

The very survival of these groups is threatened by the restructuring of social programs now being conducted by federal and provincial governments. Funds to all women's organizations have been severely decreased, and many community-based organizations have had to lay off staff, reduce their range of services, and eliminate critically needed programs like language instruction.

The board of the Working Skills Centre was required by government agencies to produce a close-out budget, and it spent 1995 and most of 1996 working on contingency plans for closing. Notices of lay-offs were given to staff. Then, since the government had not yet developed a new policy on delivering services to immigrant women, the organization was asked to continue with its core program for an undefined period of time, and some staff were rehired on three-month contracts. (The board and staff have little time to consider what to do with the records of the organization. In fact, the question has not even been raised in meetings.)

The restructuring of social programs which has been under way since the early 1990s at the federal and provincial levels will dramatically change how social services are delivered and who will be eligible for them. Many community-based groups will disappear, and those that survive will have very different mandates. At the present time, many community-based groups are trying to position themselves so that they can continue to deliver social services in the new system.

These political events increase the present study's historical significance and its potential to inform public policy on overcoming the race, class, and gender discrimination experienced by racialized women. The book is an account of the struggles of community-based groups to provide culturally sensitive services to victims of wife abuse in their ethnic and racial communities. It also analyses the implications, for the long-term feminist goal of bringing about social change, of cooperating with a patriarchal state to provide these services.

Although feminism identified the need for services for abused women, the work is done by women with varying commitment to feminist ideals. The book discusses the pragmatism that guides service providers as they help women resolve their difficulties in escaping from the abuse that they experience within the home and in facing the racism that they encounter in the shelters or in society at large. Since some abused women need to live temporarily in shelters, service providers in community-based groups and shelters have to work together to meet their needs before, during, and after the stay there.

Referrals from community-based groups to shelters and vice versa bring the workers together, and they seek to work cooperatively. Nevertheless, conflicts sometimes erupt over the racism and other difficulties that emerge when women, all of whom are in a crisis situation, have to adjust to living with others from different cultures, racial groups, and social classes, and with different beliefs about feminism and patriarchy.

The book seeks to contribute to feminist discussions of the role of the state, the dangers of institutionalization, and the politics of bringing about social change. The research presented in it draws upon reports and studies prepared by community-based groups to document their development and delivery of social services to victims of wife abuse and upon fieldwork with community-based groups and interviews with counsellors, staff, and administrators.

Policies established by the Multicultural Act of 1988 and the guarantee of equal rights by the Canadian Charter of Rights and Freedoms ground the demands by community-based groups for resources to provide social services to victims of wife abuse. However, racism in the larger society and the biases of employers make it difficult for racialized women to leave abusive spouses. The book also documents their struggles to overcome their victimization.

The literature by community-based groups on wife abuse has been written primarily for government agencies. Some of the accounts are feminist (e.g., explaining abuse as an expression of the desire by the spouse to control and dominate his wife), but most groups are less interested in conducting theoretical discussions of abuse than in making a case for social services under their own auspices. Consequently, their reports focus on those aspects of abuse which bear upon requests for resources. For example, they contend that women from their groups are unable to obtain services from mainstream social service agencies because of the Eurocentric norms of the agencies and the racism of service providers in them.

Interviews with counsellors in these organizations, excerpted in this book, document how race, class, and gender intersect in the everyday lives of abused working-class women and provide insight into the everyday work of community-based groups and shelters for abused women. In these interviews, counsellors describe the services they provide, the difficulties they have in running some of their programs, and their success in advocating on some issues.

Struggling against systemic racism is a significant aspect of the work of counsellors in community-based groups and shelters. Some of the counsellors I interviewed militantly denounced the racism of white middle-class social workers who labelled racialized women as 'traditional' or 'passive' women. Almost all felt frustrated by the racism encountered by themselves and by abused women. (Two of the six women whose interviews appear in this book were abused women.) Many of the counsellors had encountered discrimination in the hiring practices of mainstream social service agencies. Their experiences inform the counselling they provide to working-class racialized women.

In the interviews, counsellors describe some of the horrendous abuse experienced by these women. The women give the lie to the stereotype of being passive victims. They show resourcefulness and courage in surviving abuse. Nevertheless, abused women are often ashamed of their ordeal, and they are reluctant to reveal it. Cultural norms which encourage women to be self-sacrificing and to give priority to the welfare of others (including the extended family) induce guilt. Seeking help from outsiders – the police, community-based groups, or shelters – means risking the loss of sympathy and support from their families and from other members of the ethnic or racial community.

Abused women often seek help only when their own lives or the lives of their children are threatened, and they encounter many obstacles to leaving abusive homes. Even a telephone enquiry to an agency is difficult and dangerous for a woman who is under the surveillance of an abusive spouse or his relatives. A woman who does not speak English, works in a menial job, or remains at home may not have information about her legal right to stay in Canada, to obtain custody of her children, or to receive social assistance and housing. This information can be made available to her, sometimes in her own language, once contact is established with a community-based group. Counsellors in community-based groups can explain her legal rights and make legal processes less intimidating by escorting her to a courthouse and staying with her while her case is being heard. Counsellors can also help her apply for welfare, housing, and legal aid.

The most frequently repeated justification given by community-based groups for providing social services themselves is their desire to protect women from the racism of mainstream social service agencies. They note that abused racialized women encounter racism in their interactions with white social workers when they seek social assistance. They contend that mainstream social service agencies have 'monocultural models' of delivering services. European and North American cultural values and norms influence the way service providers define the problems of abused women and the solutions they offer. They often alienate women with vastly different cultural values, and the women withdraw from seeking services from these agencies. Consequently, community-based groups argue, there is a denial of effective social services.

Mainstream social service agencies have to balance the need to treat all women equally, without regard to race or ethnicity, with the need to respect women's different cultural traditions. Mainstream social service agencies have responded to criticisms by introducing new programs, described as multicultural services, and by hiring more racialized women on their staff. Still, community-based groups remain dissatisfied, arguing that such programs are mere 'add-ons,' which do not fundamentally change the structure or philosophy of the agencies, and that the agencies still lack adequate interpretation services.

Yet community-based groups that employ racialized women who understand the cultural values and norms of the women who seek their services and who can communicate with a woman in her own language pose a new problem. Racialized women who have been in Canada for several years, and second-generation racialized women, sometimes feel ghettoized and marginalized when they are working only with women from their own communities. The groups they work for value their ethnicity over their academic qualifications, and this appears to them to be another manifestation of racism.

Community-based groups and racialized counsellors claim to provide 'linguistically appropriate and culturally sensitive' social services, but cultural sensitivity may preclude exposing or criticizing values and norms that oppress women. Most cultures incorporate patriarchal biases. Nostalgia and cultural pride may make counsellors in community-based groups reluctant to acknowledge oppressive norms in their cultures. Racism in the larger society increases their desire to assert the dignity and value of their own cultures, and they may feel that criticism of their cultures only reinforces stereotypes in the dominant society of certain immigrant communities as 'traditional' or 'violent.'

Abuse exists in the countries of origin of immigrant women, and that poses a further difficulty for them. Although immigration removes women from the supportive network of their extended families, it is also true that few social services are available in most Third World countries and families there are not always willing to help abused women. Sometimes the patriarchal values of relatives or their limited economic resources make them unwilling to intervene to help abused female relatives.

Community-based groups perceive themselves as providing surrogate families or 'a home away from home' for abused women. They create a safe place for racialized, non–English-speaking, working-class abused women, where they can obtain social services (e.g., welfare, housing, or education) which facilitate their decision to leave an abusive home. However, counsellors' willingness to criticize oppression in patriarchal families is limited by their fear of losing the support of the community or of alienating the women who seek their services. Community-based groups therefore have to balance carefully the struggle against sexism in their communities with their clients' need to survive materially and emotionally in a sexist, classist, and racist society.

This study of community-based groups reveals the difficulties of reconciling feminist theories with the everyday experiences of racialized women. In many community-based groups, feminist explanations of women's oppression coexist with conventional and traditional norms. Some community-based groups describe themselves as feminist, but they seldom define the term or locate themselves in the spectrum of feminist views. The literature by community-based groups frequently identifies patriarchal norms as the primary cause of abuse, but it does not place patriarchy in any historical, economic, or geographical contexts, or discuss the ways in which patriarchy manifests itself in different cultures. Some of the instructional literature by these groups on counselling abused women repeats the mantra of 'the integrated nature of race, class, and gender oppression,' but its primary focus is on gender oppression. It does not discuss the ways in which racism limits the choices available to abused racialized women.

Some women who work at community-based organizations are committed to feminist goals of social change and transformation, but others are merely doing a job. Some are trained social workers and are guided by the norms of their profession (criticized by some feminists as androcentric), while others have 'the authority of experience.' Formerly abused women can empathize with clients in similar situations and have some insight into the dilemmas confronted by them, but a feminist counsellor may wish to put the woman at the centre of her concern while the abused women may be more concerned about the welfare of her children, the survival of her family, and even the well-being of the abusive spouse (MacLeod and Shin 1993, iii; Chinese Family Life Services 1989, 24).

Feminists have been critical of power relations that oppress and exploit women, and many therefore support collective organizations, in which there are no distinctions based on rank or status. In practice, however, community-based groups are pulled in another direction by the requirements of state agencies. The North York Women's Shelter, for example, describes itself as a collective, but it receives funding from government agencies and consequently is required to have a volunteer board of directors that assumes responsibility for the organization and the disbursement of funds. The board defines policy and hires and fires workers, while paid staff are responsible for the day-to-day operation of the shelter. A hierarchy has emerged, with full-time staff above part-time: the latter are paid a lower rate and work as subordinates to the full-time staff. Women who use the shelter have to abide by the rules dic-

tated by the staff (e.g., allocation of chores), and there are penalties for neglecting chores or breaking other regulations, including
ejection from the shelter. In practice, then, the only 'collective'
appears to be the full-time staff, who receive equal salaries and
benefits.

Despite feminist critiques of power relations, it is difficult to
eradicate the exercise of power, even between women, and power
is exercised by racialized counsellors over abused working-class,
non–English-speaking women from their own communities. Counsellors are mediators between these women and the larger society,
and the women depend on the counsellors to access information
and services. In the interviews, counsellors did not address the
power relations between themselves and their clients or talk about
the differences between themselves and the abused women. They
reiterated their claim to be better able to understand clients of
their own community than white Canadian counsellors, but they
did not describe specific ways in which this understanding helps
their clients overcome the difficulties they confront.

Community-based groups give priority to protecting women
from violence. Although the women's movement initiated public
discussion of wife abuse and asserted the need to provide services to victims of wife abuse, the fight against abuse is now conducted primarily by the state through its allocation of resources
to programs and services for victims of abuse. The dependence
of community-based groups on the state for resources makes
them temper their criticisms of racism and sexism in mainstream
social service agencies and even in the larger society. Although
the underlying philosophy of the movement against wife abuse is
feminist, there is a greater emphasis on social services that are
needed by individual women than on social change or transformation. Dependence on the state has led to compromises with
feminist ideals and has sidelined some political goals. It has
enabled community-based women's organizations to survive, and
the social services that they provide have empowered some working-class, non–English-speaking women. Nevertheless, the work
of generating wider social change has been postponed.

ONE

Immigrant Communities in Canada

Nearly all Canadians are immigrants or descendants of immigrants, but this fact does not prevent differences of race and class from dividing Canadians into separate groups. Some immigrants have been welcomed to Canada enthusiastically, while others have experienced rejection and hostility. Some have become 'Canadians' in one generation; others remain outsiders – labelled as 'immigrants.'

Wife abuse occurs in all cultures and in all social classes, but the resources that are available to victims of abuse in Canada vary greatly across lines of culture and class. Although perpetrators of wife abuse exist in every racial and ethnic group and in every social class, working-class women from Asia, Africa, and the Caribbean often find that there are far fewer choices open to them than to their more privileged counterparts.

Systemic racism informs the everyday lives of women from Asia, Africa, and the Caribbean, and it circumscribes their choices. When life in their homes becomes dangerous and intolerable, they seek help for themselves and their children, but help is difficult to find in a society that has not welcomed them as immigrants and is not sympathetic to their social or cultural norms. Community-based organizations seek to mediate with government agencies on their behalf and to provide 'culturally sensitive' social services for them.

Naming the Subject

One of the most contested issues in research on so-called immigrant women is the choice of terms to be used in identifying its subjects, particularly when they are from Asia, Africa, and the Caribbean. Most of the terms in common usage – for example, 'visible-minority women,' 'women of colour,' 'black women,' 'non-white women,' 'immigrant women,' and 'Third World women' – are associated with stereotypes that disregard the many differences among the women to whom they are applied. Some of these terms evidently originated with government agencies – for example, 'visible-minority women' (Carty and Brand 1989), while others were adopted in response to objections raised against terms that had become derogatory. However, there is no consensus about the appropriateness of any of these labels. Many women insist that they, rather than other people, have the right to name themselves and that resistance to these labels is a symbol of their struggle against the power that white middle-class men and women have exercised over them.

The term 'visible-minority women' has been criticized because it attributes significance to skin colour or other physical characteristics and implies that the women are not only different but also inferior and inadequate (Bannerji 1986). The term 'non-white women' implies that white women are the norm from which all others deviate (Khayatt 1994). Like these terms, the terms 'black women,' 'women of colour,' and 'Third World women' homogenize groups of women who have very diverse identities. One 'black woman' may have come to Canada from the Caribbean as a domestic worker, another may have come from Somalia as a refugee, and a third may be a fifth-generation Canadian born in Nova Scotia or Ontario (Bristow 1994; Hamilton 1994; Shadd 1994). Some 'black women' prefer to call themselves African Canadians, in honour of their distant roots and the history of their ancestors. Others, who have immigrated from the Caribbean, prefer to be known as Afro-Caribbean Canadians or as Indo-Afro-Caribbean Canadians. However, many women from Africa do not think that the word 'African' should be applied to people who were not born there. Some women from Nova Scotia prefer to call themselves 'coloured' rather than 'black' (Cannon 1995, 140–1).

The word 'immigrant' is often used nowadays because of its supposed neutrality and objectivity, but it has been used in the past in Canada to assign a lower status to Asian, Southern European, and Jewish women than that accorded, for instance, to Christian women from Britain or France (Agnew 1996, 108–12). The term 'immigrant women' is now in common usage as a 'polite' reference to working-class, non–English-speaking women from Third World countries and Southern Europe (Ng 1988, 15–17). Ironically, however, government reports that apply the term according to its wider, legal definition to all female immigrants have been criticized on the grounds that including women from North America, Britain, and Northern Europe in the category is a covert attempt to undermine the social programs that women from other regions provide for their own communities in Canada (Hernandez 1988; Cross-Cultural Communication Centre 1988).

The community-based groups that are discussed in this book (e.g., the Korean-Canadian Women's Group, the South Asian Family Support Services, the Chinese Family Life Services, and the Canadian-African Newcomer Aid Centre of Toronto) have adopted a variety of different terms for identifying the women they serve. Most, however, focus on their ethnic origin. They present themselves to government agencies in their proposals for funding as organizations that provide services or programs to a large constituency, but they emphasize that they differ from mainstream social service agencies in many significant ways – for instance, in being more sensitive to differences in culture and lifestyle. Although they cast a wide net, however, these community-based groups provide services primarily to working-class women from one or two ethnic groups. Some umbrella groups that have prepared reports or lobbied government agencies for additional resources also identify themselves in racial or ethnic terms.

The Canadian Panel on Violence against Women distinguishes between 'women of colour' and 'immigrant and refugee women.' Its report uses the term 'women of colour' to refer to 'women who do not identify themselves as white, whether they are from Asia, Africa, the South Pacific, the Caribbean, the Middle East, South or Central America; whether they are immigrant and refugee women of colour; or women of colour who were born in Canada and whose families have been here for generations.' It notes that 'Black women are included in the definition of women of colour, although many prefer simply to be referred to as Black women' (1993, 79).

Race and ethnicity are socially constructed categories. Dominant groups in a society select certain physical criteria and attach social and political significance to them. Physical traits such as skin colour, the shape of eyes, or hair texture are associated with social, psychological, or moral values or with behavioural and attitudinal norms. Over time the association of physical characteristics with behavioural norms and moral values may come to be widely accepted and begin to seem natural, although some of the stereotypes that are associated with such categories change (Li 1990, 5–6; Miles 1989, 11–40).

The different histories of women and their different perceptions of their own identities also make the process of naming and defining extremely difficult. Women who share a socially defined identity – for example, black immigrants, working-class whites, or South Asians – do not, after all, share the identities attributed to them by social stereotypes, and they do not share identical views on issues like immigration policy or social policy, let alone on issues affecting women.

A similar problem faces any organization's attempt to identify a 'community' of immigrant women: it is almost certain to exclude some women who consider themselves to be members of the group and to include others who do not. An organization might define 'the South Asian women's community in Canada,' for example, as comprising all women who have come to Canada (or whose ancestors came to Canada) from Bangladesh, India, Pakistan, or Sri Lanka. But this definition excludes South Asian women who have come from Africa, and it includes South Asian women who feel they have much in common with women from some South Asian regions but nothing at all with women from other South Asian regions. Moreover, it excludes women who would like to be represented by such an organization, and it includes women who would adamantly deny that the organization speaks for them.

However, all categories overlook some individual differences, and none is capable of encompassing anyone's whole personal identity. Calling into question the very possibility of identifying or defining groups of women, like the subjects of this book, threatens to undermine organized resistance to racial or gender discrimination. Indeed, it may appear to many community-based organizations that recent academic attacks on terms like 'race,' 'class,' 'gender,' and even 'subject' are aimed against groups of women who want to redefine themselves to bring about social change. Nancy Hartsock asks:

> Why is it that just at the moment when so many of us who have been silenced begin to demand the right to name ourselves, to act as subjects rather than objects of history, that just then the concept of subjecthood becomes problematic? Just when we are forming our own theories about the world, uncertainty emerges about whether the world can be theorized. Just when we are talking about the changes we want, ideas of progress and the possibility of systematically and rationally organizing human society become dubious and suspect. (Hartsock 1990, 163–4)

In this book, I identify, wherever possible, the ethnic origin and social class of the women who are served by the community-based organizations that I discuss. I use the term 'women from Asia, Africa, and the Caribbean' to refer to women who have immigrated (or whose ancestors immigrated) from those regions. This category encompasses very diverse women, with different histories of struggle in their countries of origin and different experiences in Canada. The thread of unity in the group is their common experiences of racial discrimination. In using the category 'women from Asia, Africa, and the Caribbean,' I focus on their experiences of racism rather than on their histories and origins, and this book does not present ethnographic accounts or discrete histories of these groups of women.

The term 'white women' is used in this book to provide a contrast to women from Asia, Africa, and the Caribbean, even though this term also homogenizes a diverse group of women with different ethnicities, classes, and histories in Canada. Some white women – for example, Jewish or Italian women – were racialized as non-white women in the early 1900s in Canada. At the present time, women from Southern Europe confront problems that are similar to those faced by some women from Asia, Africa, and the Caribbean; for example, the inability to speak English. The use of the term 'white women' is not meant to disparage them, but it is a reminder of the ways in which race privileges them and of the differences that race can make to the experiences of women. However, since white women are often unconscious of how race privileges them, it may create some feelings of discomfort among some readers (Spelman 1988; Frankenberg 1993).

Since this book examines community-based groups that aim to meet the special cultural needs of victims of wife abuse, it is appropriate in many cases to note the race or ethnicity and class of the workers and their clients. In order to identify women who are discriminated against on the basis of race, national origin, or class, it is necessary to mention these characteristics. Much of the thinking that underlies the discrimination is associated with stereotypical images of women whose skin colour is not 'white,' who are not fluent in English, or who 'look like immigrants.' No women want to be thought of only in these terms, but the fact that some are is one of the sources of the problems that are examined in this book.

Racialized Women from Asia, Africa, and the Caribbean in Canada: An Historical View

Race, Class, and Gender Discrimination in Canada prior to the Second World War

Feminists from Asia, Africa, and the Caribbean have described the 'silence' about women from these regions in the discourses of dominant groups as a form of oppression. Black women charge that these omissions are part of the racism that is found in the 'Canadian intellectual tradition':

The vision of Canada as an entire culture of Anglo and/or French existence is narrow and inaccurate. This Eurocentric perspective ...

fails to accommodate any other peoples in its structuring ... [W]e have been told in our attempts to recover the history of African Canadians, that the 'evidence' does not exist; and when this 'evidence' is produced it is seen as marginal to the dominant historical narrative. (Bristow 1994, 8–9)

Middle-class racialized writers from Asia, Africa, and the Caribbean have attempted to rectify their own and their foremothers' absence and marginalization from Canadian history, women's history, and ethnic history. Generally these accounts describe the lives of working-class women from their communities and the victimization of these women by race, class, and gender biases and their struggles against them. They have undertaken the task of 'giving voice' to these women in their struggles to overcome oppression and marginalization (Kogawa 1981; Brand 1991; Women's Book Committee, Chinese Canadian National Council 1992).

The experiences of racialized women from Asia, Africa, and the Caribbean in the post-1960s period have been the subject of reports such as those by Alma Estable (1986), Shirley Seward and Kathryn McDade (1988), and Monica Boyd (1989). These reports discuss gender biases in immigration policies, patterns of settlement and adaptation, and discrimination in employment. Some articles explore particular aspects of the lives of women from Asia, Africa, and the Caribbean – for example, in feminist practices or in women's studies classes (Agnew 1993a; Bannerji 1991; Silvera and Gupta 1989). The experiences of domestic workers from the Caribbean have been documented in several studies which reveal how systemic and interpersonal racism has exploited them and made their lives in Canada particularly harsh (Silvera 1983; Calliste 1989; Daenzer 1993).

The experiences of racialized women from Asia, Africa, and the Caribbean were informed by the race, class, and gender biases of society, but in the early part of this century these experiences did not create a unity among them. Only small groups of these women were allowed entry into Canada. Chinese, Japanese, and South Asian women settled primarily in British Columbia, where the racism of the larger society and the hardships of their everyday living kept them confined to their own ethnic group. Black women lived in isolated communities in Southern Ontario and Nova Scotia.

Immigration to Canada in the early part of this century was relatively easy for Europeans but was difficult for Chinese, Japanese, and South Asians (e.g., Sikhs). Racism was rampant in British Columbia at this time and found expression in the media and in the pronouncements of some politicians who sought to stop the immigration of the 'Orientals' to Canada and their settlement in British Columbia (Roy 1989a; Ward 1978). The government acceded to these racist demands by introducing legislation which had the effect of halting further immigration by Chinese, Japanese, and South Asians.

In 1885 legislation required Chinese immigrants to pay a head tax of $50, which gradually increased to $500 by 1903 (Li 1988, 29–30). The financial cost of immigration made it impossible for most Chinese women to migrate, with the exception of the wives of some merchants (and prostitutes, who also worked as waitresses) (Yee 1988). Sometimes a Chinese labourer after years of work in Canada might bring his wife to Canada, but in economically difficult times some wives were forced into prostitution to support themselves, their spouses, and their families in China (Chong 1994).

Chinese experienced systemic, interpersonal, and everyday racism, documented by several studies (Li 1988; Baureiss 1987; Bolaria and Li 1988; Anderson 1991). British Columbians considered the Chinese to be 'sojourners' rather than immigrants who had come to stay permanently. The racism of the times made social interaction between Chinese and white-Canadian women impossible, and interracial marriages were abhorred. 'The prospect of Chinese men marrying white women was so horrendous that when one British Columbian editor learned of two such cases in Halifax, he suggested that perhaps the "brides were better off in their coffins."' A journalist also observed that 'it is when we contemplate these unnatural unions that we find the kernel of the Asiatic problem – the mixing of the races. Race mixture is the essential danger of the Asiatic occupation of the country for race mixture means race deterioration' (Roy 1989b, 18). Consequently, many Chinese men lived in all-male communities and looked to each other for physical sustenance and emotional survival. Some gambled and smoked opium, which only added fuel to the racist fires of the time.

The few working-class Chinese women who managed to come as wives or concubines led harsh, lonely lives filled with unremitting work. Denise Chong in *The Concubine's Children* (1994) has poignantly described the extreme hardship of the life of her grandmother, who came in the early 1900s to Vancouver. She had been sold as a young child to a wealthy man in China. He subsequently resold her as a concubine to Chong's grandfather, who had been working in British Columbia as a labourer and wished to have a family life in Canada. During a return visit to China, he decided that his first wife should continue to stay on in his village to maintain the family home, and he purchased Chong's grandmother to accompany him back to Vancouver.

In Vancouver she was put to work as a waitress to earn the money he had borrowed for the trip and for her purchase. Their earnings enabled the grandfather to buy land in China, and he began building a lavish house in the village. They had twin daughters. The twins were left in the care of the first wife, and Chong's grandmother never saw the twins again.

The dream of a family life was never realized. When both the grandfather and grandmother had a job, they lived a meagre life, but even that disappeared during recessionary times. The grandfather found it difficult to get a job and drifted away, leaving the grandmother with another female child. The grandmother became a prostitute and worked in the gambling dens of Chinatown. She started smoking opium and drinking. For a while, the grandmother's earnings paid the grandfather's debts and financed his dream house in China, but that too was eventually abandoned.

Chong's mother lived in this environment of poverty, gambling, and prostitution, neglected and ignored by the adults. She had no companions of her own age. She did well at school and started to train as a nurse, but she encountered so much racism that she was forced to quit without completing her training. Two weeks later, she got married. She worked in her husband's dry-cleaning business, mended laundry, and later worked part-time as a seamstress from her home.

Like their Chinese counterparts, South Asian women found it difficult to immigrate to Canada. Six thousand South Asians had landed in British Columbia by 1908 (although some went on to the United States), but in response to racist sentiments, legislation was introduced which required all South Asians to come to Canada via a continuous journey. During 1911–12 two South Asians attempted to bring their wives to Canada after visiting them in India. Although the men were readmitted, the wives were ordered to be deported. After vigorous protests, they were allowed to stay as 'an act of grace without establishing any precedent' (Jensen 1988, 128). The *Komagata Maru* incident of 1914, in which a shipload of men from India attempted to challenge the discriminatory legislation which excluded them from Canada but were sent back by Canadian officials, marked the end of immigration from South Asia for some time (Johnston 1979). However, South Asian men continuously lobbied government officials to allow them to bring their wives to Canada. In 1918 Prime Minister Borden agreed to allow wives and children to enter Canada, but the law was not implemented until 1924. At that time there were only a thousand South Asians living in Canada, and by 1941 only 180 wives had immigrated to Canada (Johnston 1979, 95).

The attempts by these men to bring their wives to Canada were viewed sceptically. H.H. Stevens, a Conservative member of Parliament and an avid opponent of immigration from India, claimed:

Hindu agitation for entry of wives for those now here is a subterfuge and was only taken up when it was found to be good ground for appeal to the sentiment of Eastern Canada. This is an effort to break the immigration regulation in principle. If the privilege to bring in wives is allowed it will result in large numbers of women being brought in for immoral purposes under the guise of 'wives of Hindus here.' British Columbia is opposed to Asiatic immigration, because from experience they know they will not assimilate. It results in a large male population with much immorality, where there should exist a large community of white families. (Wagle 1993, 212–13)

Sunder Singh replied in a pamphlet, *India's Appeal to Canada; or, An Account of Hindu Immigration to the Dominion*:

> But Christian Canada denies home-life, the birth right of each human being, by shutting out the wife of the Sikh, who is a fellow citizen of the Empire. The right of the husband living with his wife is the most sacred human institution, and anything done to impair it goes at the very root of all principles of morality and social welfare. Further, the ideals of Sikh's home life are highly spiritual and monogamous. (Quoted in Wagle 1993)

There is little information on the paid work done by South Asian women at that time. The few women who were in British Columbia then are usually assumed by historians to have been wives (Chadney 1984, 37).

The Japanese, like the Chinese and South Asians, were victimized by racism, but the Gentlemen's Agreement of 1908 allowed for the immigration of Japanese women and children. Many of the Japanese men in Canada were unmarried, and they arranged through the Prefectural Association matchmaker to marry 'picture brides' (Adachi 1976, 87–108). In 1908, 566 women arrived, and between 1909 and 1929 their annual numbers usually exceeded those of men, ranging between 153 and 530 (Ujimoto 1988, 132).

The lives of working-class Japanese women were harsh and lonely. They worked in factories, in domestic service, on farms, and in family businesses. The conditions of work are described by Kobayashi (1994, 58):

> The new bride would be required to be up at dawn on the day after arrival, the day after meeting her husband for the first time, to work in a laundry or family business or perhaps to cook for a camp of labourers under conditions that were, of course, entirely foreign. She would endure the insults of a husband whose main concern in bringing her from Japan had been to provide for food and clean clothing for the men under his supervision in the bush camp, and who did not want to be embarrassed by a wife who was inept at her new work. Under such conditions, one woman recalled, 'My tears were silent and helpless.'

Paid work contradicted Meiji gender ideology, but nevertheless the women stoically endured the hardships and tried to find satisfaction in living up to the ideals of being a good wife and mother (Kobayashi 1994, 66).

Black women, like the Chinese, Japanese, and South Asians, experienced race, class, and gender discrimination, but their history is very different. The history of black women in Canada has been documented in *'We're Rooted Here and They Can't Pull Us Up':* *Essays in African Canadian Women's History* (1994). The first black women came to Canada in the late seventeenth and eighteenth centuries from the United States as slaves. Later they came as fugitives from slavery via the Underground Railroad (Hamilton 1994; Cooper 1994). Women from the Caribbean first came to Canada from Guadeloupe in 1910 as domestic workers in Quebec (Calliste 1989, 135).

Black women lived in isolated communities in Nova Scotia and Southern Ontario, eking out a marginal existence. Although race and gender located them at the bottom of the class hierarchy, they struggled to form and maintain families and establish small communities (Bristow 1994, 69–142). In the mid-nineteenth century, black women, like all women at this time, could not own land, but some worked on land near Buxton and Chatham in Southern Ontario, where they shared in all the farming tasks of clearing, planting, harvesting, and selling crops. '[T]hese women were active in all aspects of their black community. They taught school, ran businesses, raised children, worked as farmers, domestic servants, midwives and healers, and were political activists' (Bristow 1994, 125).

Gender restricted the opportunities for paid employment for all women in Canada, but racism further circumscribed the jobs that were available to black women. Domestic work was done by 80 per cent of black women in Toronto and Montreal at least up to the Second World War. Starting as domestic workers at the age of fifteen, they put in a sixteen-hour day, got paid in clothing in lieu of wages, and were 'subject to arbitrary demands' by their employers (Brand 1994, 181). Industrialization created a demand for labour, and during the war there were labour shortages. Consequently, despite the endemic racism of the times, 'things opened up' for black women. Although they encountered racism in factory jobs as well, they 'grabbed on to an industrial wage and hung on for dear life.' Brand comments:

> Racism created an atmosphere in which Black women's presence was on sufferance. So, the industrial wage (such as it was), the whole-sale war recruitment that suggested that one's chances were as good as anyone else's, the anonymity of industrial labourers, and the indications of Black progress that this opportunity signalled were all a boon to Black women and to the Black community as a whole – despite the laissez faire racism on the job in the war plants and other industries. (Brand 1994, 181)

The history of black women reveals many individual acts of courage and defiance against the race, class, and gender discrimination of Canadian society. One woman challenged the property rights of her master to her children (Hamilton 1994, 23); another challenged the colour bar prevalent in 1946 in Nova Scotia (Brand 1994, 188). Black women chipped away at the barriers that excluded them from jobs in factories or as nurses, teachers, and clerks (Bristow 1994), but the small number of blacks in Canada prior to the Second World War made organized resistance against race, class, and gender discrimination almost impossible.

Systemic Racism, Classism, and Sexism in the Post–Second World War Period

Canadian history from the 1960s onwards is marked by more frequent assertions of rights based on gender, race, or ethnicity. Ethnic minorities expressed their dissatisfaction with policies of assimilation which had marginalized their cultural norms and kept them from sharing power and authority in society (Burnet 1988). In the late 1960s, the women's movement re-emerged with greater vigour, demanding equality and liberation (Black 1988). However, the struggles of ethnic and racial groups were dominated by males, while the burgeoning women's movement was dominated by white

middle-class females (Agnew 1996). The experiences of marginalization in progressive movements and increasing understanding of
the integrated nature of their own oppressions created solidarity
among racialized women from Asia, Africa, and the Caribbean and
demonstrated that their oppressions could not be subsumed under
gender alone or under race alone.

Women immigrated to Canada in the post–Second World War
period under a variety of immigration policies and programs.
The policies were usually driven by economic needs, although
they sometimes responded with humanitarianism to the plight of
refugees. In the postwar period, the Canadian economy changed
from one primarily focused on raw materials to one with greater
industrial and manufacturing capabilities. Immigration policies
introduced in the 1960s reflected the changing needs of the
labour market. They were less concerned with the ethnic origins
or nationality of the immigrants and more with their education
and professional training. International crises – for example, the
communist revolution in China – led to increases in immigration
from particular parts of the world (Hawkins 1988; Richmond
1967).

The 1967 immigration policy aimed to establish objective criteria
(popularly referred to as the point system) for selecting prospective
immigrants on the basis of skills, education, and the needs of the
Canadian labour market. It created three categories of immigrants:
independent, sponsored, and dependent (Hawkins 1988). The policy eliminated the most blatant forms of racial discrimination, but
critics argued that some systemic biases remained. The size and
location of immigration offices, for instance, had some effect on
the number of immigrants from different parts of the world
(Malarek 1987, 253–4; Baureiss 1987, 20). Immigration policy in
the post-1967 period eliminated the racial bias of earlier times
encoded in terminology such as 'preferred nations' (Northern
Europeans), 'traditional sources' (Britain and Europe), and 'assim-
ilability.' Nevertheless, as Harney points out, although 'immigrants
from certain groups were no longer considered undesirable
because of their distance from the racial and cultural core,' they
were excluded 'because of the impact they [might] have on those

already in Canada, those "somewhat nervous about rapid ethnic change"' (1988, 55).

Some gender biases in previous policies were also identified and criticized. Earlier immigration officers had routinely selected the man as the primary immigrant or as the 'head of household'; women and children accompanied him as his dependants (Boyd 1990). This assumption discriminated against women, restricting their eligibility for language-learning classes with training allowances.

The immigration policy of 1967 was successful in attracting increasing numbers of males and females with university education from Asia, Africa, and the Caribbean (Samuel 1990), but sometimes they were accompanied by dependants (wives, children, and parents) who did not speak English and needed opportunities to learn the language, to acquire some job-related skills, or to obtain recertification as teachers or nurses. Similarly, immigrants who were supported by relatives were not eligible for welfare for several years but sometimes needed additional training to recertify or to learn English.

The range of immigrants became even more diverse with the introduction of immigration programs which targeted specific groups of individuals; for example, the entrepreneur program and the domestic worker program. There is a demand for domestic workers in Canadian households, but the work requires long hours, pays poorly, and means isolation and loss of privacy, particularly for live-in domestic workers. New immigrants who take up domestic work usually leave such work as soon as they locate other jobs.

The government has introduced several programs to bring domestic workers to Canada, and these have attracted women from Europe, the Caribbean, and the Philippines (Boyd 1989, 4). The first program, in 1955, established a quota for domestic workers from the Caribbean, but immigration officers were apprehensive that the immigration of these women would 'create future problems.' They feared that the women, who were presumed to belong to 'lower classes,' would sponsor 'unskilled workers' to join them in Canada. The women were even alleged to be immoral and promiscuous (Satzewich 1991, 141–5).

Similar biases are evident in the programs that have been adopted to bring domestic workers to Canada since 1955. The government attempted to meet the demand for domestic workers by tying them to particular employers and by restricting them to domestic work. Since domestic workers were allowed in only for limited periods and were required to renew their visas periodically to stay in Canada, they were vulnerable to exploitation by unscrupulous employers (Calliste 1989; Daenzer 1993; Silvera 1983; Arat-Koc 1990). Domestic workers had to contribute to unemployment insurance and to the Canada Pension Plan although it was unlikely that they would ever benefit from these deductions. Consequently, advocacy groups for domestic workers have protested against the programs as exploitative (Intercede 1990).

In 1987 the government of Ontario amended the Employment Standards Act to provide greater protection for domestic workers, requiring employers to pay a minimum wage and stipulating the number of hours for a work week; but advocates of domestic workers argued that such laws were regularly breached and the women felt too vulnerable to complain (Intercede 1991). Domestic workers do not have the right to organize themselves into a trade union and are therefore unable to bargain collectively for better wages or work conditions; and they are not covered by the Ontario government's health or safety legislation (Henry et al. 1995, 77).

The new Live-in-Caregiver Program introduced in 1992 resolved some problems but created new ones. Now domestic workers are automatically eligible for landed immigrant status after two years of employment. However, to work in Canada, domestic workers are now required to have grade 12 and at least six months of professional child-care training. These requirements favour workers from Europe over those from the Philippines or the Caribbean (Henry et al. 1995, 77–8).

Since 1978 the Canadian government has introduced a variety of business programs intended to attract capital, investors, and entrepreneurs to Canada. In 1980 the largest number of business immigrants came from the United Kingdom, followed by the United States, West Germany, and the Netherlands. By 1990 the top four countries from which business immigrants were drawn changed to

Hong Kong, Taiwan, South Korea, and Lebanon. Hong Kong led the group, with 1,625 immigrants, compared to 119 from England, which now placed sixth on the list (Borowski and Nash 1994, 237). Not surprisingly, business programs have attracted males as primary immigrants. Between 1979 and 1984, only 9 per cent of all entrepreneur immigrants were females, although the percentage increased slightly to 13.6 between 1986 and 1987 (Employment and Immigration Canada, 1990, cited in Borowski and Nash 1994, 243).

All these programs, too, have been dogged by controversy. Some charge that the programs in effect sold visas and placed a form of head tax on immigrants (Taylor 1991, 11). Sometimes immigrants abused the programs, gaining entry for themselves but not establishing any businesses, or settling their wives and children in Canada while they returned to work in Hong Kong. These programs were temporarily discontinued in some provinces in 1994 (Cannon 1995, 203).

Female refugees have come to Canada from several Third World countries. South Asians came from Uganda in the 1970s, and Vietnamese came in the mid-1970s (Canada, Employment and Immigration, 1982, cited in Li 1988, 91–2). More recently, women refugees have come from Sri Lanka and Somalia. The admission of refugees is guided by humanitarianism, and immigration officers do not use the point system in refugee camps, but refugees are 'screened to make sure that they can adapt to the Canadian labour market and society' (Knowles 1992, 172). Women have not done well under this system. For example, 75 to 80 per cent of the world refugee population are females, but more males than females apply and gain entry to Canada (National Action Committee 1987, 1).

Some female refugees come straight from their country of persecution and claim refugee status at their point of entry in Canada. They are then assessed by the Immigration and Refugee Board. At times, controversies have erupted over people who are thought to be bogus refugees trying to gain entry to Canada through unfair means, but at other times, the Board has been criticized for long delays and insensitivity towards individuals trying to escape years of persecution and in some cases torture (Knowles 1992; Malarek

1987). Gender persecution was not considered a legitimate basis for granting refugee status until 1993. Canada has now introduced guidelines which direct refugee boards to grant refugee status to women who have been persecuted or fear gender persecution (Valpy 1993).

These varied programs have created some major changes in Canada's immigration patterns. Unlike the pre–Second World War period, 50 per cent of immigrants are now females. The most significant change, however, is that the source countries from which Canada attracts immigrants are no longer European but Third World countries. Between 1978 and 1981, eight of the top ten countries of origin were Third World countries: Vietnam, India, the Philippines, the People's Republic of China, Hong Kong, Jamaica, Haiti, and Guyana (Boyd 1989, 42). The educational level, skills, age, and marital status of the new immigrants vary. For example, the 1981 census shows large differences in knowledge of English and French among foreign-born women. While 45.7 per cent of the women from the People's Republic of China could not converse in English or French, the comparable figure for women from Guyana was only 2.8 per cent (Boyd 1989, 47). The percentage of foreign-born women who cannot converse in English or French is nearly twice that of immigrant men (7.1 per cent versus 3.6) (Boyd 1994, 552).

Gender and racial discrimination in employment angers and frustrates women from Asia, Africa, and the Caribbean (Brand 1994; Daenzer 1993). Many studies have documented that racialized people experience discrimination at work.[1] As well, feminists have identified patterns of gender discrimination in the workplace.[2] There is, in fact, a wide consensus among a variety of scholars – including members of both the dominant culture and racial and ethnic groups, researchers for government agencies, and researchers for community-based immigrant women's groups – that ethnic and racialized women encounter race and gender discrimination in the workplace.[3]

Race and gender discrimination has the effect of stratifying women at the lower levels of the labour market. Working-class women from racial minorities in Canada are concentrated in garment manufacturing, domestic work, assembly-line work, janitorial work, and other low-paid, low-skilled jobs. Working-class women from racial minorities frequently work in non-unionized workplaces, and their unfamiliarity with the English language makes them easy prey for unscrupulous and exploitative employers. As well, working-class women from racial and ethnic groups often lack information about Canadian labour or human rights legislation, and this can lead to even greater victimization from co-workers and employers.

Middle-class women from Asia, Africa, and the Caribbean are found in professional, managerial, technical, clerical, sales, and service jobs as well as nursing (Basavarajappa and Verma 1990, 298). Statistics indicate, however, that 16 per cent of visible-minority women have degrees, diplomas, or certificates, as compared to only 12 per cent of the general population. Despite this, they earn less and are less likely to be employed in their chosen fields (Urban Alliance on Race Relations and Ontario Women's Directorate, n.d., 1).

The forms that racial discrimination takes in the workforce have also been identified. Employers may require 'Canadian experience,' which racialized minorities have argued is a tactic for excluding new immigrants. The educational qualifications and work experience acquired by women from Third World countries are devalued by potential employers. Professionals (e.g., nurses) and tradespeople may find that they are unable to become registered or licensed in Canada because no standards have been set for evaluating training they acquired in their countries of origin.[4] Immigrant women may encounter additional problems. They may have childcare responsibilities that do not allow them to participate in language training or skill training, and they may have had little or no work experience in paid employment. The discrimination that they encounter in seeking language training with benefits similar to those available to men has also been documented.[5]

There is often a vast difference between the kind of work the women did in their country of origin and the work that they are likely to get in Canada (Agnew 1991, 23). Sometimes employment agencies, even those meant to help non–English-speaking women, slot them into menial, dead-end jobs, without regard for their previous education and work experience (Ng 1988).

Frances Henry notes in her study of Caribbean people in Toronto that in the interviews she conducted 'racial harassment and discrimination was a common theme for most respondents regardless of their class position.' She describes the forms that racial harassment took:

> For some verbal harassment and name calling were cited as indicators of racism; for others discrimination meant being passed over for promotion despite having qualifications similar to or better than those of the successful employee. Earning less money than similarly placed White employees was another form of discrimination, as were salary disputes with the employer or the company. (Henry 1994, 107)

Women from the Caribbean are more troubled by racial discrimination than by gender discrimination, but unlike men from the Caribbean, they are usually reluctant to launch complaints with the Human Rights Commission. One Caribbean woman said, 'You only complain if you want to get fired' (Henry 1994, 108).

Much has been written about the victimization of women from Asia, Africa, and the Caribbean by the race, class, and gender biases of society, but there are no published accounts which examine the strategies they have adopted to overcome their exploitation. We know that governmental initiatives, such as employment equity, are nudging employers to hire and promote visible minorities, but there are no published accounts of the effectiveness of these programs for women from Asia, Africa, and the Caribbean. We have no studies, such as those available from Britain, which indicate how gender relations of racialized women are transformed when they obtain work outside the home and bring home a salary. The British studies show that when women work, even at menial, dead-end jobs, they meet other women, participate in more social activities (e.g., weddings and baby showers), and hear accounts of other women's lives. Such interactions raise their consciousness of the values and norms of their own culture. A pay cheque, however nominal, may increase their self-confidence in asserting their rights within the family. Sometimes they come together with other women to fight against exploitative employers (Westwood and Bhachu 1988; Parmar 1986).

Women from Asia, Africa, and the Caribbean have adopted a number of strategies to cope with the race, class, and gender discrimination of Canadian society. Like men in various ethnic communities, they have found that starting their own business is a way of avoiding the race and gender biases of society. Women provide labour that is essential for the success of small family businesses, such as restaurants, groceries, and clothing stores, that primarily serve members of their own ethnic group. Women who have young children or who cannot speak English have sometimes started businesses from their homes, and some of them have received help in starting such ventures from community-based groups.

The existence of community-based groups is evidence of entrepreneurship by middle-class women from Asia, Africa, and the Caribbean. Middle-class women have taken the initiative to find out about funding opportunities available from government agencies and have obtained funds for providing services to women in their communities – for example, to victims of wife abuse. These organizations hire women with similar ethnic and racial backgrounds as office staff, program coordinators, and counsellors. When funds are available, they add new programs (e.g., support groups for senior citizens). In this way, employment opportunities and volunteer work become available to women who might otherwise have difficulty in finding positions in mainstream organizations. As well, new immigrants gain valuable Canadian experience, which facilitates their entry into other jobs with diverse organizations in Canada (Agnew 1996).

One example of a government initiative used by middle-class women to create employment for women in their communities is the Jobs Ontario Community Action Program. The Riverdale Immigrant Women's Association, the South Asian Women's Group, and the Canadian Tamil Women's Association received funding to train women from their communities. The project of the Canadian Tamil Women's Association is to train Tamil women who came to

Canada as refugees but do not speak English fluently to run restaurants and gift shops. The first restaurant has now opened at a downtown Toronto location. The project manager has gained valuable experience in starting a small business, and she has created jobs for cooks, waitresses, and an assistant-manager. The profits from the first restaurant are to be rolled over to start an additional restaurant and gift shop, where the association will provide training and employment for more Tamil women.

Women from Asia, Africa, and the Caribbean have experienced race, class, and gender discrimination throughout this century. In the early part of this century, racism and sexism were openly expressed in legislation, employment, and everyday interactions, but women remained absorbed in eking out a marginal existence for themselves and did not come together in any organizations to protest the conditions of their lives.

Racism, sexism, and classism have been experienced in a different way in the post–Second World War period. Women from Asia, Africa, and the Caribbean have become more articulate about their oppressions and have organized themselves to struggle against them. Nonetheless, the lives of women from Asia, Africa, and the Caribbean are still shadowed by race, class, and gender discrimination. How they are struggling against one manifestation of it is the subject of this book.

Review of the Literature on Immigrant Women and Wife Abuse

During the 1980s the women's movement exposed the problem of wife abuse to the Canadian public. They succeeded in changing the perception of wife abuse as a personal or private matter between family members to the realization that it was just as much a crime as assault against anyone else (Pierson et al. 1993, 109–13). The federal government introduced a variety of initiatives to examine the problem of violence against women and established the Family Violence Prevention Division in the Department of Health and Welfare. By the mid-1980s the issue of violence against women was 'taken away' from the grass-roots women's movement and came firmly under the control and direction of government agencies (Levan 1996, 329).

Government agencies, pressured by the public discussion, responded by commissioning reports to study the nature and extent of wife abuse in Canadian society. A significant government initiative was the appointment in 1991 of the Canadian Panel on Violence against Women by the federal government to study the subject. Other government agencies have also commissioned reports or provided funding to study the problem of wife abuse, including the Ontario Women's Directorate and, in the federal government, Health Canada, Health and Welfare, the Department of Justice, the Secretary of State, and the Ministry of the Solicitor General. The Canadian Advisory Council on the Status of Women also published reports (1980, 1987, and 1989). These initiatives gave legitimacy to the concern of women's groups and signalled the willingness of government agencies to intervene by allocating resources to provide services to victims of wife abuse and to change legislation to more effectively prosecute its perpetrators.

The literature on wife abuse in ethnic and racial immigrant communities can be divided into two categories. First, there are reports commissioned by government agencies to identify gaps in social services for abused wives. Second, there are studies initiated by community-based groups and given financial support by government agencies to document the incidence of violence in their communities, to identify needs for services, or to explain the cultural norms of the ethnic or racial groups that they represent to service providers in mainstream agencies. While the reports are available in libraries, the studies have limited circulation and are usually not found in libraries or archives. The studies are intended to demonstrate to government agencies the special difficulties of women from ethnic and racial communities and their need for social services that are sensitive to their culture and race (Chinese Family Life Services 1989; Papp 1990; Musisi and Muktar 1992; Korean-Canadian Women's Association 1992; South East Asian Services Centre 1992; Rafiq 1991; Ocampo and Villasin 1993).

There are no full-length academic books on wife abuse in ethnic and racial communities in Canada, and there are only a few

accounts in academic journals. Shirene Razack, a South Asian professor born in the Caribbean, examines the cultural context in
which violence against aboriginal women and women of colour is
perpetrated, but her prime emphasis is on aboriginal women
(1994, 894–923). Rita Kohli, a South Asian activist, describes her
own experiences of working in shelters in Toronto (Kohli 1991a;
1993); and Aruna Papp, also a South Asian activist, has documented her personal experience of abuse as well as the experiences of six other South Asian women (1995). There is no discussion of the many theoretical issues that arise in this area; for
example, the implications of cooperating with the state in providing services to abused women or the difficulty of reconciling the
feminist view of the state as gendered and patriarchal with the
acceptance by community-based groups of the services that the
state provides to abused wives.

Research on wife abuse in immigrant communities reveals how
feminist theory has evolved since the early 1970s. In early feminist
analyses of work and social life in Canada, the experiences of
women from Asia, Africa, and the Caribbean were either omitted
or marginalized. More recent literature on wife abuse now acknowledges that racialized and ethnic women experience multiple
and integrated oppressions of race, class, and gender that make
them more susceptible to violence in their homes. This development in feminist understanding can be traced in two seminal studies by Linda MacLeod, a freelance journalist who has written
extensively on wife abuse in Canada.

The first study, a report commissioned by the Canadian Advisory
Council on the Status of Women and published in 1980, is
regarded as marking the beginning of a public discussion on wife
abuse in Canada. The report documented the severity of the problem, the hardships encountered by victims of wife abuse, and the
shortage of transition houses to provide shelter or social services to
them. The report did not distinguish between different groups of
women but treated gender bias as the primary source of oppression. A follow-up study by MacLeod in 1987, also commissioned by
the Advisory Council, explained the additional difficulties encountered by immigrant women – linguistic isolation, fear of being

deported, distrust of the police, and 'cultural mores' (26–7). In the 1980 study, wife abuse was defined as physical violence against women; it emphasized that 'wife battering can be a life-threatening problem and that immediate and decisive action [is] essential'; but the latter report broadened the definition to include psychological and emotional violence as well (MacLeod 1987, 14).

Feminists from Asia, Africa, and the Caribbean have argued that most feminist theory exhibits a racial bias, especially evident in its exclusive emphasis on gender oppression and in its relative indifference to race and class as oppressors of women. These feminists also object to the appropriation of leadership roles by white middle-class feminists (Agnew 1993a; Bannerji 1987; Silvera and Gupta 1989). Recent discourse on wife abuse shows sensitivity to these issues. White feminist discussions of wife abuse now refer to the special difficulties of immigrant women from Aisa, Africa, and the Caribbean (Randall 1989; Walker 1990; Guberman and Wolfe 1985). They explain that wife abuse can result from both patriarchy and racial inequality and note that the integrated oppressions of race, class, and gender keep women in abusive environments. These analyses of wife abuse are similar to those by women from Asia, Africa, and the Caribbean, but the latter emphasize institutional racism in Canadian society, particularly in the delivery of social services and in legislation that tends to keep women trapped in abusive homes (Rafiq 1991; Kohli 1991a, 1991b; Razack 1994). The work by feminists from Asia, Africa, and the Caribbean also raises issues of voice appropriation and lack of representation (Pierson et al. 1993, 202–10).

A conflict arose concerning the composition of the Canadian Panel on Violence against Women. Many women's groups asserted that it was not representative of Canadian women. Although all panel members had experience working in the area of violence against women, nevertheless women's organizations argued that these women were tokens chosen by the government and not representative of their groups. Some women's organizations found it unacceptable that the panel, for which they had lobbied for years, was not accountable to the women's movement but to the government that had appointed it (Levan 1996, 338–51). Although the panel attempted to resolve some of these problems by setting up an advisory body which would better represent the diversity of Canada's population, women's organizations remained dissatisfied.

Mobina Jaffar, a lawyer of South Asian origin, was a panel member, but groups of women from Asia, Africa, and the Caribbean argued that she did not represent them but was a nominee of the government. The panel was unable to resolve this disagreement, and the Congress of Black Women and the National Organization of Immigrant and Visible Minority Women, along with the National Action Committee and two other women's groups, refused to participate in its proceedings or to support its work (Levan 1996, 338–51). The panel acknowledged that 'women from cultural and visible minorities, as well as women with disabilities, were inadequately represented in the panel's makeup' (1993, B3). It admitted that its failure to resolve the issue resulted in 'disarray and a sense of powerlessness within both the panel and the feminist community' (1993, B5).

The panel contracted for two studies: 'Violence against Immigrant Women of Colour,' by Fauzia Rafiq, a lesbian feminist activist, immigrant from Pakistan, and editor of *Diva: A Journal of South Asian Women*; and 'Violence against Women of Colour,' by Rozena Maart (1993, F1).

The panel's report identifies problems concerning sponsorship, immigration status, and the exploitation of women who come into Canada as domestic workers. Chapter 11 of the report is on women of colour, and chapter 13 is on immigrant and refugee women and foreign domestic workers. The report strongly reflects the perspective of activist feminists from Asia, Africa, and the Caribbean. It states unequivocally that 'efforts to overcome violence against women can no longer be dissociated from the struggle against sexism, racism, intolerance and inequality' (1993, B4). It notes that some people think that violence is part of other cultures but argues that this belief betrays a racist attitude:

Racism, cloaked in the more respectable mantle of 'cultural considerations,' results in the stereotypes about violence being part of the 'culture' of a people. This can be an excuse for non-intervention within the legal system and other services based on the misinformed fear of interfering with the practices of another culture. However, no cultural practices or norms can be used to justify violence. (1993, 80)

The report found that there were 'three major impediments' to women who experienced violence and sought help from social services:

> racism from those involved in service delivery; a lack of services specifically focused on their needs, even when the demographics of the community would demand such availability; and the peripheral role women of colour play in the structuring and delivery of mainstream services ... A lack of specialized services leaves women of colour isolated and more likely to return to the violent situations from which they were seeking escape. (1993, 82)

The panel acknowledged the work of community-based organizations of immigrant women in providing social services to women from their communities, but it noted that they had to work with inadequate funds:

> The chronic underfunding of these organizations precludes co-ordinated and consolidated work in creating real changes regarding sexism, racism and poverty. Provincial and territorial policies seem to be based on the belief that the federal government has exclusive responsibility for funding services. At the federal government level, government departments often believe that Employment and Immigration Canada will fund the total range of services. These jurisdictional confusions leave immigrant and refugee women 'falling through the cracks.' Governments have a responsibility to initiate and participate in co-ordinating efforts to ensure that funding to immigrant women's organizations is sufficient to provide not only responses to violence but also preventive outreach services. (1993, 95)

There is some literature on immigrant women in Canada. Monica Boyd has examined the impact of public policy on immigrant women (1989, 1990, 1991, 1994). Shirley Seward and Kathryn McDade (1988) have provided an overview of the difficulties that immigrant women face in finding employment, and Alma Estable has discussed their paid-work experiences (1986).[6] The racism experienced by immigrant women has been documented in Agnew 1993a; Bannerji 1986; Dhruvarajan 1991; Srivastava and Ames 1993; Brand 1991, 1994; and Ghosh 1981. Calliste 1989, Daenzer 1993, and Das Gupta 1996 focus on racism in employment. Giles 1987, Boyd 1990, and Go 1987 examine discrimination against women in the provision of language training, but much less work has been done on racism as an obstacle to women seeking social services.

Three studies have been published by government agencies. Linda MacLeod and Maria Shin prepared *Isolated, Afraid and Forgotten: The Service Delivery Needs and Realities of Immigrant and Refugee Women Who Are Battered* for the National Clearinghouse on Family Violence, of Health and Welfare Canada (1990). MacLeod and Shin also co-authored *Like a Wingless Bird: A Tribute to the Survival and Courage of Women Who Are Abused and Who Speak Neither English nor French* for the Department of Canadian Heritage (1993). Joanne Godin wrote *More Than a Crime: A Report on the Lack of Public Legal Information Materials for Immigrant Women Who Are Subject to Wife Assault* for the Department of Justice (1994).

Isolated, Afraid and Forgotten explains that immigrant women who are victims of abuse experience all the difficulties of non-immigrant women, but their problems are 'magnified many times by the loneliness, strangeness, and newness of their environment' (1990, 7). They need information about immigration policies, their legal status in Canada, and their rights according to Canadian legislation, and they are sometimes afraid to report the abuse to the police because they are apprehensive of being deported.

The authors argue that victims of wife abuse who are members of racial and ethnic groups need a 'supportive network to provide understanding and caring' when they are leaving the abusive environment. They need the 'opportunity to discuss and reassess their beliefs and assumptions concerning wife abuse' and to discuss them 'with women and men who understand their culture and who can communicate in their language.' The women need additional help in finding jobs through 'subsidized language-training classes with training allowances and free day-care facilities.' The report identifies a need for more job-training courses for women who do not speak English or French and for 'affordable good housing' (1990, 11–12).

Similar issues and problems are discussed in *Like a Wingless Bird*, but the authors give more prominence to the perceptions and views of the victims of abuse. They make recommendations similar to those in *Isolated, Afraid and Forgotten* but discuss them in greater detail.

More Than a Crime was commissioned by the Department of Justice as 'part of its Public Legal Education and Information program.' The report addresses the need identified in earlier reports for providing information to victims of wife abuse on 'their rights and responsibilities under the law.' They need this information for several reasons. They must consider the repercussions of calling the police to report abuse, and 'they need to understand the terms of Canada's assault laws, the ways in which the operation of the justice system may or may not protect them from further abuse, and the implications of a separation under family law.' They must consider the consequences for 'the custody of their children, the division of matrimonial property, their property and other rights if their union is common-law, and the ability of the police to restrain the actions of the spouse' (1994, 3). They need to know the law pertaining to immigration status, sponsorship breakdown, and deportation.

Community-based groups provide counselling for victims of wife abuse. Deborah Sinclair's *Understanding Wife Assault: A Training Manual for Counsellors and Advocates* aims to 'equip workers to intervene effectively in families that are torn apart by violence' (1985, 12), but her book does not examine the special problems of immigrant women. Sinclair argues that 'the basic principles [of counselling] apply to all women's lives regardless of background' and says only that counsellors and advocates have a responsibility to sensitize themselves to the unique situation of specific groups of women whenever possible (1985, 12–13). Similar statements appear in other studies.[7] In contrast, Monica Riutort and Shirley Small's *Work-*

ing with Assaulted Immigrant Women: A Handbook for Lay Counsellors
attempts to counteract some common stereotypes and to explain
legislation on social assistance for immigrant women (1985).

Community-based groups have been critical of the Eurocentric
norms of counsellors in mainstream agencies and have argued
that their groups are better able to provide the culturally sensitive services needed by abused women (Papp 1990; Korean-Canadian Women's Association 1992a; South East Asian Services
Centre 1992; Chinese Family Life Services 1989; Mederios 1991).
Some community-based groups have come together to develop a
model of this type of counselling.[8] The Toronto Advisory Committee on Cultural Approaches to Violence against Women and
Children was funded by the Ontario Ministry of Citizenship's
Wife-Assault-Prevention Training Programs to document 'anti-racist and culturally appropriate approaches to combatting women
assault.' The preliminary report emphasized the need for 'cultural sensitivity and anti-racist training for mainstream direct service workers' and 'increased training for ethno-racial minority
women to work in this area' (1992, 18). An additional grant from
the Ontario Ministry of Community and Social Services funded
a more extensive document on culturally sensitive counselling.
This study, written by a new immigrant from India, Smita Tyagi
(1993), is a lengthy description of psychological theories of wife
abuse. Tyagi consulted with only four community-based groups,
and her report leaves many important questions unanswered; for
example, whether culturally sensitive counselling may perpetuate
patriarchal norms.

Some of the reports initiated by community-based groups on
wife abuse are valuable resources for explaining their communities
to the larger society, but they do not circulate through libraries
and archives. Although there is literature on blacks in Canada,
much less is known about recent immigrants and refugees from
African countries such as Ethiopia and Somalia (Musisi and Muktar 1992). Some of the reports describe common misunderstand-
ings between mainstream service providers and their ethnic and
racial clients and suggest ways to deal with them (Chinese Family
Life Services 1989). Others describe the inhibitions that women

from those communities may have in approaching mainstream service providers or the police for help (Pinedo and Santinoli 1991). The reports by community-based groups on wife abuse do not include much information about the groups or about their culturally sensitive services.

Ng has studied one community-based group which attempts to locate jobs for immigrant women (Ng 1988). The present author's *Resisting Discrimination* (1996) discusses the origins of community-based groups, who funds them, their structure, and their advocacy work. One chapter analyses their responses to the problem of wife abuse in their communities and looks at difficulties in living at the shelters for abused women.

Immigrant-serving agencies and their services are the subject of *Legal Information and Wife Abuse in Immigrant Families*, written by San San Sy and Sudha Choldin and funded by the Research and Statistics Directorate (1994). The authors recommend greater cultural sensitivity to the needs of immigrant women and more training for translators and service providers in 'the area of legal information affecting wife abuse.' They call for greater cooperation among agencies that serve immigrants, such as the legal system, Employment and Immigration Canada, ethnic associations, and mainstream public and non-profit social service agencies and shelters (1994, 29).

The objective of most discourse on wife abuse in immigrant communities is practical solutions to problems. The reports by community-based groups do not explore underlying, systemic racism or patriarchy; and even though they are critical of the Eurocentric norms of mainstream social service agencies, they do not describe how these are manifested in the agencies' counselling sessions or their services. Nor do community-based groups specify how they overcome biases in their own practice.

The reports by community-based groups seldom try to identify the class of the clients they serve. Usually they circumvent the issue by pointing out that wife abuse is found in all groups and classes, which gives the impression that community-based groups serve clients from all social classes. However, most of the women who come to these groups are working-class, non–English-speaking women who are unable to obtain or reluctant to seek services from main-stream social service agencies. The administrators and counsellors of community-based groups are middle-class women, but their reports do not explore the question of whether class differences may pose obstacles to the provision of social services or lead to mis-understandings in the groups.

This book interprets through a feminist lens the work of com-munity-based groups that provide services to victims of wife abuse. It locates the social and political contexts in which community-based groups operate and assesses the extent to which they are able to meet the needs of the women who come to them. Its analy-sis is based on observation of the operation of several of the groups and on documents about the groups which are not avail-able from libraries or archives. Excerpts from interviews are included to give voice to service providers and to document how they perceive the problems encountered by women seeking to escape abusive homes.

TWO

Wife Abuse

Violence against women is a significant area for feminist theory and activism. Feminists have exposed and documented forms of violence which until very recently remained largely unacknowledged – for example, wife abuse and date rapes. However, while feminists have increased public awareness of violence against women and have successfully lobbied for more stringent penalties for its perpetrators, questions have been raised about the extent of violence against women and even about the definition of violence (Sommers 1994; Roiphe 1993). Some, like the distinguished law professor Catherine MacKinnon, have defined violence as endemic to almost all sexual relations between men and women and as infiltrating almost all activities of human beings (MacKinnon 1989). Others object to such sweeping claims, arguing that they risk trivializing serious acts of violence against women (Sommers 1994; Roiphe 1993).

Naomi Wolf has criticized 'victim feminism,' arguing that in speaking of themselves as victims, 'women identify with powerlessness even at the expense of taking responsibility for the power they do possess.' She advocates, instead, power feminism, which 'examines closely the forces arrayed against a woman so she can exert her power more effectively' (Wolf 1994, 136–7). Rather than focus attention on situations in which women are victims, she recommends that women celebrate the victories of past struggles and exercise their power to realize more positive feminist goals and objectives. Nevertheless, the experience of working-class, non–

English-speaking women indicates that there is till a pressing need to address violence against women in order to empower women to overcome it.

The first section of this chapter examines several competing definitions of wife abuse; the second section analyses statistics on wife abuse; the third discusses methodologies used in investigating it; and the fourth discusses feminist theoretical underpinnings of the literature on wife abuse. The last section presents some personal accounts of wife abuse from women who have survived it.

Problems in Defining Wife Abuse

Language, as feminist epistemologists have demonstrated, encodes power relations. Those who define a 'problem' or elucidate its characteristics are enabled 'to project an interpretation, a definition, a description of their work and actions, that may not be accurate, that may obscure what is really taking place' (hooks 1994, 62). Dorothy Smith has discussed the power of professionals to 'construct' an event by giving significance to some details and not to others. The way in which an event or incident is described in professional discourses (e.g., police reports) frequently differs from the way it was actually experienced by the people involved (Smith 1990, 73–80).

Feminists reject the use of terms such as 'domestic violence' or 'family violence' in describing the abuse of a woman by her spouse because these terms tend to suggest that both partners share responsibility for the violence. Feminists argue that 'family violence' and 'domestic violence' are the terms of professional social workers and bureaucrats who tend to discount the social context in which violence occurs (Barnsley 1985; Pierson et al. 1993; Walker 1990). Discourse on 'family violence' and 'domestic violence' is informed by psychiatric, medical, and therapeutic models which often place the blame for the violence on the behavioural, temperamental, or attitudinal characteristics of the women involved (Dobash and Dobash 1992, 213–50). Larry Tifft (1993, 7) cites several examples:

In disbelief many battered women have faced the accusation that they were battered 'because they had deficiencies' (Flitcraft and Stark, 1978) or 'had asked for it.' Or they had been told that their injuries and bouts with depression were the result of interpersonal disputes, with one or both persons to blame. Many of these professionals have intervened in the belief that by doing so they could 'restore harmony' in the relationship and preserve the family (Martin, 1981:190). 'Restoring harmony,' however, has frequently meant asking these women to accept relational inferiority and the social arrangements that would likely continue to foster their feelings of injustice, dependency, and repression. (McGrath 1979, 16)

Gillian Walker sees a conflict between feminists and professional counsellors:

> [T]he struggle becomes one of contestation over whose knowledge will define the situation, who is to be held to be to blame, and what kind of action will be taken by whom. It breaks down into a struggle between professionals who are the 'experts' mandated to deal with problems in terms of individuals and families, and women's groups who are attempting to develop solutions that dispute male domination through the use of violence and challenge the organization and structuring of family relations. (Walker 1990, 18)

Feminists prefer terms such as 'wife abuse' or 'woman abuse.' 'Wife abuse' emphasizes the fact that women are usually, though not always, victims of violence in the home. 'Woman abuse' emphasizes the experience of the woman, whether she is abused by a spouse or another person. Walker explains that 'a feminist position starts with a validation of women's experience, expresses anger at the range of victim-blaming stances put forward in many varieties of the other models, and is determined to locate the abuse of women in its historical and political context as part of the systematic subjugation of women' (1990, 83). Many feminists also object to the term 'victim of wife abuse' because it 'evokes an image of a helpless, dependent creature, while the reality may be that women who experience abuse demonstrate a great deal of resourcefulness in surviving the violence directed against them' (Dobash and Dobash 1992, 39–40).

However, the term 'wife abuse' can be used in a very narrow sense, which includes only physical assault or battery of a spouse, or in a very broad sense, which might include a harsh glance directed by a man at his spouse. Feminists who give priority to the concepts of subjectivity and experience sometimes suggest that 'abuse' should include whatever a woman experiences as abuse. Judith Grant traces this line of thought to early feminists who could point to 'no theory that proved that women as women were in an *objectively* oppressed situation' and who resolved the problem by defining oppression as 'anything that women *experienced* as oppression' (Grant 1993, 30). This approach was grounded in a justified mistrust of conventional social and political doctrines that was articulated early in the Redstocking manifesto of 1969:

> We regard our personal experiences and our feelings about that experience as the basis for an analysis of our common situation. We cannot rely on existing ideologies as they are all products of male supremacist culture. We question every generalization and accept none that are not confirmed by our experience. (Quoted in Grant 1993, 31)

We may not be able to rely on 'experts' to decide what counts as abuse, but too broad a definition has several disadvantages. Adopting a broad definition of 'abuse' still leaves the task of distinguishing among types of abuse, and although physical, psychological, and even economic acts can do harm to a woman, the variable degrees of severity with which they are felt may not be the best indicators of the differences. Christina Sommers, a professor of philosophy who has questioned feminist research on wife abuse in the United States, argues that broad definitions have been used by 'gender feminists' to inflate numbers and sensationalize the problem of violence against women (Sommers 1994, 188–208); and Linda MacLeod argues that a broad definition of abuse can lead workers in the field to believe that violence is so widespread that nothing but a 'massive structural change in our society' can prevent it, and therefore they can do little about it (MacLeod 1989b, 3). However, Walter DeKeseredy, who has studied abuse in dating relationships, is critical of narrow definitions because they fragment women's experience of abuse by isolating physical, sexual, and emotional abuse from each other and do not convey the reality of abuse as it is actually experienced by women. Some incidents seem trivial, but when located in the context of an ongoing relationship, reveal a pattern of abuse. He supports a broad definition because it better captures women's subjective experience of abuse and does not create a 'hierarchy of abuse based on seriousness' (1995, 159–60).

'Wife abuse,' 'wife assault,' and 'battering' are terms that are often used in the literature on this subject. 'Assault' is part of Canadian legal terminology, which distinguishes between assault, sexual assault, and aggravated sexual assault. Legal definitions are required for laying charges and prosecuting perpetrators of wife abuse (Statistics Canada 1994, 105). They include several kinds of physical assault. Statistics Canada reports that

> the most prevalent forms of wife assault were women being pushed, grabbed, and shoved, followed by threats of hitting, slapping, throwing objects, and kicking, biting, and hitting with fists. A significant number of women also reported being beaten up, sexually assaulted, choked, hit with an object, and having a gun or knife used against them. Rarely was only one type of violence reported. (Statistics Canada 1994, 12)

Studies by MacLeod, the 1993 report by the Canadian Panel on Violence against Women, and the 1994 report from Statistics Canada on family violence define 'abuse' broadly to include physical, sexual, economic, and spiritual acts of violence. The report of Statistics Canada defines 'abuse' to include 'physical and sexual assault, intimidation, mental or emotional abuse, neglect, deprivation and financial exploitation' (1994, i). Physical and emotional abuse often occur together. The report identifies five signs of emotional abuse by a husband:

He is jealous and doesn't want her to talk to other men; he tries to limit her contact with family or friends; he insists on knowing who she is with and where she is at all times; he calls her names to put her down or make her feel bad; he prevents her from knowing about or having access to the family income, even if she asks; and any emotional abuse. (Statistics Canada 1994, 11)

'Battering' usually suggests extreme physical violence in which a woman is subjected to serious physical attack and is a helpless victim. However, one African-born victim of abuse objects to the term. She says, 'I hate the word "battered." Battering has the connotation that he [my spouse] physically deformed my face or me and that I am finished. I am not yet finished – and I am ready to fight on; he will not destroy me' (Musisi and Muktar 1992, 20). Jones finds that the term 'battered,' which identifies women primarily as victims, is at odds with their own perception of their situation. She notes that women who have been battered and know 'the immense daily expenditure of strength and attention and self-discipline it takes to survive, rarely identify themselves as "victims." They think of themselves as strong women who can somehow "cope"' (Jones 1994, 83). MacLeod, who studied abused women in shelters, accepts the term but defines it very broadly:

Wife battering is the loss of dignity, control, and safety as well as the feeling of powerlessness and entrapment experienced by women who are the direct victims of ongoing or repeated physical, psychological, economic, sexual and/or verbal violence or who are subjected to persistent threats or the witnessing of such violence against their children, other relatives, friends, pets and/or cherished possessions, by their boyfriends, husbands, live-in lovers, ex-husbands or ex-lovers, whether male or female. (MacLeod 1987, 16)

The report of the Canadian-African Newcomer Aid Centre of Toronto considered formulating an 'African' definition of abuse but concluded that 'since we are in Canada, we must use the Canadian legal definition and refine it in our own African context.' Such a definition, they noted, should include 'intentional physical and psychological abuse' and 'sexual manipulation/abuse,' particularly if it was 'directed by men towards women with the sole purpose of intimidating' or controlling their behaviour (Musisi and Muktar 1992, 20–1).

A report 'on anti-racist and culturally appropriate approaches to combatting women assault' gave a list of things that service providers counted as instances of assault on women. Forcing a wife to engage in activities against her will topped the list, along with forcing her into a lifestyle alien to her or against her values. Also included were not allowing her to visit relatives or friends; 'violence in the name of love'; using her as a 'tool' to work or care for aged in-laws; being dominated by sisters-in-law; and requiring her to ask permission to go out. In many of these cases, the husband was not the perpetrator but another member of the husband's family, as when a wife was verbally humiliated and belittled by the man's family. But a woman's own family might be abusive, for also included in the list were 'forced marriages' (Toronto Advisory Committee on Cultural Approaches to Violence against Women 1992, 12).

None of the instances on the list fits a legal definition of 'assault,' and it would be difficult to determine a common characteristic in all of them. Different counsellors had different things in mind, and they reflected different conceptions of gender roles and different cultural norms.[1] Consequently, some caution is required when discussing a community-based group's work with women whom it describes as victims of 'wife abuse' or 'assault.'

Most of the community-based groups studied in this book use the term 'wife abuse,' and this book follows their lead, but without attempting to impose either a broad or a narrow definition on the term. Instead, it attempts to explain what each group means by the term. When a woman goes to a community-based group seeking help, issues of definition and labelling have practical consequences. If a man has physically struck his wife, the situation is fairly clear. However, patriarchal norms in a culture may give a man authority, power, and control over his wife. When their relations are exposed to the scrutiny of service providers because some kinds of behaviour have become intolerable or some acts have become life-threatening, counsellors may characterize other aspects of the man's behaviour as 'abuse.' If the perceptions of the woman differ from those of her service providers, the question arises as to whose interpretation of what occurs at home is to be privileged. Such a question raises the issue of power and authority. Counsellors are exercising power when they define a woman as abused, even when the consequences are beneficial and enable the woman to gain access to a range of social services. For example, a feminist counsellor may think that requiring a woman to wear a veil counts as wife abuse, but a Muslim woman may not think of it in that way at all. She may simply not want to attract attention to herself by dressing differently, or she may believe that the veil would be an obstacle to getting a job. Her resistance to wearing the veil cannot be assumed to symbolize rejection of patriarchal norms or of traditional gender roles.

Women who go to community-based groups are usually more interested in stopping the violence than in disputing the hierarchy of their family relations. Counsellors also want to serve the immediate needs of the women, but doing so postpones achieving the larger feminist goals of social transformation to a future date.

Problems in Quantifying the Incidence of Wife Abuse

In contemporary society, few Canadians would deny that there is violence against women although they might disagree about its extent. Given the ambiguity of the term 'wife abuse,' however, it is difficult to judge feminist claims that wife abuse is widespread (Walker 1990; Barnsley 1985). The data that are available are based on a variety of different definitions of wife abuse (DeKeseredy and Hinch 1991, 7–15). Since services for abused women and education programs for preventing abuse compete for resources with programs against child abuse, pornography, and other social problems, service providers may cite figures that overestimate its occurrence.

It is difficult to document the extent of wife abuse in Canadian society, let alone its prevalence in any one ethnic or racial group.

Legislation now requires professionals such as doctors to report suspected abuse, but the extent to which they comply with the new regulations is unknown. It is also difficult to determine whether incidents of wife abuse have increased in recent times or whether reports of wife abuse have increased.

There are similar difficulties in measuring the extent of assault or 'battering,' and they may result in underestimates or overestimates of its occurrence. Linda MacLeod found that 'counting battered women was not always simple':

> Battered women did not want to be counted, did not always see themselves as 'battered women,' did not always accept the idea that they are somehow different from other women or even that their experiences are so far apart from those of other women. And then there were women who had never been physically struck or threatened but defined themselves as battered women on the basis of psychological battering. (MacLeod 1987, 4)

Social, cultural, and political inhibitions make women reluctant to reveal abuse that they encounter in their homes, and even more reluctant to report it to the police or to lay formal charges. Gender socialization tends to place responsibility for the smooth functioning of the home on the woman, and when abuse erupts she may feel that revealing her situation will bring shame to her, to her family, and to her friends. For Filipino woman, for instance, reporting abuse 'would cause the person, her family and community embarrassment' (Cervantes 1988, 5).

Immigrant women may be reluctant to involve people who represent what they consider an alien culture. Sometimes language is a barrier between a woman and the police, and her abuse may never be communicated and recorded. A Filipina might 'feel too intimidated to phone the police partly because she would have to express herself totally in English, to a male foreigner, in uniform' (Cervantes 1988, 5). As another study indicates, 'many women belonging to racially or ethnically oppressed minorities "have come to mistrust the police" and the courts and to fear their intervention in domestic conflicts' (Pierson et al. 1993, 111).

Some working-class, non–English-speaking women may fear that if they report abuse by their spouses, their entire family will be deported (Musisi and Muktar 1992, 16); or that the spouse will either refuse to sponsor their relatives or withdraw his sponsorship of them. A woman who has entered Canada as a fiancée but has not married the man who sponsored her may become a victim of abuse (e.g., mail-order brides). She may be reluctant to involve the police for fear of being deported. Sometimes the spouse has deliberately misinformed the woman, and she may fear that her children will be removed from her care. The woman's lack of job-related skills is an additional impediment to reporting the abuse.

One of the estimates of the occurrence of wife abuse most frequently cited in the literature and by service providers in community-based groups is that one in ten women is a victim of wife abuse. Linda MacLeod, for instance, estimated in 1980 that in 'each year one in ten women in Canada are psychologically, physically or sexually battered by their husbands or live-in partners.' She derived this figure from her study of transition homes (MacLeod 1982, 1). When these figures were first published, women's groups across the country demanded that resources be allocated for public education and services to help abused women and their children (Pierson et al. 1993, 111). In a 1987 study, MacLeod noted that there are 'at least 600,000 battered women across Canada [who] may have sought some sort of outside help.'[2] In addition, there are women who do not report their battering to any official agency or front-line service. She concluded that 'even if we "guess-timate" that two out of three women report their battering to some official agency – a very conservative estimate according to front-line workers interviewed – this would mean that almost one million women in Canada may be battered each year' (1987, 7).

Walter DeKeseredy and Ronald Hinch are critical of MacLeod's estimates, arguing that since the shelter population is not representative of Canadian society at large, her figures on wife abuse in Canadian society are no 'better than guesses' (DeKeseredy and Hinch 1991, 14). MacLeod acknowledges that her 1980 figure was 'not derived from a random sample of all women, but rather was extrapolated from the number of women who stayed at transition houses and women's emergency shelters, the number of women who filed for divorce on the grounds of cruelty and estimates of the proportion of battered women who need help but do not stay at transition houses' (MacLeod 1989b, 13).

Other studies suggest an even higher incidence of abuse. Melanie Randall and Lori Haskell's Women's Safety Project was prepared for the Canadian Panel on Violence against Women. They selected their sample of 420 women living in Toronto from 'a list of all the residential addresses (including houses and apartments in highrises and other buildings).' They used this method to 'include [a] diverse group of women somewhat resembling the female population in the city.' This method of selecting respondents meant that 'women did not need to be officially registered as voters or taxpayers to be included in the sample, nor did they have to be listed in the telephone book. Women did not have to be Canadian citizens or meet any other such criteria for participation in the study.' The sample included women on landed immigrant visas and on student/work visas (Canadian Panel on Violence against Women 1993, A3).

The Women's Safety Project defined 'physical assault / physical abuse' as 'any act of physical force and/or violence used against a woman, ranging from slapping, hitting, shoving and punching to repeated beatings as well as attempts on a woman's life' (Canadian Panel on Violence against Women 1993, A12). It also included in its definition the phrase 'or being hurt in any other way.' The project found that 'one in four women has experienced physical assault (or ongoing physical assaults) in an intimate relationship with a man'; that is, 27 per cent, or 115 women, reported 'an experience of physical abuse in an intimate relationship with a husband, live-in partner, boyfriend or date' (Canadian Panel on Violence against Women 1993, A7).

Statistics Canada, in *Family Violence in Canada* (1994), reports even higher figures, based on what it describes as the first 'national survey on violence against women that is statistically representative of all Canadian women living in the ten provinces and generalizable to the population at large.' It defines abuse very broadly to include 'physical and sexual assault, intimidation, men-

tal or emotional abuse, neglect, deprivation and financial exploitation' (1994, 2). The survey interviewed 12,300 women eighteen
years of age or over by telephone about their experiences of 'physical and sexual violence, experiences of sexual harassment, and
their perceptions of their own personal safety.' The women were
selected using the random digit dialling method of contacting, in
which every household has a chance of being selected (1994, 3).
The survey found that '29% of ever-married women have experienced either physical or sexual violence by a current or previous
marital/common-law partner ... In 1992, 92% of victims in cases of
spousal assault were women, and 93% of the accused were men'
(1994, i–ii).

   There is violence against women in immigrant communities, but
the extent of the violence cannot be determined. Reports from
coalitions of community-based groups are sometimes based on surveys conducted by just one or two organizations, so that it is difficult to measure its incidence for any one ethnic or racial group
(Tyagi 1993). Also, some of the reports are based on surveys only
of clients of the organizations, who are likely to differ in important
ways from those who did not use these services. Their surveys cannot be used as a measure of wife abuse in the community as a
whole (Papp 1990; Chinese Family Life Services 1989).

   Academics, service providers, and feminist activists point out
that wife abuse is found in all communities, ages, classes, and races;
however, Statistics Canada's 1994 report notes some variations. For
instance, there is a higher rate of wife assault among 'newer marital partnerships (of two years or less).' Although it found wife
assault at all income levels, those with incomes of less than $15,000
had rates that were twice the national average for other groups.
Women between the ages of eighteen and twenty-four reported
four times the national average of incidents of wife assault. However, there was no distinction in the rates of wife assault according
to the educational level of the victim (1994, 8).

   One study which surveyed a broad range of immigrants from
Africa who live in Toronto found that a victim of abuse is likely to
be a relatively new immigrant. She is likely to be young, that is,
below the age of thirty-five. She is likely to have been sponsored to

Canada by her spouse. The family's income tends to be under $30,000 a year, and the woman contributes slightly less to it than her husband (Musisi and Muktar 1992, 165).

The Chinese Family Life Services surveyed 54 women who were using their services. The report lists the kinds of abuses this sample of women encountered. Physical abuse included 'pushing, slapping, punching, choking, pulling hair, kicking, stepping, pointing, forcing a bar of soap into the wife's mouth, and pouring hot soup on the wife.' Verbal abuse included 'the use of abusive language, belittling of wife's personality/integrity, housework, parenting skill and country of origin.' The list also included 'destruction of property,' 'neglect/isolation,' 'financial control,' 'forcing wife to leave the home,' and the 'harassment of the wife's parental family and friends.' 'Sexual abuse included forced sex and forcing the wife to perform sexual acts portrayed in pornographic movies and magazines.' Threats, homicidal and suicidal, were also included (1989, 12).

This survey found that length of residence in Canada did not alter the pattern of abuse. Abuse occurred among those who had been in Canada only a couple of months, but a large proportion of the women had been here between two and forty years. Some victims of wife abuse had university education; others, only some high-school education. Only three of the women were in professional and managerial jobs; thirty were in sales, clerical, or factory jobs; twenty of the women were not working outside the home; and one was a student. There are no statistics on how many of these women spoke English (Chinese Family Life Services 1989, 4–11).

A report prepared by the South Asian Family Support Services, based on the women who called the organization for help, found abuse among those who had chosen their own partners and those who had had marriages arranged for them. Most of the women had been married and lived in Canada for several years (Papp 1990, 22–3). Such findings confirm the claim that victims of wife abuse come from all socio-economic backgrounds.

It is difficult to measure how many women in immigrant communities are victimized and to determine their socio-economic characteristics. Women who speak English and work in middle-class jobs have the choice of accessing services from mainstream social service agencies or from community-based groups. They can more easily obtain legal information, particularly regarding immigration policies, and make informed choices. Even so, they may experience alienation and isolation from white-Canadian society and may be reluctant to break their ties with their ethnic and racial communities. Working-class women, especially those who do not speak English, are trapped in abusive homes. How community groups are responding to their situation is the subject of the next chapter.

Methodology

Identity and Social Context

Feminists have critiqued 'androcentric' research for failing to acknowledge the 'locations' of the researchers and for presenting interpretations of social phenomena as a 'god's eye view' or as a 'view from nowhere.' They have argued that studies presented as objective, rational, and neutral accounts of social phenomena have been biased by the race, class, and gender identities of their authors. 'Androcentric knowledge' presents universal explanations of phenomena, not as interpretations, but as the only 'truth.' In contrast, feminist methodology argues that all accounts are historically situated and their interpretations are informed by the race, class, and gender of their authors (Di Stefano 1990; Harding 1990).

I am a South Asian woman who was born in India and immigrated to Canada in 1970. However, such an identification of myself by race invites an essentialist or stereotypical judgment of my identity (Alcoff 1988), and it suggests that the racial identity I shared with the respondents in my interviews created a greater commonality of interests and understanding than what really existed. During my research, I found that, despite my being a South Asian woman, my respondents did not always think of me as an insider. Yet, at academic meetings and conferences on Canadian campuses dominated by white middle-class professors, my race almost always located me as an outsider. At academic conferences, I was expected to discuss racism, but when I did, white middle-class feminists refrained from making any comments or engaging me in any discussion. I spoke, but I do not know whether I was heard.

My South Asian respondents viewed me as an assimilated immigrant and a feminist, who might be knowledgeable about their values and norms but not necessarily share them. Nevertheless, our ethnic identity did create a bond, and they would confide in me, describing what they thought about the racism of Canadian society or about Canadian norms concerning personal relations, and revealing their own histories.

One day a Sikh woman at a community-based organization invited me for a coffee at the local cafeteria. During the next two hours, she told me her story. She recounted twenty-two years of abuse from her spouse, whose behaviour only grew worse over time. Though he began his career as an engineer, he became an alcoholic and a manic depressive, and extremely violent. When the violence became life-threatening, the woman sought help. Although she had a bachelor's degree and spoke English well, the years of abuse had eroded her confidence and self-esteem. She described her struggle to support her four children on welfare and eventually her successful attempt to find a minimum-wage job. Her spouse had isolated her for years, and now that she was single, the stigma of being a victim of wife abuse still kept her from mixing freely with the Sikh community. She has made significant gains in normalizing her situation, and her children are all university students, but she intensely regrets the fact that her children had to spend their childhoods witnessing abuse and subsequently became isolated from the Sikh community.

My Chinese and black respondents interacted more cautiously with me and often asked about my ideas about feminism before they talked freely. They were open with me, however, when we discussed the prevalence of racism, the Eurocentric biases of social service agencies, or the racism of service providers.

My respondents perceived me, a university professor, as a privileged individual who had a permanent job, while many of them worked on short-term contracts with no guarantee of continuation. This was revealed to me by a South Asian Muslim, a one-time victim of wife abuse who worked as a counsellor at a community-based agency I had visited several times and whose staff I had come to know. Twice, just before the appointed time for an interview with me, she called to postpone our meeting. Finally she came to my house, and as we sat at the kitchen table making casual conversation before the formal interview, she confessed that she had cancelled our meetings because she thought it would be 'scary' to talk to a professor. Then a friend told her that it was flattering that a professor wanted to listen to her, and this persuaded her to do the interview.

My research with community-based groups was conducted at a time when there was some acknowledgment that racism and sexism mar the lives of some Canadian women. Throughout the 1970s and 1980s, reports commissioned by state agencies and other studies documented the problem of widespread racism in Canadian society, particularly in the media and in the areas of policing, education, housing, and social services (Henry and Ginzberg 1984; Henry et al. 1995; Doyle and Visano 1987).

One state response to racism is the promotion of a multicultural ideology which acknowledges the place of all ethnic and racial groups in the Canadian mosaic. The ideology is enshrined in the Multiculturalism Act of 1988 and the Charter of Rights (Fleras and Elliott 1992). But some critics have argued that a multicultural policy is only intended to 'contain' the discontent of ethnic groups who are resentful of the distribution of power and prestige in Canadian society (Anderson and Frideres 1981). Others argue that the multicultural policy ghettoizes racial and ethnic groups and slows their assimilation into Canadian society (Bissoondath 1994). Margaret Cannon argues that racism persists in everyday life despite the rhetoric of multiculturalism:

We may not be calling people nigger or chink or kike or raghead on the street, but we make it clear that the values we want enshrined in our institutions are the values of the founding races – white, Catholic, Protestant, European culture, Western philosophy. We might add an African author or two to a reading list or take kids to a Spike Lee film. We can drop in on the Chinese Cultural Centre in Vancouver and walk through a Ming garden and then stop off at the mall to buy a Thai silk scarf for Grandma. But if a Sikh war veteran shows up at some Legion Halls, he won't be welcome if he wears a turban. We can buy, eat, and consume the multicultural mosaic without ever believing in it at all. (Cannon 1995, 271)

Frances Henry and Carol Tator (1994) note that although lip service is paid to the need to eradicate racism, organizations and institutions are far more committed to maintaining the status quo in order to stabilize or increase their power.

In the 1980s middle-class women from Asia, Africa, and the Caribbean criticized the ethnocentric theories and practices of white middle-class feminists who tended to attribute all problems to gender discrimination. They argued that women from Asia, Africa, and the Caribbean experience multiple and integrated oppressions of race, class, and gender (Agnew 1991; Carty 1991; Daenzer 1993). During the 1980s feminists successfully raised public consciousness about the problem of wife abuse, and state agencies demonstrated their commitment to abused women by commissioning reports and allocating resources to provide services. They have recognized the integrated oppression of women from Asia, Africa, and the Caribbean and acknowledged the additional barriers encountered in trying to escape abusive relationships (Canadian Panel on Violence against Women 1993; Randall 1989).

The writing of this book occurred at a time when some feminist principles and research were being questioned by scholars such as Christina Sommers (1994), Katie Roiphe (1993), and Donna Laframboise (1996). These writers are part of what has been termed the backlash against feminism. A common criticism of the women's movement, supported even by feminists (e.g., Naomi Wolf), is that it has become divorced from the everyday lives of women. These writers are critical of feminism at several levels, including the issues that the movement advocates and supports, and its increasingly academic and abstract language.

Sommers, Roiphe, and Laframboise deny the extent of violence that the woman's movement claims is experienced by women. Sommers notes that the frequently cited story of an increase in incidents of violence against women on Super Bowl Sunday is derived from data which have been seriously distorted and misrepresented (Sommers 1994). Roiphe has questioned the truthfulness of some accounts presented in 'Take Back the Night' marches on American university campuses. She argues that women traumatized by male violence are reluctant to reveal their personal tragedy in a public forum and that the women who participate in public rallies and demonstrations are probably seeking attention by exaggerating their ordeals in dating relationships or retaliating against a male for a presumed slight (1993). Such works make one wary of statistics that are now commonly accepted – for example, that one in ten women experiences some form of violence in Canada.

Laframboise, a Canadian journalist who describes herself as a 'dissident feminist,' believes that North American feminism is giving 'female equality a bad name' and that 'mainstream feminism' espouses many of the same extremist ideas about patriarchy and violence against women as its 'lunatic fringe' (1996, 7). She particularly criticizes 'popular feminist spokespersons' such as Catherine MacKinnon and the feminist magazines that have eagerly and unquestioningly embraced and publicized her view that 'all sex is rape' (1996, 25–33).

Laframboise labels the Canadian Panel on Violence against Women as a 'national embarrassment' (1996, 41) since it has reproduced uncritically 'feminist dogma' about patriarchy and asserted that 'in a society whose very structure condones male violence, all men, whether or not they are violent, derive substantial benefit from its institutionalization' (1996, 41–4). She argues that although men benefit from a patriarchal ideology, individual men cannot be held 'morally responsible' for its existence. Laframboise argues that feminist discourse focuses not on violence, but on the gender of the male perpetrators. This perspective denies 'real female suffering' and understanding of 'the whole truth of women's lives' in favour of advancing a dogma (1996, 45).

The political climate in which the writing of this book took place was relegating to history some of the work that was being documented in it. A conservative agenda encoded in terms like 'family values' had moved beyond rhetoric and was finding expression in spending cuts that were being imposed on women's organizations and in reductions of the social services available to them. In Ontario a Conservative government was elected on the platform of a 'common sense revolution' that promised to give priority to reducing the provincial debt by eliminating those programs that were increasingly perceived by some middle-class people as unnecessarily generous – for example, welfare. In 1995 the provincial government announced cuts to all women's organizations that were providing educational programs, although it allowed these groups to continue to provide social services to women. In April 1996 the government cut an additional $2.9 million from programs relating to violence against women and closed the Ontario Advisory Council on Women's Issues (*Globe and Mail*, 12 April 1996, A1).

Fieldwork

Investigation of the everyday realities of women's lives, often ignored or devalued by androcentric research, reveals that what is termed 'normal' or 'routine' is often based on special power relations. Dorathy Smith and Sandra Harding suggest that feminist researchers must ask questions which arise from women's lives and experiences so as to expose the social order and gender relations (Smith 1987; Harding 1987). A 'neutral' observer might ask why a victim of wife abuse does not simply leave her home. This question places the responsibility for her difficulties on the woman. However, when questions are allowed to emerge from women's experiences, a researcher is more likely to ask, for instance, what barriers are encountered by women which make it difficult for them to leave their abusive homes. Such questions direct our attention to the race, class, and gender biases that sometimes limit women's choices, especially when they live on the margins of mainstream society. The answers may not lie in 'problems' in their experiences or lives, but 'in the beliefs and activities of people at the centre who make policies and engage in social practices that shape marginal lives' (Harding 1993, 54).

Traditional research methodology tends to transform subjects into objects of knowledge by 'assimilating those subjects to physical objects, reducing their subjectivity and specificity to interchangeable, observable features' (Code 1993, 32). Feminist research methodology, in contrast, engages the subject of the enquiry in the research process, acknowledges the expertise of the subject, and provides a forum in which suppressed and subordinated voices can be heard. Feminists contend that in conventional methodology the researcher exercises control, authority, and ownership. The research belongs to the researcher, who appropriates the experiences of others to prove theories or to serve personal goals. Such research subordinates the voice of the subject and makes the researcher the expert (hooks 1988, 42–8).

Feminist research methodology serves the needs, goals, and objectives of the subject as well as those of the researcher. Subjects of an enquiry collaborate with the researcher in determining the questions that will guide the study. Questions are not imposed upon the subject by an individual who assumes the role of expert. Equal participation transforms the power relations between the subject and the researcher and makes the research non-exploitative (Acker, Barry, and Esseveld 1991; Nielsen 1990). The research in this book gives voice to middle-class service providers from Asia, Africa, and the Caribbean and discusses from their perspectives the barriers encountered by women from immigrant communities in accessing social services and the attempts of community-based organizations to provide services and advocate on behalf of abused women.

When I began my fieldwork on community-based organizations of immigrant women in 1990, I found that although the initial objective of community-based groups was to provide settlement services such as language-learning classes for immigrant women, some had responded to emerging needs by adding services for victims of wife abuse (e.g., the South Asian Women's Group and the Korean-Canadian Women's Association). Other community-based groups were organized specifically to provide services to victims of wife abuse (e.g., the South Asian Family Support Services). My focus on wife abuse emerged out of discussions with women from Asia, Africa, and the Caribbean which were initially intended to document how race, class, and gender intersect in their lives. I subsequently included research on shelters for women as part of my fieldwork.

My fieldwork included participant observation of the work of ethno-specific and immigrant women's groups that provide services to victims of wife abuse. I observed the interactions of their personnel with state agencies and with other women's organizations. Since 1990 I have attended conferences and workshops organized by immigrant women's groups on wife abuse. I also attended the three-day professional retreats for service providers organized by the Ontario Council of Agencies Serving Immigrants in 1993 and 1994. At those retreats, I attended workshops on wife abuse and had informal interviews with service providers from various parts of the province. I served a two-year term (1992–4) as a volunteer board member of the South Asian Family Support Services. Since 1993 I have been elected a board member of the Working Skills Centre and am currently serving a two-year term (1996–8) as its president. In 1996 I was elected for a two-year term to the board of the North York Women's Shelter. I am also on the advisory board of the Canadian Tamil Women's Association. As a board member, I have accompanied executive directors to state agencies that fund these groups' programs, reviewed their applications for funds, participated in their staff-development days, and attended their annual general meetings.

My research was intended to be collaborative and non-exploitative. Traditional research methodologies of fieldwork have sometimes adopted the stance of doing 'research on' a particular group of people. If the researchers were outsiders to the society that they were researching, they were considered neutral observers and their research an objective reporting of facts (Westkott 1990; Cook and Fonow 1990). But feminists argue that feelings and emotions are as significant as reason in research, although their role is usually unacknowledged or criticized by androcentric approaches (Jaggar 1983, 377–89). Feminists have been critical of the value system underlying such research techniques and have argued for the use of methodologies of 'research with' the subject (Harding 1987; 1990).

Despite my desire to collaborate, the research was perceived by the respondents as my project. My respondents had taken time from providing services and counselling abused women to discuss their work with me. However, although they encouraged me to attend their workshops and other community events, they were not keen to have ongoing discussions on a one-to-one basis. Some of the reasons were pragmatic and related to their work and family schedules. The women often worked in organizations that were short-staffed, and were thereby compelled to fulfil their obligations to provide services to abused women on tight schedules. Sometimes the women were required to attend evening meetings of their board or were asked to participate in events organized by other community-based organizations or governmental agencies. Some of the women had young children and other family obligations. All of these reasons made them reluctant to commit additional time to the project of identifying how race, class, and gender informed the provision of social services to abused women. My suggestion that they review the transcripts of their interviews was usually declined, with an expression of confidence in my discretion.

The women's reluctance to engage in ongoing collaboration in this project also revealed different priorities that women in different locations assign to academic research. Community-based groups undertake research, but from a 'utilitarian' perspective (Ristock and Pennell 1996, 34). Often the goal of their research is to document the need for a particular service or to make a case for additional funds. My respondents were wary of my research, wondering whether it would compete with theirs for funds from government agencies or whether it might overlap with their studies and reports. Some asked me about my motives for doing the research. I explained I wished to document their work with the hope of informing public policy and creating some understanding of how race, class, and gender discrimination impinged on the lives of abused women. These long-term goals contrasted with their focus on the immediate work of providing services.

Power was not eliminated from the interview process. Power, in fact, is not static but shifts and changes in different contexts, and power relations 'form and reform in various combinations' (Ristock and Pennell 1996, 4). The respondents and I exercised power at different points. The respondents had the power to grant me some time to discuss their work, and they could terminate the interview at any given time (although none did). They had knowledge and information which I needed. They were the 'knowers' and the 'experts,' and their views guided my enquiry. In writing this book, I exercised the power to give greater or lesser significance to some interviews than others and to use the information provided to me to answer the questions that I thought most relevant in a discussion of abused women.

I interviewed approximately seventy-five service providers who were working as administrators, counsellors, program coordinators, and office staff. In addition, I interviewed volunteers on the boards of directors of community-based organizations and activist women from Asia, Africa, and the Caribbean involved with these organizations. I began my interviews by locating women who were active within immigrant women's service organizations. After each interview, I asked for the names of three other women and subsequently asked them to meet with me. Interviews were usually recorded at the workplace of the respondent and lasted approximately two hours. Some women declined to be recorded, and I made notes after these interviews. I began the interviews by asking some open-ended questions but did not impose a research agenda on my subjects. Questions were used as 'openings, as pathways ... in which they would feel free and able to speak their thoughts and their feelings' (Brown and Gilligan 1992, 19). Instead of leading the interview, I let the respondents' interests and expertise guide it.

During the interviews, women only rarely identified themselves as victims of wife abuse, but some personal histories were revealed to me by third parties. I observed victims of wife abuse during conferences on wife abuse, at workshops, and in the offices of community-based organizations. The histories of many women who have left their abusive homes tell remarkable stories about their resourcefulness and courage against all odds. They confronted and overcame the obstacles of not knowing English, having no job-related skills and little or no money, lacking information about their legal rights, being unfamiliar with Canadian social assistance programs, and feeling alienated from Canadian society.

It is difficult for counsellors to enquire into a woman's personal and intimate life. Attempting to raise her consciousness of injustice in her personal relations may generate resentment and anger, and intervention may risk disrupting a relationship that is necessary for her personal survival. For example, women may find some satisfaction in the traditional gender roles of being good wives and mothers, however oppressive these might be, and may wish to preserve a relationship even though it is structured according to patriarchal values and norms.[3] A non–English-speaking woman from Asia, Africa, or the Caribbean may find the prospect of making it on her own, in a society informed by racial inequality, a daunting and intimidating one. If she has no parents or siblings in Canada, she may only want to reduce the violence of her spouse.

Almost all my respondents spoke of abused women's desires to maintain their relationship with their spouses and to preserve their marriages. One counsellor explained that she gives her clients a variety of information about their legal rights and the social services that are available to them. However, she compared sending a woman back to the abusive family to setting a 'time-bomb': the woman is empowered by the information and it makes her less tolerant of abuse, but she risks retaliation from her spouse for seeking help.

It is also difficult to facilitate the oppressed in coming to voice. Women have a right to their privacy and may not wish to expose their relationships to the scrutiny of outsiders. Telling their stories can be painful and humiliating, and it requires them to relive experiences and to feel again forgotten and perhaps repressed emotions. Coming to voice could be the beginning of a healing process, but abused women suffer from lack of self-esteem after years of abuse. Telling their stories, even to service providers, requires a great deal of courage and confidence, and they may reveal the full extent of the abuse that they have experienced only after many months. Few of the victims of wife abuse who were receiving services at the time of my research participated in the conferences or workshops which they had been encouraged by their service providers to attend.

There were some occasions when a 'safe space' was created by service providers to enable the victims of wife abuse to speak of their experiences. One workshop that I attended was held at a public-housing complex in downtown Toronto. Service providers from community-based agencies brought one or two of their clients with them. They were working-class women with limited ability to speak English, but the organizers tried to get the women to share their experiences across cultural and linguistic barriers with a variety of innovative techniques.

One strategy was to ask the women to act out scenes of wife abuse from their past lives with the help of the service providers whom they had come with. The women participated in these scenes with much less enthusiasm than the service providers. Another strategy was to ask the women to draw a scene of abuse. One woman drew scenes of a man behind bars, and another a house surrounded by trees and enclosed by a fence. A facilitator collected these drawings and made a collage of them on the blackboard. The service providers then interpreted the collage in an effort to explain the significance the women attached to various aspects of their experience.

The interviews conducted with the service providers generated important information, but they also gave me an insight into how the women felt about their work and the women whom they were helping (Oakley 1981; Geiger 1990; Anderson et al. 1990).[4] My respondents saw themselves as knowledgeable front-line workers engaged in valuable work, and they saw me as an academic collecting data for research. This does not mean, however, that they valued academic research or thought that it had much relevance to their day-to-day work. They were sceptical and asked questions: why was I doing the research and who would benefit from it? They gave priority to their everyday work rather than to collaborating in the research project, and they were not always persuaded by my arguments about the value of constructing a knowledge base that could be used to inform public policy about immigrant women from Asia, Africa, and the Caribbean. Their concern was with the here and now, with how to protect the women from abusive spouses, how to help them obtain social services and resources like housing, welfare, and employment, and how to help them cope with isolation and alienation.

The interview sometimes provided an opportunity for a respondent to reflect, away from the incessant demands of her day-to-day work, and to express her frustrations. It was often a safe place (at least when the recorder had been shut off) where a respondent could confide her views of 'feminists' (by which was meant white middle-class feminists) and discuss how her own ideas diverged. A commonly cited point was the desire of abused women to preserve their marriages, which respondents felt is not given importance in feminist research. Sometimes, in the course of the interview, there would be a moment when several ideas suddenly fell into place, and a respondent would say, 'I had never thought of it that way before' or 'I didn't realize that before.'

The ideology of the counsellors whom I interviewed emphasized the moral or political rights of women, but they defended some social or cultural values that might conflict with these rights. They said that women have the right to live in a violence-free home, and that women have a right to be treated equally without discrimination on the basis of race, class, gender, and immigration status. Nonetheless, they defended arranged marriages, and they were not sure that women should have an equal voice in making decisions within the family, or should share responsibility for the family's economic welfare and care of the children. Their ambivalence was evident in their attitudes towards a woman leaving the family home or seeking a divorce. Only some of the service providers took an uncompromising view against patriarchy, exercise of authority within the home by males, or males' attempts to control the women.

Some of my respondents were feminists; others were satisfied with traditional gender roles. Some were professional social workers; others had training in fields unrelated to their work at community-based agencies. Some of the women were lesbians. Some were articulate and militant about sexism and racism in Canadian soci-

ety; others were happy to have overcome their own personal difficulties and to be making a new life for themselves. The different
identities and locations of these women gave them different understandings of wife abuse, and this raises a difficult issue: should some
of their views be privileged, or can they be integrated into one? And
should the views of the counsellors be privileged over those of their
clients?

Some feminists argue that although there is no single position
from which alone knowledge can be developed, some locations are
better than others (Hartsock 1987, 159). Women who are engaged
in the practical tasks of everyday living, for instance, may be better
positioned than men who are freed from this work and whose
thinking is characterized by more abstractness and impersonality
(Smith 1987; 1990). Helen Longino explains that women 'who
become self-conscious agents' in their work 'are able to incorporate men's perspectives as well as their own and hence to develop
a more accurate, more objective, set of beliefs about the world'
(1993, 106).

Uma Narayan, a South Asian feminist living in the United States,
argues that the oppressed have an epistemic advantage because
they have the knowledge of their own social context and of that of
the dominant group. She would privilege the perspective of the
oppressed (in the present case, of victims of wife abuse):

> It is *easier* and *more likely* for the oppressed to have critical insights
> into the conditions of their own oppression than it is for those who
> live outside these structures. Those who actually live the oppression
> of class, race, or gender have faced the issues that such oppressions
> generate in a variety of different situations. The insights and emo-
> tional responses engendered by those situations are a legacy with
> which they confront any new issue or situation. (Narayan 1990, 264)

In contrast, Bat-Ami Bar On denies that marginality is a ground for
claiming epistemic privilege (Bar On 1993, 87).

An abused woman is an authority about her lived reality, but
experience by itself needs to be ordered and interpreted before it
can generate knowledge. For Judith Grant, 'experience by itself

leaves too much unexplained,' and it does not provide much basis for imagining a liberated future. Moreover, 'experience is always contaminated by ideology,' and one must step outside ordinary experience in order to critique lived reality (1993, 100). The feminist researcher does not merely describe incidents of oppression but interprets that reality (Acker, Barry, and Esseveld 1991). Therefore, I have concluded that both counsellors and clients must be given voice in this work, and I have not tried to resolve the issues that arise in their work together, but only to show how and why they arise. Neither victims nor counsellors have the last word on wife abuse, and neither mainstream feminists nor their critics have come up with the ultimate explanations or solutions. I do think, however, that the victims and counsellors have the advantage of practical experience over the theoreticians, and theirs are the most prominent voices here.

The counsellors are engaged in feminist work, although they do not all share feminist goals of social transformation of gender relations. Their goals are more immediate and entail finding solutions for women here and now. Most counsellors attempt to find workable compromises which give priority to women's rights but maintain some of the culturally sanctioned privileges of their spouses. This research is feminist, therefore, to the extent that it allows the women who are victims of abuse and the women who counsel them to speak for themselves, and it draws on feminist theory to try to explain some of the phenomena that they encounter firsthand.

Feminist Theoretical Underpinnings of the Literature

The literature by community-based groups on wife abuse defines feminism broadly in terms of practices that place women at the centre of their concern, aim to empower them, and try to bring about social change. Feminism, though, embodies a range of different theoretical and political perspectives, each of which identifies different sources of women's oppression and different strategies for overcoming them. Feminist theories have been categorized as liberal, Marxist, radical, and socialist. At the present time, postmodern feminism has challenged many of the political goals of other forms (Nicholson 1990; Barrett and Phillips 1992), and individual theoreticians differ over the importance to be assigned to various aspects of women's oppression (Lupton and Gillespie 1994, 2). The feminism which informs the literature on wife abuse does not conform rigidly to any one feminist theory. It discusses some basic precepts of liberal and socialist-feminist theories but does not integrate the developments in feminist theories of the 1980s and 1990s (such as postmodern feminism and discourse analysis).

Feminist theories have evolved over a period of time, and theorists have adopted and built on insights from each other; for example, the articulation of the relationship between the public and private spheres of women's lives (Grant 1993). Radical feminists during the 1970s argued against the traditional separation between the 'political' and 'personal' realms of women's lives. Every area of life is a sphere of 'sexual politics': 'All relations between women and men are institutionalized relationships of power and so constitute appropriate subjects for political analysis ... [M]ale power is revealed through such "personal" institutions as childrearing, housework, love, marriage and all kinds of sexual practices from rape, through prostitution, to sexual intercourse itself' (Jaggar 1983, 101). Socialist feminists sought ways of understanding sexuality, childrearing, and housework in political and economic terms, particularly through their analysis of patriarchal capitalism.

Liberal feminists now recognize the links between women's private and public lives. Before the 1970s, however, abuse of women in their homes was generally considered to be a personal and private issue. Now it is generally regarded as a manifestation of women's inequality and lack of power in society. Deborah Sinclair, a white social worker, criticizes the attitude which regarded the family as a 'sacred place,' in which no one had a right to intervene, as an 'excuse for irresponsibility and inactivity' on the part of family, friends, and professionals. It encouraged women to 'suffer in silence' (1985, 26). Current literature on wife abuse agrees that the 'personal is political' and that the abuse of women in their homes is an appropriate issue for public debate.

The literature on wife abuse tends to treat the patriarchy that oppresses women as a universal and unchanging system. For example, the instructional literature on how to counsel victims of wife abuse acknowledges the interconnectedness of race, class, and gender oppression, but it discusses only gender oppression. Deborah Sinclair's *Understanding Wife Assault: A Training Manual for Counsellors and Advocates* (1985) and Monica Riutort and Shirley Small's *Working with Assaulted Immigrant Women: A Handbook for Lay Counsellors* (1985) are two handbooks on counselling abused women that are cited often in the literature on wife abuse. The authors acknowledge the need to examine social contexts in order to understand abuse, but they remain silent on racism. There is no discussion of class in the literature or of the difficulties encountered by women in locating employment.

The literature identifies gender oppression as the primary cause of abuse, assuming that it is a common denominator in all women's lives, unmediated by differences of class, ethnicity, or race. Thus, for example, Sinclair focuses on what she takes to be the 'traditional female role' of all women:

> A woman is taught from an early age to passively accept what life brings her. She often goes from her father's home to her husband's home ... She is socialized to believe that her worth as a person will be measured by her ability to 'catch a man' and to 'keep him.' She grows up believing she will be taken care of economically and socially by a man in exchange for caring for his home and children ... She is expected to assume a dependent, helpless, child-like stance in the world, while the men in her life make decisions affecting her future. (Sinclair 1985, 25)

Liberal feminists during the 'first wave' argued for equality between men and women but treated the lives of middle-class women as the norm against which to direct their arguments for equal political and economic rights. During the 1970s radical feminists used Marxist class analysis to explain the oppression of women. They said that women constituted a class whose membership was defined by gender, and that distinctions of gender structured virtually every aspect of women's lives (Jaggar 1983, 85).

Women from Asia, Africa, and the Caribbean criticized both of these approaches as racist because neither reflects their own life situations (Davis 1983; hooks 1984; 1988; Agnew 1996). Socialists accepted the point that race, class, and gender intersect in complex ways to oppress women, but they directed most of their attention to trying to demonstrate how patriarchy and capitalism intertwine to oppress women (Ramazanoglu 1989).

The explanations of wife abuse in the literature by community-based groups are ahistorical, and they imply that patriarchal domination is experienced in similar ways by women from all ethnic and racial groups. Riutort and Small simply say that wife assault is 'one way men have of controlling women' and that it is 'related to the traditional male attitudes towards women – ideas such as wives should obey their husbands, women are the property of men.' It is 'most likely to occur in marriages where husbands have a strong sense of "rightful" control, feel they are entitled to dominate their wives' (Riutort and Small 1985, 3).

Other literature by community-based organizations on wife abuse generalizes in a similar way. Rosa Maria Pinedo and Ana Maria Santinoli say that 'men exert dominance over women at all levels of society' and that the 'family values' of 'most cultures' include 'the control of husbands over wives, fathers over daughters, brothers over sisters, and even sons over their elderly mothers.' They cite examples from India, Africa, and the Philippines to demonstrate the 'world-wide repression of women' (1991, 72). Similarly, Rita Kohli argues that patriarchy renders women 'powerless globally.' She explains that men 'beat women' to exercise domination over them and that violence against women is 'nothing but a manifestation of the sexist and patriarchal system of social control of women' (Kohli 1991b, 82).

Radical feminists defined patriarchy as a 'universal system of male domination' in which men receive concrete and material benefits from the oppression and exploitation of women. Characterization of patriarchy as a broad and 'transhistorical social structure' enabled radical feminists to perceive a strong element of commonality in 'Indian suttee, Chinese foot binding, African genital mutilation, European witchburning, and American gynaecology' (Daly, quoted in Jaggar 1983, 101). Other feminists argued, however, that men dominate women through different social structures. The socialist feminist Heidi Hartman defined patriarchy as a set of 'hierarchical relations between men and solidarity among them which enable them in turn to dominate women.' 'The material base of patriarchy is men's control over women's labor power. That control is maintained by excluding women from access to necessary economically productive resources and by restricting women's sexuality' (quoted in Kemp 1994, 105–6).

The sexual division of labour assigns household tasks and the care and maintenance of children to women, and their unpaid work in the home is used as a rationale to consign them to lower paid and less desirable jobs. The combination of domestic work and paid work creates a 'double day of labour' for many women. As well, the need to care for children limits many women's paid work, and the assumption that women are primarily housewives economically dependent on males has been used as a rationalization for ghettoizing them in low-paid jobs or denying them employment or promotion (Adamson et al. 1988, 110–11). Their work is 'either unpaid domestic labour or underpaid clerical and service employment' (Chunn 1995, 182).

Hartman argues that the relations of patriarchy are incorporated into labour-market processes through job segregation:

> Low wages keep women dependent on men because they encourage women to marry. Married women must perform domestic chores for their husbands. Men benefit, then, from both higher wages and the domestic division of labor. This domestic division of labor in turn acts to weaken women's position in the labour market. (Hartman 1976, 139, quoted in Kemp 1994, 108)

Hartman does not acknowledge, however, that women belonging to different classes have experienced varying degrees of control and domination by men, or that the extent to which men control women's labour has varied throughout history. Alice Kemp says that it would be a mistake to view 'patriarchy as a universal social construction' rather than 'changing historically with changes in modes of production' (Kemp 1994, 113). Judith Grant argues that socialist feminists are unable to show how patriarchy 'can exist across so many different modes of production, except by resorting to radical feminist assumptions about transhistorical male domination' (Grant 1993, 57).

A woman's experience of the sexual division of labour and the double day also depends upon her class and race, which often determine 'the kind of paid work she does, the wage she receives, the status attached to this work as a female employee, the physical environment in which these different forms of labour take place, and the resources she has to manage and carry out the organization of the domestic household and child care' (Day 1992, 14). Literature that focuses on patriarchy without fully considering the impact of race and class on an abused woman's potential for employment can only partially explain her situation.

The literature by women from Asia, Africa, and the Caribbean on wife abuse also emphasizes the liberal feminist principle of women's equality, their right to be free from discrimination, and their right to maintain the norms of their own culture. The conventional liberal view of equality has been challenged on the grounds that it denies the historical disadvantages of many women and perpetuates the status quo. Scholars argue that a recognition of the different histories of racial and gender oppression and introducing affirmative action policies would go some way towards ensuring justice and equality for women from Asia, Africa, and the Caribbean (Abella 1984). Some right-wing critics argue, however, that recognition of ascribed characteristics of race and gender undermines liberal principles of equality and equal opportunity and contradicts the ideal of a meritocracy (D'Souza 1991). When groups seek funds from state agencies to provide services to abused women from Asia, Africa, and the Caribbean, they often assert both the right of abused women from their communities to equal social services and their right to conform to the norms of their own culture.

Personal Accounts of Wife Abuse

Reliable statistics on wife abuse would be valuable for documenting the seriousness of the crime and for persuading state agencies to allocate resources to provide services to victims of wife abuse. Statistics, however, do not record the pain, indignity, and trauma that accompany wife abuse. Victims of wife abuse often suffer in silence for years.

During the course of my research, I met many abused women, but most of them did not speak of their experiences of abuse, choosing instead to discuss their work or their life since they left the abusive situation. Some counsellors and service providers are formerly abused women, but only some of them are willing to discuss their experiences publicly. There is no typical victim of wife abuse. Some have encountered more trauma than others have, and some have had a more difficult time in leaving.

Some personal accounts of abuse have appeared in Canadian publications. A Korean woman described the situation she faced at home in the following excerpt from *The Voice: Korean Canadian National Magazine* (1991), 20:

My husband keeps me up all night. During the night, I get pushed, beaten, kicked, threatened and humiliated. If I happen to fall asleep for a minute, he puts ice cold water on my face to carry on the unshakable nightmare. I get very terrified. You don't get used to it no matter how often it happens.

Once he dragged me out to some field at two in the morning. He tied me to a tree and told me that he was going to kill me. He didn't kill me that night, but I really believe he will one day.

A South Asian woman in her late twenties, at a conference on wife abuse organized by the South Asian Family Support Services (26 April 1992), described her struggle to escape:

I waited for over a year for my husband to change to a nice person. I hid from everyone that I was being abused and our newborn son was being assaulted. Not even my brother and sister, with whom we lived in the same apartment, knew of how I was being treated. Every time I would go to the washroom I would come back to the room and find my son lying on the icy cold window [sill]. [My husband] would take off all the baby's clothes and put him there all naked. I would come back to find him shivering.

When you are upset and you see your own baby treated this badly by his own father, it is just very confusing.

My husband told me that if I always obeyed him, then he would, out of gratitude, be good to me and stop hitting our son. So I figured that since he is going to change, there is no use in letting anyone know about how he is treating me or what he is doing. But things just kept getting worse.

My sister and friends told me that he had told them that he had only married me to come to Canada and he's going to leave me after he got his Canadian citizenship. You wouldn't know how hurt I was. So that night when he started fighting with everyone, I called the police. The police took him away and later on he got out of jail on bail. We had a mistrial the last time at court, because all the witnesses were not present and his lawyer declined to proceed with the trial. The judge asked the police to interview some people. The police interviewed my aunt, brother, sister, and brother-in-law. [The police] wanted to find someone who saw my husband hitting the baby or me. And I am saying, how is this possible when he did it in a room that was always locked, and we were always in the room, and he had the door always locked? I was too upset to get mad ... The police told me I'd be lucky to send my husband to jail for a while, let alone deport him.

It's very difficult knowing what to do even though you know you have your family support. And now, even though we are separated, I always feel that he is out there waiting for a chance to grab my son and kill him. He didn't show up for the [hearing] of child custody and no one knows of his whereabouts. I feel [scared] even more.

I used to be so scared to go out alone that I always went out with my brother or friend. Just when I thought I had got control of my fear, I had to go to the court to see my coordinator. I made myself go on the bus and I prayed all the way there that I wouldn't see my husband anywhere. But my horror increased when I got to the court. I found out that one of the charges against my husband was dropped. The police had told me that they would be adding more charges from the evidence they had received. I asked my coordinator how this is possible – that a charge can be dropped. She said I will have to wait and talk to the crown attorney about it. So I guess I will have to wait and see. But this is very frustrating.

I have been attending a support group, and it has helped me a lot, but

it is just not enough. I don't think I will ever be able to get over this experience.

The story of Amina, born in Africa, is told through her fifteen-
year-old daughter, Ram:

[Ram remembers] her father as always drunk and 'causing trouble in the
house.' She remembers her father locking himself and their mother in a
room after supper and hearing her father's shouts and her mother's
screams. She did not know what the cause was nor how or where her
mother was assaulted ...

Since age ten, Ram came to know that for any small thing that went
wrong in the home, her mother could be 'spanked' ... Ram says that initially her mother tried to explain to them that their father was under
stress and that he was sick and that he could not control himself, but that
he would be alright soon and they would all be happy. Ram also remembers her mother begging them not to let anyone know because it might
have consequences that might split the family.

Ram [eventually] told her teacher ... The school informed Children's
Aid Society ... [but] since there was no physical abuse directed towards
the children, the children were [allowed] to stay with their parents.

Amina never sought any help from the police nor shelters ... She does
not believe that anyone has a solution for her, and therefore she would
rather keep all the information to herself. (Musisi and Muktar 1992,
76–7)

The experience of Amba, a woman born in Africa, is described
in this way by researchers:

Amba does not have a steady source of income but she works in a service
industry where she could earn [additional] money [through commis-
sions] ... Chris [her spouse] demands that all the money Amba makes
must be handed to him as he is the head of the family. At times he will
give her only twenty dollars as pocket money or none at all. Amba resents
this but she continues to hand over all the monies she makes because ... if
Chris ever found out [that she was withholding some money] she will be
in more trouble.

The first beating did not come as a surprise because [there had been] several ... outbursts ... Chris does not talk, rather he just commands and when Amba does not do as he commands, Chris just bursts out exploding with anger. [Amba] adds that the fact that she does not have any children aggravates the whole problem. Chris blames Amba for their not having any children.

[Amba] wrote to her family and Chris's family ... they are willing to intervene. [Amba's family is] trying to convince Amba that it is her fault and that she needs to pray and trust in God. In fact, they have even tried to send her some self-help literature to teach her to cope with the situation. On the other hand, Chris's family promises to talk to him to change his behaviour, but they tend to take his side of the story that minimizes the nature of violence he inflicts on Amba.

On more than one occasion, after assaulting Amba, Chris has felt remorseful and he has called his friends to arbitrate. He has apologized and promised not to do it again [but the cycle repeats itself]. (Musisi and Muktar 1992, 80–1)

A Korean woman describes her situation:

I came to Canada through my husband's sponsorship. I met him when he came back to Korea to find someone to marry. Although he was married before and had a child, he never told me this until we went to register for the marriage. I was disappointed ... but I decided to follow him to Canada.

I never thought that he would abuse me ... The violence started right after I came to Canada ... I [lived] ... in a one-bedroom apartment with his nine-year-old son and his mother. My mother-in-law and the child slept in the living room. The emotional abuse by my mother-in-law began right away.

I enrolled in an English language program, but to attend it I had to go through many difficulties at home. I had to get up every morning at 5:30 a.m. to prepare breakfast for my mother-in-law and my husband before I went to school. I was never given any money for lunch, so I often went hungry at school. Because of the abuse at home, I avoided people, especially Koreans in the class. My husband told me not to talk to any Koreans at the school and not to associate with them ... As soon as I [returned] home, I made dinner for the family, but I was only allowed to eat whatever was left over after my husband finished eating. After dinner, I did the laundry by hand until nine p.m. I was not allowed to use the laundry machine to wash the clothes. After all this, I would try to do some studying, but my husband didn't like me to study and we used to fight about it until we went to sleep. I got $50 a week for grocery shopping, but he always made me spend it all at once on the groceries so that I had no extra money on me.

Once I was hit and threatened with scissors by my husband in front of his son and mother. I got very scared and I grabbed the scissors and threw it away from my husband. My mother-in-law got very angry and accused me that I tried to kill her. She forced me to kneel in front of her and my husband and beg for forgiveness. I felt very humiliated. The five months of my life with my husband was like hell and I felt like I was going insane. (Korean-Canadian Women's Association 1992b, n.p.)

In the following, a Korean-Canadian woman describes her experience of racism at a shelter:

Due to problems with my family, I was living at a shelter with my three children. During my stay, I faced many incidents which I felt were cases of racial discrimination. I'd like to share some of my experiences.

1. It was May of 1991. One day, my daughter, on her way to the shelter from school, had been badly hurt. I found out that the child-care worker who brings kids home from school had pulled my daughter's ponytail. As a result, my daughter's neck was twisted and she fell.

The child-care worker seemed to treat my children differently. She was fine with the other children but not mine. My daughter, in grade 4 at the time, was crying after her fall but the child-care worker thought it was amusing and only laughed.

I was very upset. I tried to get an explanation with the help of the shelter workers, but they only said the child-care worker was trying to save my daughter from a dangerous situation. The child-care worker had absolutely no intention of apologizing.

It wasn't until the KCWA [Korean-Canadian Women's Association] intervened and disclosed the matter, that the child-care worker apologized to my daughter. If KCWA had not been involved, this incident would have ended with my daughter being at fault. I had wanted a formal apology. I was not satisfied with this outcome, but, seeing my daughter's neck healing, I thought I'd be better to forget the whole thing.

2. Living in a shelter is like communal living: everyone had to take turns on various duties of cleaning, taking out garbage, etc. Because I was an immigrant in an unfamiliar country, I didn't want to be blamed for anything. I made sure my children were well-behaved and put in extra effort to give a good impression, sometimes by taking on other people's duties.

Despite all my efforts, I clashed with this one woman. A woman who I thought held an attitude of superiority and looked down upon me. Once, it was my turn to clean up the cafeteria. I finished all my duties, even took out the garbage, and went to bed. But the next morning the woman yelled at my kids, 'It was your mom's duty but she didn't do it!' My angry children replied that I had finished my duties but that it was the people who came out to use the cafeteria during the night who didn't clean up. At this the woman mimicked them and called them racist names. The upset children burst into tears as they replied, 'We are Korean.'

3. Another woman comes to mind. A woman by the name of Maria. She had a 14-year-old and a very young daughter. I thought about the hardship she must be going through and wanted to help her. I offered to babysit her children, gave her some clothes, and did her a lot of favours.

However, the woman only discriminated against my children. She would yell at my kids to get up when they were watching TV, made sure my kids wouldn't approach her even to compliment her cooking, and threateningly asked my daughter if she hid any food in her room. When my children made snacks, her kids would come and steal them. But she ignored all this among many others. There were many other children but she would only pick on my children, making their lives miserable.

Though my children were relatively well-behaved in the shelter, the woman's harsh treatment of them makes me feel victimized and unfairly treated. (Korean-Canadian Women's Association 1992a, 12–13)

THREE

Settlement Services and Community-based Organizations

Immigrants to Canada since the mid-1960s have increasingly been drawn from Asia, Africa, and the Caribbean rather than Britain, the United States, or Europe (Samuel 1990). The 1967 immigration policy eliminated biases of race and nationality and encouraged professionals from all over the world to come to Canada, while other immigration policies targeted specific kinds of people; for example, domestic workers and entrepreneurs (Simmons 1990). There is therefore no stereotypical immigrant. Immigrants are found at both ends of the labour market; while some are professional people, others work for minimum wages at menial jobs (Boyd 1990). Immigrants from Asia, Africa, and the Caribbean have settled all over Canada, although a large proportion of them have made Toronto, Montreal, and Vancouver their home (Balakrishnan and Selvanathan 1990).

Canadian society makes social services available to immigrants when they first arrive. These services are meant to last from one to three years and to smooth the immigrants' transition from their countries of origin to Canada. Settlement services were originally intended to ensure the entry of certain kinds of skilled workers into the labour force. Consequently, services for non–English-speaking people, such as language training or skill upgrading, were given secondary importance. However, since the 1960s, the Canadian government has moved from being a '*laissez-faire* overseer of immigration flows' to becoming 'actively involved as an agent in the resettlement process' (Lanphier and Lukomskyj 1994,

342). The ideology underlying settlement policies is multiculturalism, which symbolically affirms the 'cultural entitlement' of newcomers and offers them some long-term prospects for viable
settlement. The Canadian Charter of Rights and Freedoms further
protects the citizenship rights of new immigrants and entitles them
to social services similar to those available to white English- and
French-speaking Canadians.

Communities from Asia, Africa, and the Caribbean have argued
that their access to settlement and social services provided by
mainstream social service agencies is impeded by systemic and
everyday racism. They have formed their own organizations as an
alternative to the services offered through mainstream social service agencies. The community-based organizations formed by
women from Asia, Africa, and the Caribbean illustrate the enterprising and dynamic nature of ethnic and racial communities in
Ontario. Their advocacy on behalf of the most disadvantaged
immigrant women has led government agencies to allocate
resources to them to provide services that are specially geared to
the needs of women in their communities.

The first section of this chapter discusses the policy of multiculturalism and the Charter of Rights and Freedoms, and the second
analyses some settlement and social services. The third and fourth
sections examine how community-based groups emerge and how
they obtain funding. The final section analyses the dependence of
women's organizations on the state.

The Entitlement to Multicultural Social Services

The work of community-based organizations derives its legitimacy
from the principles of equity and access in the policy of multiculturalism introduced in 1971 and in the Charter of Rights and Freedoms of 1982. However, community-based groups have argued that
women from Asia, Africa, and the Caribbean are ensured equal
access to social services only when institutions recognize these
women's right to conduct themselves by the social and cultural
norms of their ethnic and racial groups. When the values underly-

ing social services are Eurocentric, or communication is only in the English language, access and equality are being denied to non–English-speaking women from Asia, Africa, and the Caribbean.

The policy of multiculturalism was first introduced in 1971 and became law in 1988. By 1971 the assimilationist philosophy that had previously characterized Canadian policies and legislation had become largely discredited. Ethnic minorities found that despite their attempts to become 'Canadian,' they remained mostly on the margins of mainstream cultural, political, and social institutions (Harney 1988). Spokespeople for ethnic minorities pressed the Royal Commission on Bilingualism and Biculturalism, set up to resolve the discontent of the French population with English Canada, to find some resolution to their frustrations as well. The result was the announcement of a multicultural policy within a bilingual framework (Burnet 1988).

The multicultural policy introduced in 1971 emphasized the right of ethnic groups to maintain and preserve their cultures. In introducing the policy in Parliament, Prime Minister Pierre Trudeau argued that multiculturalism within a bilingual framework was the 'most suitable means of assuring the cultural freedom of Canadians.' He said that 'such a policy should help to break down discriminatory attitudes and cultural jealousies. National unity, if it is to mean anything in the deeply personal sense, must be founded on confidence in one's own individual identity; out of this can grow respect for that of others and a willingness to share ideas, attitudes and assumptions ... It can form the base of a society which is based on fair play for all.' Trudeau promised the support of the government to 'assist members of all cultural groups to overcome cultural barriers to full participation in Canadian society' and to learn at least one of Canada's official languages (Fleras and Elliott 1992, 282).

The policy of multiculturalism has often been criticized for reducing the task of providing equal access to power and privilege to that of simply becoming 'sensitive' to the values and norms of ethnic and racial groups.[1] A social service agency may 'add on' a multicultural approach to providing services without questioning the fundamental assumptions which characterize its organizational structure and philosophy. It may recruit a few 'ethnic' workers to deal with clients from cultural or racial minorities, translate some of its literature, and provide linguistic interpretation to clients when needed (and if resources permit). These changes do not address inequality; they do not give equal access to social services to all women (Tator 1996, 155).

Although the policy of multiculturalism accorded respectability to ethnic groups, the economic recession of the early 1980s and the growth of a racialized population through immigration during that time 'provoked negative reactions [to the new immigrants] that no multicultural policy could overcome' (Dorais, Foster, and Stockley 1994, 387). The growing consciousness of the pervasive nature of racism and its deleterious impact on racialized people led the minister of multiculturalism and citizenship to see that multicultural programs and funding could not be 'disassociated from the broader issue of equal participation of all citizens in a united Canada.' Gerry Weiner declared that the emphasis of the multicultural policy should be on civil and human rights, and that programs and funding should be provided which would help Canadians 'achieve a greater degree of equality and then use that equality to participate fully in the life of our country' (Dorais, Foster, and Stockley 1994, 374). The Multiculturalism Act of 1988 was intended to promote racial and ethnic equality and to foster anti-racist policies (Lanphier and Lukomskyj 1994, 355)

The Charter of Rights and Freedoms (1982) guarantees equality to all and explicitly forbids discrimination based on race, national or ethnic origin, colour, religion, sex, age, or mental or physical disability. It asserts the 'right of all individuals to *share* equally in the opportunities provided by Canadian society' (Fleras and Elliott 1992, 86). The Charter does not assert a right to preserve one's ancestral language or culture, although section 27 says that the Charter 'shall be interpreted in a manner consistent with the preservation and enhancement of the multicultural heritage of Canadians.' Disadvantaged populations may be helped through affirmative action, and the Charter 'does not preclude any law, program, or activity that has as its object the amelioration of conditions of disadvantaged individuals or groups' (Fleras and Elliott 1992, 86).

Judge Rosalie Abella notes that equality under the Charter is 'a right to integrate into the mainstream of Canadian society based on, and notwithstanding, differences. It is acknowledging and accommodating differences rather than ignoring and denying them' (Abella 1984, 13). She explains:

> Formerly, we thought that equality only meant sameness and that treating persons as equals meant treating everyone the same. We now know that to treat everyone the same may be to offend the notion of equality. Ignoring differences may mean ignoring legitimate needs. It is not fair to use the differences between people as an excuse to exclude them arbitrarily from equitable participation. Equality means nothing if it does not mean that we are of equal worth regardless of differences in gender, race, ethnicity, or disability ...
>
> Ignoring differences and refusing to accommodate them is a denial of equal access and opportunity. It is discrimination. To reduce discrimination, we must create and maintain barrier-free environments so that individuals can have genuine access free from arbitrary obstructions to demonstrate and exercise fully their potential. This may mean treating some people differently by removing the obstacles to equality of opportunity they alone face for no demonstrably justifiable reason. (Abella 1984, 3)

Judge Abella's report recommended adopting a systemic approach to discrimination to address the problems that groups (women, visible minorities, native people, and the disabled) rather than individuals encounter. She urged Canadian employers to examine the outcome of their policies rather than focus merely on their intent and principles. If the outcome consistently showed a pattern of exclusion, then, she noted, the policy was systemically discriminatory (Abella 1984).

The right to equality and the respect for cultural diversity encoded in legislation are reflected in the philosophy of settlement services. By the late 1970s, a 'multicultural settlement policy' had evolved with an implicit set of principles which acknowledged that all immigrants were eligible 'for services prior to and immediately after arrival in Canada,' and which recognized the need to respect the ethno-cultural background of immigrants while providing access to acquisition of English/French-language ability. Nevertheless, settlement services focused on economic rather than on social or cultural adaptation (Lanphier and Luko-mskyj 1994, 354–5)

The Multiculturalism Act and the Charter of Rights and Freedoms transform access to social services from a privilege to a right of all immigrants, and they have prompted a variety of government agencies and mainstream social service organizations to draw up antiracist plans and allocate some resources to provide social services to abused women from Asia, Africa, and the Caribbean. However, willingness to draw up plans to bring about changes does not by itself indicate that the changes are actually being implemented (Minors 1996; Johnson 1996); and while agencies may be willing to introduce 'multicultural services' or hire more women from Asia, Africa, and the Caribbean, they are reluctant to introduce structural change to overcome racism (Sunderji 1996, 185).

Some agencies have initiated projects for affirmative-action hiring or for 'multicultural services' when special funding was available. They were seldom financed by the ongoing operational expenses of the organization. That seems to reflect the resistance by organizations to systemic and structural change (Sunderji 1996, 185; Multicultural Coalition for Access to Family Services 1991). Fears about the vulnerability of multicultural services are corroborated by a Decima Research report, *Canadian Attitudes towards Race and Ethnic Relations,* prepared for the Canadian Council of Christians and Jews, which found that funding for 'multicultural, anti-racism, diversity, or access issues is not considered nearly as important as other political priorities and is therefore an easier target for government cut-backs in these times of fiscal restraint' (quoted in Desai 1996, 249).

Mainstream agencies have become more sensitive to cultural diversity, but despite the rhetoric of multiculturalism and equal rights, social services offered through mainstream agencies present a variety of barriers for women from Asia, Africa, and the

Caribbean wishing to utilize them (Lawrence 1990, 72–3; Tator 1996; Doyle and Visano 1987; Agard 1987; James 1996).

Settlement and Social Services

The responsibility for providing settlement and social services is shared by federal, provincial, and municipal governments. At the federal level, the Department of Employment and Immigration offers services which aid the economic settlement of immigrants (e.g., the Immigration Settlement and Adaptation Program, which funds language classes). The Department of Multiculturalism of the Secretary of State is responsible for the social, political, and cultural integration of immigrants and funds services through, for example, the Community Support and Participation Program (Employment and Immigration Canada 1992, quoted in Lanphier and Lukomskyj 1994, 346). In Ontario, the Ministry of Community and Social Services is responsible for the design and delivery of social and financial assistance programs to eligible Ontario residents (Lawrence 1990, 58); and the Ministry of Health at the provincial level provides resources for counselling abused women. In addition, various other government agencies may fund particular programs; for example, the Ontario Women's Directorate has funded the translation of brochures on wife abuse and information pamphlets about shelters.

The division of responsibility between different agencies of government for the settlement and adaptation of immigrants fails to meet the needs of immigrant women. Their status as sponsored immigrants further impedes their access to some social services. As sponsored immigrants, women have limited access to employment counselling or job training provided by the Department of Employment and Immigration, and programs available through the Secretary of State have failed to consider women's need to earn an income while attending language classes or job-training programs (Fincher et al. 1994, 167–9).

Settlement services are offered through mainstream agencies or are 'contracted-out' to community-based groups.[2] Community-based groups rely on funds received through several programs to provide social services for abused women. For example, education is a shared federal and provincial responsibility. Community-based groups receive funds for running English-language classes for women from the federal government through its Immigration Settlement and Adaptation Program, which pays for training allowances for women who attend the classes, but the teacher is paid by the local school board, and daycare for the children of participants is funded through a municipal program or by obtaining funds from private agencies (e.g., the Canadian Women's Foundation or the Levi Strauss Foundation). English-language classes indirectly subsidize other programs by paying for a large proportion of the administrative costs of the community-based groups. When these classes are eliminated, the entire range of services offered by a community-based group is jeopardized.

An abused non–English-speaking, working-class woman from Asia, Africa, or the Caribbean usually needs social assistance and public housing, but her access to them is determined by her immigration status. Over 50 per cent of women who immigrate to Canada come as 'family class' immigrants; that is, they are sponsored by their spouses and come as his dependants (Stairs and Pope 1990, 214). The sponsor is responsible for his dependants, and sponsored immigrants are normally not entitled to receive welfare or other forms of government assistance for ten years (Pope 1991, 38–9). Most sponsored women's applications to immigrate are processed while they are outside Canada, and they enter Canada as permanent residents (i.e., landed immigrants). When a landed immigrant can prove the existence of abuse (e.g., through police statements, the report of a medical doctor, or a statement by her lawyer), the sponsorship is considered to be severed, and she is entitled to welfare and other forms of social assistance (Stairs and Pope 1990; Riutort and Small 1985).

Social assistance in Ontario consists of two programs: general welfare assistance, which provides for short-term or emergency assistance; and family benefits, which provide for long-term financial assistance. The primary objective of these programs is to provide basic subsistence in the form of 'food, shelter, fuel, clothing, personal needs, utilities, medical coverage through OHIP, prescription drugs, dental coverage and special needs like those associated with pregnancy and special diets' (Barbara Schlifer Commemorative Clinic 1991, 112). An abused woman can apply for welfare or family benefits from the Department of Welfare. She is then interviewed during a home visit by a social worker, who determines 'the validity and degree of need' (Agard 1987, 26). This route to gaining access to social assistance is obviously difficult for a non–English-speaking woman.

The *Transitions* report of the Ontario Social Assistance Review Committee (1988) noted that the present 'social assistance system is highly complex, adversarial in its approach, stigmatizing, and inequitable' (quoted in Lawrence 1990, 73). Racialized people may be discriminated against when social workers have discretionary authority in the application of rules regarding social assistance (Lawrence 1990, 57–76). Biases may appear during interviews with counsellors for social assistance when some cultural mannerisms (e.g., avoiding eye contact) are interpreted in an ethnocentric manner (Agard 1987, 32). Consequently, 'significant disparities exist in the help available to people in similar situations' (Lawrence 1990, 73). A South Asian service provider described her encounter with welfare officers in this way:

> I see a lot of racism in social work agencies, for example, welfare and metro housing. The other day, I went to the welfare department and the worker was asking the [abused] woman what her husband's date of birth was. I was the interpreter, so I asked the abused woman, [but] she didn't know. The welfare worker said to me that's strange, this woman is married to him and she doesn't know his date of birth. So I told her that [there] was a cultural reason.[3] The welfare worker was just very impatient. She wouldn't even let me finish interpreting. She would just interrupt and say, this is the question I am asking, can you hurry up [and answer]? So that was really upsetting and this happens quite often as well. (Interview, 4 Aug. 1989)

A woman who comes from a Third World country may be unfamiliar with the concept of social services or be reluctant to use them to resolve her financial difficulties. Many racialized communities 'loathe the stigma attached to social assistance,' and their 'sense of independence and pride' motivates them to seek alternatives. Welfare is often the last resort (Agard 1987, 30–1). A non–English-speaking woman is bewildered by the multiplicity of organizations and agencies, with their complex and confusing eligibility rules and their changing sets of programs and services (Doyle and Visano 1987, 24; Agard 1987, 35). One abused woman said, 'It is frightening to have to do it all yourself when you don't know what is happening, supposed to happen, what to say or how to handle things' (Ontario Association of Interval and Transition Houses 1991a, 27). However, a community-based group can help a non–English-speaking woman from Asia, Africa, or the Caribbean overcome the difficulties of applying for welfare and family benefits, and a counsellor can help her through the maze of rules and regulations.

One of the most critical needs of an abused woman is to find safe housing.[4] In an emergency, an abused woman may go to a shelter, but the shelter has funds for housing a woman for only six weeks. Within these six weeks, the woman must find alternative housing. Finding good affordable housing is difficult for all people, particularly in large urban metropolitan centres like Toronto. The abused woman's search for housing is impeded by discrimination that she encounters from landlords who are biased against her if she is from Asia, Africa, or the Caribbean or on social assistance. The rent allowance available through welfare is frequently not sufficient for housing in the open market, and she may not have the first and last months' rent demanded by most landlords. Consequently, many abused women have to rely on public housing. In 1989 there were seventeen thousand people on the waiting list for subsidized housing in Ontario. Of these, one-third were 'mother-led' families (Ontario Association of Interval and Transition Houses 1989a, 26–9).

In recognition of the difficulties of abused women, the Ontario Housing Authority established a Special Priority Program in 1986, which gives an abused woman 'top priority' for the first available appropriate public-housing unit. The policy is intended to 'offer permanent affordable housing for women wanting to separate from their abusive spouses on a permanent basis' (North York Women's Shelter 1995, 5). The rules of the Special Priority Program are complex and restrictive, and vary from one region to another. The program recognizes only physical abuse as the basis of establishing eligibility for housing, and the presence of abuse in a woman's life has to be corroborated by a letter from a shelter worker, a physician, a lawyer, or another 'professional' that 'outlines a woman's current living situation, specific indicators of assault, and any pertinent information regarding special needs the woman and/or her children may have' (Ontario Association of Interval and Transition Houses 1989a, 26–9). Once the letter is received by the Housing Authority, a special-needs worker schedules an interview with the applicant to assess her eligibility (North York Women's Shelter 1995, 5).

Although a significant number of abused women have found housing through this program, difficulties remain because of the shortage of public-housing units. The Ontario Association of Interval and Transition Houses has recommended that the Ontario Housing Authority extend the program to cover women victimized by emotional and psychological abuse. They have protested that regulations which require that a woman prove her intention to separate to a lawyer are discriminatory. Some women, they point out, are fearful of seeking legal recourse, although they intend to separate from their spouses permanently (1989a, 28).

The Emergence and Organizational Structure of Community-based Groups

New immigrants have received some help from government agencies and volunteer organizations in their settlement and adaptation to Canadian society. They have been helped in locating employment, finding English-language classes, and coping with cultural alienation and conflict. However, the Eurocentric norms of the agencies and of social workers have often left a trace of bitterness and resentment (Iacovetta 1995). Consequently, immigrants have organized groups to provide services to members of their own communities. Although community-based groups began as volunteer organizations, they now seek and receive funds from government agencies to provide social services to their clients.

Immigrant women's groups from Asia, Africa, and the Caribbean, along with other women's organizations, have argued that there are now two major problems with mainstream social services. First, there are insufficient social services available to abused women. For example, a report on abused South Asian women noted that although 'reports from shelters, police records, newspapers, and social agencies' indicated that wife abuse existed in the South Asian community, South Asian women were not receiving social services:

> Attempts at granting assistance to these women were being foiled by the dearth of information on their situation. It has been noted that South Asian families very rarely become known to existing social service [agencies] until very serious problems have developed ... Alternatively, South Asians are unaware of the services available to them and are reluctant to come forward to mainstream agencies for help in dealing with family issues. (Papp 1990, 6–7)

Second, when these services are available, the racism of the service providers or of the norms of the organization make them relatively inaccessible to working-class women from Asia, Africa, and the Caribbean. As a South Asian counsellor in a community-based agency explained, service providers in mainstream agencies do not fully understand the cultural and social norms of clients (e.g., hijab, caste, extended families) from Asia, Africa, and the Caribbean, and women are reluctant to seek help there:

> Women from ethno-racial groups are being labelled 'traditional,' 'less liberated,' and 'resistant clients' by counsellors [in mainstream agencies]. Of course, a woman is going to resist if she is going to find out that [the counsellors] are judging her culture, her family, the way she behaves, the way she does things [from the perspective of] mainstream values. Anything that doesn't fit that standard is devalued – in a way, it becomes very racist. (Interview, 6 Oct. 1992)

A survey done by the Ontario Association of Interval and Transition Houses found that inaccessibility of social services was the 'number one issue' for 'racially diverse women.' A 'partial' list of barriers included:

- racism in all areas, including in social services, police response, court interventions, child care and education, employment, health care, as well as in shelters and women's services
- continuing lack of interpretation services
- continuing inadequacy of English-language classes
- cultural insensitivity and lack of education of all community workers on diverse cultural values and customs
- lack of counsellors and advocates who represent a range of communities
- lack of services specifically designed to address a diverse population of abused women; for example, circle of healing for Native abused women
- lack of information on services [and] legal rights and [lack of] information about abuse and its effects on children in all languages and from all cultural perspectives
- lack of education for shelter and women's services advocates on racism and cultural issues, designed and provided by culturally diverse women
- inadequate funding of existing services which show commitment to improving accountability and service provision to culturally diverse abused women so that access can happen (Ontario Association of Interval and Transition Houses 1991a, 17)

A number of community-based organizations of immigrant women from Asia, Africa, and the Caribbean have emerged in recent years. Some organizations focus their activities on advocacy (e.g., Women Working with Immigrant Women, the Ontario Immigrant and Visible-Minority Women's Organization, and the Ontario Association of Interval and Transition Houses). Others provide specific kinds of services to victims of wife abuse, women who do not speak English, and women who have limited marketable skills. These organizations may focus their activities on a particular ethnic

group (e.g., the South Asian Women's Group, the Korean-Canadian Women's Association, the East Asian Family Support Services,
and the Chinese Family Support Services); or they may serve a
more diverse population (e.g., the Working Skills Centre, which
primarily serves 'disadvantaged immigrant women' with limited
language facility and trains them for entry-level jobs through its
Mailing Room Operator Training Program and its Bridging Program for Immigrant Women on Social Assistance).

Community-based groups emerge in many different ways, and
their goals evolve and change over time. A group of volunteer
women, usually middle-class, may mobilize other women around
the issue of providing services to women. For example, Education
Wife Assault was started in 1978 by a group of women who organized support groups for abused women, but it subsequently
expanded its activities to include publishing educational material
and providing training seminars on wife abuse (interview with staff
of Education Wife Assault, 12 Jan. 1996). Other community-based
organizations originally aimed to provide settlement and adaptation services for members of their own communities, but when
government agencies introduced programs to eliminate violence
against women, they began to offer services to abused women, as
well. A case in point is the Korean-Canadian Women's Association.

The Korean-Canadian Women's Association was started by volunteers in 1985 to help other Korean women settle in Canada, but
over the years it expanded its mandate to providing social services
to victims of wife abuse. Plans to start the organization emerged
out of the realization that Korean women were 'experiencing
many serious difficulties in their new linguistic, economic, cultural
and social life.' The group identified the primary difficulties as
inability to speak English, social isolation, and economic hardship.
They noted that all Korean women, regardless of their educational
qualifications, experienced discrimination in finding employment.
In fact, they argued, women with an 'advanced educational background or professional training' were even more disadvantaged
Korean women had to work at convenience stores or in factories as
unskilled workers. It was hard for individuals to struggle against
racism, but a group could provide a 'network' and give them

'strength' to 'improve [their] lives' (Korean-Canadian Women's Association 1986, 3). The group now provides interpretation services and 'shelters for battered women (in members' homes).' It holds workshops on how to prevent family violence, counsels victims of abuse, and runs support groups for them (Korean-Canadian Women's Association 1988, 9).

The Riverdale Immigrant Women's Centre was organized by middle-class Asian women in the heart of a district in the east end of Toronto which has a high concentration of South Asian, Chinese, and Vietnamese immigrants. A South Asian woman described how the Riverdale Centre emerged as a means to fight racism in the neighbourhood:

> There was the Riverdale Intercultural Group, which was looking at racial issues in Riverdale because they believed that the Ku Klux Klan had an office there. This was a loose group of people from different agencies who were trying to struggle with what we should do [about racism]. [They conducted research on the need for social services of women from different cultural groups in the neighbourhood.] When the project [was completed], there was the need to do something. But we had no money. The two staff, a South Asian woman and a Chinese woman, were working without pay. [Then] the United Church said they would give us a room in the basement and a couple of desks. That's where we moved. (Interview, May 1992)

In the first year, just nine women visited the office, but it was the only place they could turn to. In order to determine whether they could reach more women, the group organized a meeting with about fifty immigrant women who were working with the Working Women's Community Centre, the Immigrant Women's Job Placement Centre, and the Immigrant Women's Centre on College Street:

> We talked, and the ultimate conclusion was that it doesn't matter whether you have a lot of money, and it doesn't matter if you have the statistics, or if you have a huge advertising campaign. The issue

was that if you provided a service that was truly needed and was appreciated, somebody was going to tell somebody else about it, and you're going to get somebody to call. At the time, I was convinced in my mind – I still am – that there is a need for this kind of service in the community, particularly South Asian women. They need help. [At that point] we put together a report of everything we had done to date [and applied for funding]. We called ourselves the Riverdale Immigrant Women's Centre, and we served the Chinese and the South Asian communities. (Ibid.)

At the present time, the Riverdale Centre offers a range of services, such as English-language classes, referrals to other social service agencies, and escorts to various institutions.

Some community-based groups have come into existence primarily to provide services to victims of wife abuse. A group of women may ask a government agency (such as the Ministry of Community and Social Services or the Ministry of Health) for funds to conduct a need-assessment study to document the problem of violence against women in their ethnic or neighbourhood community. Sometimes the completed report is favourably received by government agencies, which allocate additional funds for the provision of social services, and a community-based group is established (e.g., the South Asian Family Support Services).[5] At other times – for instance, if the women who conduct the study want to become part of the paid staff of the organization – government agencies may view their report more sceptically and decline to provide additional funds to them; in that case, the group may disappear.

One group, called Education Sexual Assault, received funds from the Women's Health Bureau of the Ministry of Health to conduct a conference and to assess the needs of 'immigrant and refugee women who have been sexually violated' (Education Sexual Assault 1992, F-7). They documented widespread racism in the provision of services to immigrant and refugee women and recommended increasing funds for providing services through community-based organizations, introducing 'employment equity policies' in mainstream social service agencies, and allocating funds more evenly to different social service agencies (Education Sexual

Assault 1992, F10–12). The Danica Women's Project received funds from private foundations and government agencies to conduct a need-assessment survey for a safe house for women who were victims of sexual assault (Danica Women's Project 1993). Neither of these groups received any additional funds, and they disbanded. However, in 1986, the case of a black woman who left a shelter and was subsequently killed by her husband created a responsive environment, and government agencies allocated funds for a special shelter for immigrant and refugee women – the Shirley Samaroo House (Shirley Samaroo House 1988).

Community-based groups have also established umbrella organizations to advocate on their behalf. Some umbrella organizations seek to coordinate many different groups serving similar ethnic communities (e.g., the Council of Agencies Serving South Asians). Others coordinate groups that provide similar services (e.g., the Ontario Association of Interval and Transition Houses). These groups, too, need the financial support of government agencies to operate. The idea of forming an umbrella organization of shelters was proposed in 1977 after conferences on 'family violence' in Toronto and Vancouver. In Ontario, shelters in Kingston (Interval House), Toronto (Women in Transition), and Windsor (Hiatus House) obtained funding from the Women's Program of the Secretary of State to hold a meeting to discuss the possibility of establishing a provincial organization of shelters. The provincial deputy minister of community and social services addressed the meeting and supported the idea of a provincial body. A steering committee prepared a constitution, and the organization was launched in 1978. In 1981, with funding from the Secretary of State, it hired a full-time staff coordinator. In 1991 it had fifty-nine full members and twenty-one associate members (Ontario Association of Interval and Transition Houses 1991b, 3–5).

The original objectives of this umbrella organization were primarily to lobby governments to allocate resources and to introduce or amend legislation, and to 'initiate a dialogue with the Provincial Attorney General and the Federal Minister of Justice in regard to family violence and violence against women' (1991b, 5). Between 1977 and 1991 it identified several areas for advocacy, such as the funding of services under the General Welfare Assistance Plan, Second Stage Housing, and Family Law Reform; and the treatment of abused women by the justice system. In addition, over the years it has developed a code of ethics to guide shelter workers in the performance of their duties (Ontario Association of Interval and Transition Houses 1991b, 7).

The need to provide services to abused women forces community-based organizations to look to governments for resources. When a government allocates funds, it requires that a voluntary board of directors, composed of from twelve to twenty members of the community, take responsibility for the organization and its disbursement of funds. Board members may be volunteers and activists who are interested in the work of the organization, professionals in mainstream agencies whose work requires knowledge and interaction with the local community (e.g., social workers or hospital outreach coordinators), or self-employed professionals (e.g., lawyers or doctors). These individuals may tell the nominating committee of the board or current board members of their interest in participating in the work of the group, or the board may invite individuals with useful experience to sit on the board. Sometimes an organization holds an open house to introduce its work to the community and to identify individuals willing to become members of its board. After a trial period of a few months, if the new member and the board find that they can work together, the individual is formally invited to join the board.

The executive director of the organization and the president of the board play critical roles in determining the organization's direction. The board formulates policy and hires and fires staff. It appoints the executive director to administer its policy. Usually the board and executive director can work harmoniously, but sometimes there is conflict and there may be a struggle for power. Then both parties seek to consolidate their positions within the organization. They may bring in new members who support them, or they may lobby existing members. Sometimes the board splits into two factions, and each side seeks to bring its supporters onto the board.[6]

Conflicts between the executive director and the board or

between members of the board threaten the work of the organization and endanger its survival. If there is a struggle for power, both sides may approach government personnel and ask them to mediate. Government personnel may recommend that the organization consult professionals trained in conflict resolution, or they may suggest that an outside agency conduct a review of the organization. At the same time, however, they tighten the purse strings, fearing that the organization has become unstable, and wait to see how the matter is resolved. Community groups therefore try to keep their conflicts within the organization.

The ideology of the board and staff, which informs the direction of the agency, will also change with new board members and staff. A case in point is the changes that occurred in the South Asian Family Support Services. Aruna Papp, the founding member of the South Asian Family Support Services, had adopted a feminist analysis of wife abuse in her report and located its roots in patriarchal gender relations within the family. Papp wrote:

> Although there are many causes of wife abuse in all societies, perhaps the major cause among the South Asian community is the system of patriarchy. The South Asian family is very traditional, authoritarian and patriarchal in structure. This structure leads not only to incidence of wife assault, but it also complicates the process of assessing and assisting victims. The barriers to accessing services are not just language and culture but socialization. There is also total lack of community, family, and financial support for South Asian women who leave their husbands. (Papp 1990, 7–8)

By 1995, however, the South Asian Family Support Services had no strong political ideology to distinguish it from other government-supported agencies. Its focus had shifted from feminist activism to the provision of settlement services to immigrants. This shift paralleled changes in the composition of the organization's board of directors and of its office staff. In 1991 the executive director and the board disagreed about hiring policies, and in the ensuing power struggle, Papp was ousted and a retired Sikh man emerged as the president of the board. Since then, three executive directors have been hired, all of whom are committed to community work but not all to feminism.

By 1995 the staff of the South Asian Family Support Services had increased from two workers, a wife abuse counsellor and a receptionist, to approximately ten workers, including administrators, program coordinators, counsellors, and office staff. Sometimes additional workers were obtained through job-creation programs of government agencies (e.g., Welfare Canada), or sometimes students were allocated to the agency. The twelve members of the board of directors have also kept changing, and all have different beliefs about gender inequality.

The organization remains committed to helping abused women, but it has begun to turn its attention to helping a wider range of women in their roles as wives and mothers. In 1995 its largest program was introductory English-language classes under the new policy of Language Instruction for Newcomers (LINC). Its support groups invite guests to lecture on nutrition, health, and postnatal care. The organization provideds after-school tutoring to South Asian children in neighbouring schools, and the board has discussed the desirability of starting youth groups or providing services to men. In its board meetings, members now emphasize that the organization is meant to help families, not just women.

Government Funding of Community-based Groups

Community-based groups in Ontario are almost entirely dependent on government agencies for funding of their programs to provide services to victims of wife abuse. The groups survive by combining funds from several government agencies, such as the Ministry of Community and Social Services, the Secretary of State, the Ontario Women's Directorate, and the Ministry of Health. Government agencies typically fund particular services but also provide some money for renting space, hiring administrators and office staff, and starting new programs. One survey found that 88 per cent of all immigrant community groups in Ontario received federal funds, 87 per cent received provincial grants, 65 per cent received municipal funding, 45 per cent received funds from the United Way, and 70 per cent raised income from other sources (Ontario Council of Agencies Serving Immigrants 1991, 1–13).

Some observers have noted disadvantages of government funding. They see the allocation of resources by government agencies to community groups as a way to 'contain' the discontent of racial and ethnic groups outraged by the gender, race, and class discrimination experienced by their members. Dependence on government agencies structures the services offered by community-based groups and encourages the adoption of government priorities. As well, coordinating their work with existing social assistance programs requires community-based agencies to voice the needs of women in their ethnic and racial groups in more moderate terms than they believe the needs demand.

The nature of the relationship between community-based groups and government agencies makes it difficult to distinguish causes and effects: does the advocacy of community-based groups lead to allocation of resources, or does the availability of resources encourage women to organize themselves in community-based groups to provide services to victims of abuse? Community-based groups continually lobby politicians and government personnel either directly or through their umbrella organizations, such as the Ontario Council of Agencies Serving Immigrants (OCASI) or the Ontario Association of Interval and Transition Houses (OAITH), to allocate more resources for programs for victims of abuse. The allocation of additional resources encourages groups of women in other neighbourhoods or racial groups to seek funding for establishing new community-based groups to help abused women.

It is difficult to determine how many community-based groups are providing services to abused women from Asia, Africa, and the Caribbean at any given time. Community-based groups emerged in the late 1970s in a political and social environment in which the problem of violence against women had gained some recognition by government agencies. In the expanding economy of the 1980s, many community-based groups came into being. Some organizations expanded over the years, while others disappeared because of internal problems or loss of funding or both (e.g., the South

Asian Women's Group). As government agencies reduce or cut some programs in the 1990s, community-based groups are losing part or all of their funding and are forced to reduce their services or discontinue them.

There are no published statistics to indicate how many community-based organizations there are in Ontario. The Ontario Council of Agencies Serving Immigrants found that of the seventy organizations surveyed by them in 1990 a quarter were women-focused (i.e., 70 per cent of their clients were women), and one-third provided services to 'visible minority women' (OCASI 1990, 1–3). These community-based groups offered a variety of social services: language classes, individual and family counselling, interpretation and translation, information and referral, advocacy, legal assistance, employment counselling and job training, and health care services (OCASI 1990, 13). As needs changed and governments allocated resources for specific issues, community-based groups extended their services to incorporate antiracist sensitivity training and programs to eliminate violence against women.

Programs to eliminate violence against women have received support from all three major political parties in Ontario. In 1981 the Ontario government established a standing committee on social development to examine the problem of wife assault. Its report, 'Family Violence: Wife Battering,' was tabled in the legislature in December 1982, and many of the recommendations were implemented by the government. In 1983 the government established a Family Violence Unit in the Ontario Women's Directorate with a mandate to 'take a lead role in developing government initiatives on wife assault, as well as a public education campaign on the issue.' The government allocated funds to programs to eliminate violence against women throughout the 1980s and early 1990s (Ontario Women's Directorate 1991, 1). NDP premier Bob Rae announced a $20.3 million program, which included special funding for improving access to services for women of 'diverse cultures and races' (OAITH 1991a, 34).

In 1990 the main sources for funding women's community-based groups were the Secretary of State's Women's Program and its Citizenship and Community Participation Program, at the federal level, and the Ontario Women's Directorate, at the provincial level (OCASI 1990, 60). In addition, federal and provincial governments have allocated resources for programs intended to educate the public about the problem of violence against women or to offer services to women who are victims of violence. Government agencies (e.g., the Ontario Women's Directorate and the National Clearing House on Violence against Women, Health and Welfare Canada) must distribute their resources equitably and in a way which can withstand scrutiny from groups that can file complaints with the Human Rights Commission, institute legal cases under the Charter of Rights, or publicize allegations of racism.

The Ontario Conservative government, elected on a platform of fiscal restraint in 1995, severely cut funding to all women's groups. Although some services to abused women survived the budget cuts, education and prevention programs were sometimes completely eliminated (e.g., Education Wife Assault).[7] The Ontario Association of Interval and Transition Houses protested against these cuts, arguing that 'the Ontario government was sending women and children back 50 years to a time when they had no choice but to live and die at the hands of male violence.' They threatened to complain to the United Nations Human Rights Commission about the cuts and 'were contemplating taking legal action against the government on the grounds that cuts in funding for services to battered women constitutes a violation of the Canadian Charter of Rights and Freedoms' (Philp 1995b).

Community-based groups almost always find that the funds assigned to them are inadequate for their needs. Government agencies allocate most funds annually, although some well-established groups may have a proportion of their funds renewed automatically. Even the latter, though, must constantly search for additional funds to maintain or to expand their programs, and new groups also compete for annual funds. This situation generates insecurity and uncertainty in the staffs of the groups, and they perceive the constant application for funds as a diversion of their energies from the essential tasks of providing services to women.

Funds are obtained by making an application to a particular program within an agency. (For example, the Women's Directorate, until recently, provided funds for conducting workshops for women who were victims of violence or for sensitizing service providers to cultural differences.) Funds are allocated for providing specific services within a given time frame. If funds are required again, a new application must be made. Some community-based groups have 'core funding': they have been allocated funds which are automatically renewed each year and are sufficient for their most essential services. (They can apply for additional funding for new services or specific programs.) However, most community-based groups have to apply annually for funds, and they survive by obtaining funds from a variety of government agencies to cover their services and administrative costs.[8] For example, the Korean-Canadian Women's Association was established in 1985 with funds from the Secretary of State, but it now receives funds from a variety of government agencies to offer social services to women from its ethnic communities. Its executive director explained:

> We get a lot of project grants which go to support the agency. Our most stable funder [is] the Multiculturalism Department, which gives us an annual grant. [This year] we got some money from COMSOC [Community and Social Services] to hire a wife abuse counsellor. We have been getting wife abuse and sexual assault grants from the Ontario Women's Directorate. We have a one-time project grant from Metro Toronto. We also get donations and we do some fund-raising.
>
> United Way gave us a community initiative grant for five years but we don't have that anymore. They said they thought the Korean community is well established now – we have [access to enough] resources. United Way [supports an] antiracism policy and ethno-specific agencies. But the reality is that among the ethno-specific agencies, they are targeting the larger, more established ones. Our community has been cut off. (Interview, 28 June 1993)

The process of annual applications ensures accountability, and government agencies impose few special requirements; but the processes of requesting funds and seeking their renewal also encourage community-based groups to provide only services which will be favourably viewed by the agencies.

Community-based groups argue that the process of applying for funds is time-consuming and makes them perpetually fearful of having their funding cancelled (OCASI 1990, 45–7, and 60–3). The Chinese Family Life Services argued that although the number of cases they handled increased from May 1986 to March 1989, they never obtained core funding for their services from any government agency and remained chronically underfunded and understaffed. It was unfair for them 'to raise awareness about wife assault but be unable to help women who came to the agency for counselling' (Chinese Family Life Services 1989, ii).

Dependence on the government for funds compels groups to design their programs and services so that they can receive a positive recommendation from personnel in government agencies. They must show government agencies that their services are used by a large number of women and that the 'cost per unit' for their services is low in comparison to that of other groups. This creates a dilemma for service providers. On the one hand, they need time to talk with victims of abuse, to reassure them and to win their confidence; but, on the other, they also need to show 'good numbers' to government agencies in order to have resources reallocated to them.

An abused woman needs time to build up her own confidence and develop a trust in service providers before she will reveal the violence in her home, and she may wait even longer to reveal the full extent of the violence perpetrated against her. In one case, it was only during the several months between the laying of charges and the scheduling of a hearing that the victim came to know service providers in the community-based group and in the crown attorney's office well enough to be willing to reveal the full extent of the violence she had endured. That information led to more charges being laid.

Dependence on the government for funds influences the direction of an organization and the kinds of services it offers. Community-based groups seek funds from all government agencies, but funds are allocated for specific services – for example, for after-school tutoring, support groups for isolated senior citizens, or English-language classes. Each program allocates a percentage of its total funds to administration, and a community-based group has to design enough programs to meet its financial obligations to the office and staff. Offering a variety of different programs also ensures that a community-based group can survive over a period of years even if resources for any one program disappear.

The difficulty is that dependence on government for resources sometimes compels a group to compete for a share of the resources that are available by designing programs that will attract funding rather than meet its own priorities or political agendas. Moreover, since all these services are needed by ethnic communities, groups hesitate to forego the opportunity to provide them. These difficulties are compounded by the fact that the jobs of the service providers (who are frequently hired on contracts for specific programs) also hang in the balance.

The dependence of community-based groups on government agencies sometimes creates a tension between fulfilling their original goals and expanding their mandate to meet other needs. For example, the availability of resources for introductory English-language classes encouraged many groups to include them in their ongoing programs. These classes met a basic need of non–English-speaking women, and the resources that these classes generated helped subsidize other programs. However, funding for Labour Market Language Training (referred to as LMLT) was eliminated in 1995, thereby also placing several other programs offered by community-based groups in jeopardy. Some organizations seek to protect themselves by diversifying their services and their clients (e.g., by aiming to serve not only women but whole families).

Although the compromises that community-based groups make to survive are driven by short-term political expediency, in the long run they change the character of the organizations. Service providers in these groups may become more circumspect in their criticism of state and society, hide their militancy, and address their problems in non-confrontational ways. They may become more moderate in articulating their feminism and in voicing their feelings about the extent of racism encountered by women in employment and in the provision of social services.

The State and Women's Organizations

The relationship between the state and community-based organizations that provide services to victims of wife abuse raises some difficult issues for feminist theory. Feminist theory interprets abuse as a form of patriarchal domination and sees the state as reflecting patriarchal values and embodying male power. Community-based groups, however, depend on the state for resources to provide services to victims of abuse. Their collaboration with the state has not led them to abandon their goals of eliminating race, class, and gender discrimination, but their strategies for social change are tempered by pragmatism.

The day-to-day activities of community-based groups are providing services and helping women in their communities survive the trauma of wife abuse. Working with these women generates solidarity with them, and the groups sometimes raise a woman's consciousness about gender and racial inequality and encourage her to engage in political struggles. However, dependence on the state makes community-based groups wary of using militant rhetoric about racism, classism, and sexism. Rather, they assert women's rights as Canadians to equal access to social services and equitable treatment.

Marxist feminists argue that the state is an instrument of the ruling class and functions to perpetuate the dominance of one class over another. This function does not entirely preclude the provision of social services: the state may sometimes act in the short-term interest of disadvantaged groups in society. Nevertheless, the state's role in facilitating capital accumulation makes it complicit in perpetuating the exploitation of women.[9] Socialist feminists argue that patriarchy and capitalism are inextricably linked and oppress and exploit women.

Catherine MacKinnon argues that the values and norms which underlie much legislation, even in a liberal society, reflect a male perception of experience and reality. She explains that 'state power, embodied in law, exists throughout society as male power at the same time as the power of men over women throughout society is organized as the power of the state.' Laws, she argues, reflect the standpoint of males (MacKinnon 1989, 170).

Liberal feminists believe that the state is a neutral arbitrator amongst competing interests that should protect all its citizens. Liberal ideology distinguishes, however, between a public and a private sphere in an individual's life and argues that state intervention should be minimized in the private and familial lives of its citizens. How, then, can feminists of any of these kinds look to the state for transformation and change in unequal gender relations?

In Canada, as in Britain and the United States, feminists have chosen to work with the state to provide services to women (Dobash and Dobash 1992; Schechter 1982, 185–208). Women's groups have been successful in lobbying state agencies and politicians to acknowledge the severity of wife abuse in Canadian families and allocate resources to support women (Barnsley 1985; Walker 1990). Slogans popularized in the mass media refer to the right of women to live in a violence-free society, but that right can only be guaranteed by the state. Counsellors in the community-based organizations advise immigrant women that wife abuse is a crime in Canada and will be punished. The women are given information about their immigration status and about their right to public housing, welfare, and legal aid. The implicit message is that the state will protect and to some extent provide for them.

Feminists can defend working with the state by pointing out that they are making the best of a bad situation and that furthering women's interests in this way may incrementally contribute to transforming the state. The first priority must be assigned to women who need services and support to survive the abuse which threatens their lives.

In *Family Violence and the Women's Movement* (1990), Gillian Walker notes that the issue of violence against women was first brought to the public's consciousness by the women's movement. Resources were needed to provide support services to women, to set up shelters, and to advocate changes in legislation for women who were victims of violence. However, once the issue of violence against women entered the realm of public policy, emphasis shifted away from the theme of the general imbalance of power between the genders throughout society, and towards the theme that individual women had to be protected from violence and that individual men had to be prosecuted for perpetrating violence against women. This 'rearticulation' of the problems tended to erode feminist arguments for the need for social transformation (Walker 1990).

Cooperation between community-based women's organizations and the state risks the co-optation and absorption of feminist issues in the state's agenda (Wine and Ristock 1991; Shragge 1990; Ng, Walker, and Muller 1990). Yet isolation from the state risks marginalization and invisibility (Briskin 1991, 30–1). Sue Findlay identifies the dilemma that women's organizations face:

> To refuse to play by the state's rules and ideology, to refuse to accept the state's response as good enough, is to risk loss of credibility and visibility for women's issues and women's experience. Yet accepting the state's values and frameworks produces the same result: the institutionalization of women's issues and invalidation of women's experience. (Findlay 1988, 8)

However, the emphasis on individual problems and solutions has provided much-needed services and helped women to understand how and why things went wrong for them personally and what solutions are available to them. The process of seeking resources or services can make women conscious of unequal gender relations, or encourage them to question the inequities of gender, race, and class.

The reports of community-based groups do not discuss the issue of collaborating with the state or depending on it for resources. Many, if not all, of the reports on wife abuse by community-based groups have been written with the help of resources obtained from the state. The reports adopt a pragmatic stance and focus on documenting evidence of wife abuse and the lack of services to the victims. Some of the reports adopt feminist explanations of abuse (e.g., patriarchal domination), but they nevertheless assert that the state has the responsibility of providing social services and that women from their communities have the right to equal access to them. They want, not less, but more intervention from the state in supporting victims by its allocating resources and introducing more stringent punishment for perpetrators of abuse.

The Ontario Council of Agencies Serving Immigrants works with state agencies as a pragmatic strategy for achieving equity for women in ethnic and racial communities. The council participates in hearings held by state agencies to introduce new legislation or restructure existing programs, lobbies ministers for antiracist social services, and advocates for greater resources for member agencies. Sometimes it requests that joint committees be established with senior personnel from state agencies to ensure implementation of antiracist and anti-sexist policies and to 'develop appropriate program criteria' (OCASI 1992, 9). The physical presence of racialized representatives can in itself serve as a reminder to a committee to consider the needs of racialized groups. Their advocacy in these committees and in the media keeps the issues of racial and gender equality on the agenda of state agencies.

The Ontario Council of Agencies Serving Immigrants aims to integrate its member agencies as essential components in the delivery of social services that are offered by the state.[10] In a brief to Marion Boyd, Minister of Community and Social Services, OCASI recommended that in 'policy development and program design' the ministry 'recognize the crucial role of community-based immigrant servicing agencies as an essential part of the community and social services system of Ontario' (OCASI 1992, i). The desire of community-based agencies to be part of the system is one aspect of their struggle to gain equal access to social services for women from Asia, Africa, and the Caribbean.

Conclusion

The support of community-based organizations by the federal government is informed by the Multiculturalism Act and the Canadian Charter of Rights and Freedoms. Theoretically, the multicultural society ensures ethnic and racial groups some cultural parity with members of dominant groups (of British and French origin) and entitles them to social services that are sensitive to their values and norms. Although there have been problems in implementing a multicultural ethos in mainstream social service agencies, nevertheless the Charter and the Multiculturalism Act have given legal force to principles in terms of which groups from Asia, Africa, and the Caribbean can articulate their complaints and demand social and political change. These groups have used their cultural differences from the dominant group to develop organizations with funds received from government agencies to provide social services to women in their communities. Although such a relationship poses the threat of co-optation and conformity, at the same time it offers some hope for emancipation and empowerment of abused women from Asia, Africa, and the Caribbean.

FOUR

Social Services and Advocacy by Community-based Groups

Groups of immigrants from Asia, Africa, and the Caribbean have documented the racism, sexism, and classism encountered by them in Canadian society, in general, and in their relationships with the police, employers, and the women's movement, in particular. Such documentation has forced white Canadians to acknowledge as myth the image of a non-racist Canada and has served the useful purpose of compelling government agencies to allocate some resources to racialized communities (Brown and Brown 1996, 49; Agnew 1996). Documentation of wife abuse in these communities is another means by which they overcome their victimization by race, class, and gender biases.

Abused immigrant women are entitled to settlement services provided by mainstream social service agencies. However, immigrants from Asia, Africa, and the Caribbean often find that 'the prevailing ideology of the human services is exclusionary and racist':

> It is based on the provision of appropriate service to all, regardless of colour or creed, yet its delivery is inconsistent with these principles. The assumption of a common set of needs among very different groups, which is usually accepted as a basic requirement for the equal and accessible provision of services, can have a negative impact on minority clients. People of colour often find the traditional mainstream human-service delivery system inaccessible and inequitable. (Henry et al. 1995, 311)

Racism in the service system is manifested in different ways. Sometimes it is 'lack of access to appropriate programs and services.' Some counselling practices are ethnocentric, and some mainstream agencies have 'monocultural models of service delivery.' The educational credentials of immigrants from Third World countries (e.g., social workers) are frequently devalued, and their consequent exclusion from mainstream agencies constitutes racism. 'Inadequate funding for ethno-racial community-based agencies' is also sometimes racist (Henry et al. 1995, 154).

Immigrant women have additional difficulties. Some women from Asia, Africa, and the Caribbean have problems obtaining English-language training. Some have become ghettoized in menial jobs. Problems in employment and skill training are exacerbated when the women also experience violence from their spouses in their homes.

The first section of this chapter discusses how the feeling of being an outsider generates solidarity among immigrant women and creates a community; the second section analyses the reports by community-based organizations on wife abuse; and the third examines racism in mainstream social service agencies.

The 'Community' in Community-based Groups: A Case Study of South Asians

The word 'community' is used in a number of different ways.[1] It can refer to a geographical area (e.g., a neighbourhood), an ethnic group (e.g., the Italian community), or to a group whose members share a common interest (e.g., the gay community or the medical community). A community may be identified by people who wish to be spokespersons representing certain social or political interests, yet not all the people included in the community may feel that they belong to it or that the spokespersons truly represent them. A term like 'the immigrant community' might be used to include both recent and past immigrants or both immigrants and their children born in Canada, but it is unlikely that all of the people in such broad groups would share identical interests.

Ambiguities in the idea of a community are sometimes reflected in immigrant women's community-based groups. Some of these groups want to provide services to a particular neighbourhood (or borough) that reflect the needs of many ethnic and racial groups in that area. Others wish to provide services to a particular ethnic group and locate themselves in a neighbourhood in which many members of the group live. Sometimes, too, there are differences between a group's perspectives on the problems it addresses and those of its clients.

Community-based groups seek to distinguish themselves from mainstream social services by offering services that meet specific needs of members of their communities. For example, they provide services in languages other than English. They also claim that their services reflect values and norms that are different from those of mainstream agencies. For instance, they provide informal work environments and flexible procedures and practices to counteract the alienation experienced by working-class, non–English-speaking women in mainstream social service agencies. The familiarity of these groups with the culture of their clients helps them respond to a woman, not just as an immigrant or even just as a woman, but as a woman of a particular race and culture.

The term 'community' may connote a geographical location, but it sometimes also connotes shared social or political interests or a shared culture, that is, shared values, norms, and way of life. Consequently, a number of new questions arise. Is there a way of life shared by all members of the group a community-based organization aims to serve? Do both middle-class and working-class women in the community share the same values and norms? If there are differences between the perspectives on gender, race, and class of service providers and those of their clients or other members of the community, can they be resolved in the course of providing help to the clients? Identifying people as members of an ethnic community gives the impression that the people are homogeneous, but in practice an ethnic community in Canada is often fragmented along lines of class, religion, regional affiliation, time of arrival in Canada, and ideology. Community-based groups may 'represent' only a segment of that community.

The dynamics of a group's overcoming internal divisions and developing a sense of community are revealed through an analysis of the South Asian community-based groups in Toronto. South Asian women in community-based organizations share some similarities (national origin, history, race, class, and gender), but these characteristics do not ground their unity. Rather it is their shared location as outsiders, immigrants, non-whites, and women, and the process of engaging in struggles against gender and race oppression, that may be more effective in creating a sense of community between workers in the group and between them and their clients.

South Asia includes a number of sovereign nations – India, Pakistan, Bangladesh, Sri Lanka – with ethnically diverse populations: in Sri Lanka, Tamils and Sinhalese; in Pakistan and Bangladesh, Hindus and Muslims; in India, Sikhs, Tamils, and Parsees (to name only a few). Immigrant women in Canada from South Asia exhibit vast social, cultural, regional, religious, and linguistic differences. Some have immigrated directly to Canada from South Asia; others are second- or third-generation immigrants who have come from the Caribbean, Africa, or Europe. In addition to regional differences among South Asian women, there are differences in class, political ideology, and sexual orientation. Members of such a diverse population are unlikely to have very strong feelings of being part of a 'South Asian community.'

A third-generation South Asian immigrant coming to Canada from the Caribbean Islands will probably not have much familiarity with the culture of a woman who comes from a small town in Punjab. A second-generation woman brought up in a traditional Sikh environment in Vancouver may feel little cultural similarity with an immigrant who comes from a westernized Hindu family in New Delhi. Women from India and Pakistan, because of the historical relations between the two countries, may be reluctant to establish close social relations with each other, even though they have some cultural norms in common.

The identity of South Asian women in Canada is partly a social construction by hegemonic practices and processes. South Asian women are often categorized as a group on the basis of physical appearance (especially skin colour), with the cultural differences among them disregarded. The mass media sometimes suggest that certain cultural norms – for instance, arranged marriages – distinguish South Asians, in general, from white Canadians (Abel 1989; Bannerji 1986; Agnew 1993b). The experiences of some South Asian women in Canada are presented as if they were shared by all (Das Gupta 1994; Ghosh 1981; Srivastava and Ames 1993; Dhruvarajan 1991). Some South Asian women internalize such stereotypical perceptions of themselves, and these become part of their idea of a South Asian community.[2]

South Asian women in Canada experience racism in different ways. Working-class women may receive verbal abuse in the factory and may be excluded from informal groups that form there, while middle-class women may encounter more subtle, systemic discrimination that limits their career aspirations (Ghosh 1981; Khosla 1983; Dhruvarajan 1991; Srivastava and Ames 1993; Das Gupta 1994). South Asian women who do not speak English or who wear South Asian clothes may experience greater exclusion than others.

Encounters with racism can create a sense of community with others who experience it, but it is a sense imposed from outside. Buchignani and Indra explain:

Popular stereotypes and widespread ignorance of South Asia [have] created a certain degree of commonality in the lives of South Asian Canadians. One result has been a made-in-Canada consciousness of being South Asian among people who might not have thought much about it before. In this sense South Asians are those whom others call South Asian. (Buchignani and Indra 1985, 122)

A national conference was held in Toronto in June 1993 for South Asian service providers; as well, there is a feminist magazine, *Diva*, for South Asian women and an umbrella organization for social agencies across Ontario, the Council of Agencies Serving South Asians – all of which were or are inclusive, inviting participation by South Asian women regardless of national origin, religion, or class. However, it is not clear what the unifying factor is besides the conventional Canadian view that skin colour and geography make all South Asian women pretty much alike.

Among the several community-based South Asian groups in Toronto are the Riverdale Immigrant Women's Centre, the South Asian Women's Group, the South Asian Family Support Services, and the India Rainbow Association. None of these groups is large enough to have members from all the nations of South Asia or to reflect all their cultural, religious, and linguistic diversity. There are at least a dozen major linguistic groups among South Asian nations, and few organizations could claim to represent all of them. Moreover, even when wide representation is achieved, it is temporary since workers move in and out of jobs with these organizations.

The women who created the South Asian organizations came together initially in pursuit of resources from government agencies to fund social services. They argue that their organizations are needed to counteract South Asian women's alienation from white Canadian norms, to help women avoid the racism of social service agencies, and to ensure equity for all women needing social services (Agnew 1991; Kohli 1993; Valiante 1991; Papp 1990). Sometimes individuals in the South Asian population who desire to start a new organization, which will compete for resources, point to an older organization's lack of a particular language or allege that it has biases against a particular religion. The new organization aims to be more representative of a specific ethnic group or more representative of the entire South Asian community.

A second-generation Hindu woman whose parents came from Punjab and who is a worker at one of the agencies explained what sometimes happens when an organization addresses the problems of a group of South Asian women:

> You do outreach, you try to find out what the group says it needs, what are the problems. And you bring these problems to the organization and say to them to address it. We may have the same skin colour, but we may approach [a problem] slightly differently. We may advocate different solutions ... One may be an advocate of the community, but to say one is representative of the community is a sticky question. (Interview, June 1989)

In practice, questions of the representativeness of the organizations do not often pose serious problems. The goal of these groups is to help South Asian women, and the issue is not so much whether they speak for a community, but whether they can provide services to a community. Here, however, another question arises because they are particularly committed to providing 'culturally sensitive' services. To *which* culture or cultures are their services 'culturally sensitive'? The answer depends on the personnel working in these organizations and their familiarity with South Asian cultures, although the groups can make a good argument that they are better equipped than mainstream agencies in this regard.

Further insight into the organizations' views on these questions can be gained by looking at some of the reasons the groups' members give for working in them. Volunteers are motivated by personal reasons: they 'remember how it was to feel all alone' and 'not have anybody' (interview, May 1992). Others seek to establish closer ties with other immigrants in Canada. A Hindu woman who came from United Province in Central India observed:

In 1980 I'd already been in Canada for fifteen years [but in that year] I decided to live here for the rest of my life. That's when I had an identity crisis. It suddenly struck me that I was an immigrant, and I felt I had to understand myself and had to establish my roots.

There was the need inside me that I had to do something, somehow, to become part of the community. Even though I am a [city employee] there isn't a sense of belonging.

I have always found it difficult to see [my]self as a victim rather than somebody who is in control. You can do something about changing your circumstances. One day somebody said to me, 'Would you like to be involved [in setting up Riverdale Immigrant Women's Centre]?' I was ready to get involved, I felt the need for it. Then for the next seven years that's all I did. (Interview, May 1992)

The staff of the South Asian groups are almost all middle-class women. They have educational and work experience in social work, and most feel a political motivation to work with women from their own groups. Some have experienced racial discrimination in seeking employment (Das Gupta 1994; Henry et al. 1995).[3] As a Muslim woman from Hyderabad, an administrator at one of the agencies, pointed out, 'What mobilizes people is their personal experience.' Anger at racism in Canadian society continues to motivate her: 'Advocacy gives me a way of channelling my anger and being able to get something constructive out of it' (interview, October 1992).

Although the term 'South Asian' imposes a socially constructed identity on a diverse group of women, the women's organizations can turn this to their advantage. Organizations that are perceived as representative of the 'South Asian community in Canada' are asked to participate in groups organized by government agencies; they are also consulted by a variety of institutions wanting to eliminate Eurocentrism from their services and programs, and asked to explain and interpret South Asian culture to service providers in mainstream agencies and to other professionals.

Service providers from the South Asian Family Support Services have been asked to tell crown attorneys about the culture of South Asian women and to help attorneys whose South Asian women clients are victims of abuse. Interactions such as these strengthen the organizations' claim that they represent South Asians in Canada. However, such claims have been challenged both by members of the diverse South Asian immigrant population and by members of the dominant society.

Sometimes funding agencies cite the different linguistic and religious identities of the women in these organizations as reasons for denying resources to the organization and for questioning their credibility. For example, when the South Asian Family Support Services applied to the United Way for funds, its staff and board members were asked about the representation of Muslims among the staff and the board. (The organization's wife-abuse counsellor and one of the members of its board were Muslim at that time.)

The two most frequently noted themes in the discourse about South Asians in Canada are the cultural, regional, and linguistic diversity of the group and their experience of racism. Despite their diversity, the general public perceives them as constituting a community, even though an organization that attempts to speak on behalf of South Asians can be challenged for not being representative of all groups of South Asians. The struggle against racism has created a sense of solidarity and unity among women in the organizations, and they perceive themselves as representing South Asian women and providing a legitimate voice for them. The process of documenting for government funding agencies the struggles of South Asian women deepens their awareness of racism, and advocacy on their behalf strengthens their sense of community with South Asian women.

Reports by Community-based Groups on Wife Abuse

Throughout the 1970s and 1980s, women and racialized groups became better organized and more articulate about their experiences of race, class, and gender discrimination. Their complaints were reinforced by several studies which documented interpersonal and systemic racism in various aspects of Canadian society, including the police, the media, educational institutions, housing, employment, and social services (Henry et al. 1995; Henry 1986; Bolaria and Li 1988; Canada, House of Commons 1984). Other studies revealed various forms of gender oppression. A number of community-based groups began to provide services to victims of wife abuse in their communities.

Literature by community-based groups concerning wife abuse has almost entirely been produced with the financial support of government agencies. The groups have been funded by federal agencies such as Health and Welfare Canada, the Department of Canadian Heritage, the Secretary of State (Women's Program and Multiculturalism), and the Research and Statistics Directorate. In Ontario, at the provincial level, they have received funds from the Ministry of Citizenship, the Ministry of Community and Social Services, the Ministry of the Solicitor General, and the Ontario Women's Directorate; and at the municipal level, they have been funded in Toronto by Metro Multicultural and Race Relations.

Government agencies have allocated resources to community-based groups to identify gaps in social services for victims of wife abuse (Canadian-African Newcomer Aid Centre of Toronto 1992; Toronto Advisory Committee on Cultural Approaches to Violence against Women and Children 1992; Tyagi 1993; Papp 1990). They have funded workshops and seminars on wife abuse subsequently recorded in reports (Ontario Immigrant and Visible-Minority Women's Organization 1991; Parkdale Committee to End Wife Assault 1994). Occasionally groups have been funded to write handbooks to explain to service providers in mainstream agencies how to avoid cultural misunderstanding between themselves and victims of wife abuse from ethnic and racial groups (Rafiq 1991; Chinese Family Life Services 1989; South East Asian Services Centre 1992; Korean-Canadian Women's Association 1992a). Some groups have been funded to write guides for service providers in their own agencies on how to identify a woman who is a victim of violence, and what steps service providers should take to ensure the safety of their client and themselves (COSTI 1993; Harris 1987).

Sometimes consultants have prepared reports for the community-based groups. The report by the Ontario Immigrant and Visible-Minority Women's Organization (1991) was prepared by Monica Riutort, while the report by COSTI (1993) was written by Marina Morrow; phase one of the report of the Toronto Advisory Committee on Cultural Approaches to Violence against Women and Children (1992) was prepared by Doris Rajan-Eastcott, and phase two, by Smita Tyagi (1993).

Sometimes the reports reflect a feminist orientation, focusing on the woman and her rights (Papp 1990; Rafiq 1991; Ontario Immigrant and Visible-Minority Women's Organization 1991), while other reports are more conservative and advocate a family-oriented approach (Chinese Family Life Services 1989; South East Asian Services Centre 1992; Valiante 1991). Several of the reports recommend including men in the search for a solution (Musisi and Muktar 1992; Canadian-African Newcomer Aid Centre of Toronto 1992; MacLeod and Shin 1993), and some reflect a more militant perspective on sexism and racism (Education Sexual Assault 1992; Kohli 1993). All advocate the adoption of antiracist policies in the provision of social services.

The quality of these reports varies. Some, like the report by Musisi and Muktar on the African community (1992) and the Chinese Family Life Services report (1989), provide insight into the ethnic group concerned and into the ideology of the community-based group. Others, like that by Education Sexual Assault (1992), are simply verbatim transcripts of remarks by service providers at workshops. Many reports review the steps followed in organizing workshops or conferences and list the names and addresses of participants (Ontario Immigrant and Visible-Minority Women's Organization 1991; Citizenship Development Branch, Wife Assault Team 1988; Parkdale Committee to End Wife Assault 1994). Many present their findings and recommendations in point form, but others extend them to two or three pages and present what is akin to a wish list that takes little account of the social, economic, or political contexts in which such complaints or demands will be read (Ontario Immigrant and Visible-Minority Women's Organization 1991, 26–31; Parkdale Committee to End Wife Assault 1994; Mederios 1991; Toronto Advisory Committee on Cultural Approaches to Violence against Women and Children 1992; Canadian-African Newcomer Aid Centre of Toronto 1992; Gogia 1994).

The recommendations are sometimes idealistic expressions of the hopes of the organizations to eliminate race, class, and gender discrimination and to transform the values and norms of society. For example, the Canadian African Newcomer Aid Centre of Toronto recommended a 'campaign to stop degradation of African women in family work and community' (1992, 169). Education Sexual Assault recommended that 'white mainstream and feminist agencies prioritize anti-racist education' for their staff, implement employment equity policies, and ensure that these policies go 'hand-in-hand with changes in organizational structures and procedures such that immigrant and refugee women who are hired are fully and respectfully integrated into the organizations' (Education Sexual Assault 1992, F-12). Many of the recommendations reflect the desires of community-based groups for increased funding for their work, for more job opportunities for women from Asia, Africa, and the Caribbean, and for counselling and other services for the women whom they serve. Sometimes, however, the reports recommend that women themselves assume responsibility for preventing 'sexual assault and other forms of woman abuse.' A report of the Filipino-Canadian community recommended that women 'be assertive; report the abuse; educate [themselves] about violence against women; change anti-woman attitudes; seek out community services and police assistance; advocate for changes in laws, policies or institutions that maintain barriers for women' (Ocampo and Villasin 1993, 49).

The primary objective of community-based organizations in applying for funds is to make a case for providing services to victims of wife abuse from their communities under their own auspices. They may want to start a new organization (the South Asian Family Support Services), to extend the programs of an existing one (the Chinese Family Life Support Services), or to set up an umbrella organization to address the concerns about wife abuse of many different groups (Toronto Advisory Committee 1992; Tyagi 1993; Education Sexual Assault 1992). The community-based groups must therefore justify their claims that there is a need for services for victims of wife abuse.

Aruna Papp, a formerly abused woman, successfully argued for establishing an organization for South Asian women in Scarborough in a report funded by the federal Department of Secretary of State. In making her case for providing services for South Asian women, she argued that she had found in her fourteen years working with South Asian women that they lacked information about the services available to them, and service providers in mainstream agencies did not understand their social and cultural background and therefore could not help them (1990, 7).

Reports on wife abuse by community-based groups generally do four things. First, they document that there are victims of wife abuse in their communities. Second, they argue that victims of wife abuse are unable to access social services from mainstream social service agencies.[4] Third, they assert or imply that women from their communities are entitled to the same social services as white Canadian women and that their lack of access to them is unjust and discriminatory. Fourth, they assert that they can offer 'culturally sensitive and linguistically appropriate services.'

Reports by community-based groups do not try to explain why wife abuse occurs, and they do not focus on gender inequality in their own or any other culture's values and norms. Rather, they emphasize the racism of the larger society that they feel is manifested in social services or in employment practices that keep women from their communities trapped in abusive families. They seek to demonstrate shortcomings in services provided by mainstream agencies and to highlight the distinctive nature of the services provided under their own auspices. For instance, the mission statement of the South Asian Family Support Services states these goals:

- To reduce the incidence of violence in South Asian families.
- To determine needs and provide services in order to support, integrate, decrease isolation [of] and empower South Asian battered women.
- To train and sensitize mainstream agencies to the linguistic and cultural needs of the South Asian community and assist them in developing appropriate responses.
- To promote and develop active participation of community volunteers in [a] pro-active effort to develop community leadership.
- To advocate on behalf of South Asian battered women and the community as a whole to ensure access to essential services that are culturally and linguistically appropriate.
- To promote and develop [a] public education strategy for the South Asian community and the community at large about the issue of family violence.
- To promote the commonalities among the diverse South Asian cultures and religious groups. (Annual Report 1991, n.p.)

The reports usually acknowledge that there is inequality between men and women in families, but they tend to discuss gender roles (e.g., motherhood) in an idealized way (Valiante 1991; Musisi and Muktar 1992). Family structures and values in one culture are sometimes contrasted with white Canadian norms (e.g., nuclear versus extended families, and individualistic versus collective communities) (Canadian-African Newcomer Aid Centre of

Toronto 1992; Chinese Family Life Services 1989; South East Asian Services Centre 1992). A report on the African community in Toronto defines the African family unit as comprising 'close and distant relatives as well as other members of the clan.' It explains African family values in this way:

> In many traditional African cultures, the family members have clearly defined roles along gender and age lines. Power, privileges, respect and the general division of labour both in the home and in the larger society are based on this hierarchical structure ... Men generally tend to have more public power, while women exercise tremendous power at home. Married women tend to be more respected than single mature women. Women with children are more valued than childless women. Hence, society puts pressure on women to make marriage and motherhood their ultimate goals in life. At the same time, marriage is ... a contract between two families sealing [a] long-term friendship ... In most cases arranged marriages are the norm. The parties concerned will take into consideration the needs of both families in question rather than the needs of the couple per se. Gifts are offered by the man's family to the woman's family as a sign of goodwill and as a guarantee for the future good relations between the two families rather than as a 'bride price.' (Musisi and Muktar 1992, 8–9)

Some reports from community-based groups include more analysis of gender oppression. The former executive director of the South Asian Family Support Services explains that South Asian cultures impose a 'heavy burden on women' and encourage them to suffer wife abuse and sexual abuse in silence. Some cultures perceive women as 'property' and give husbands the right to punish wives. Religious 'prescriptions that exalt men and demean women' further oppress them and make them feel guilty for wanting to disclose the abuse:

> We believe that the crucial variable in the explanation of violence against women is patriarchal power and the resulting social inequality between men and women. Capitalism has encouraged the posses-

sion of material property and women are also considered property to be possessed and dispensed with. Gender socialization has always emphasized that man is the 'head of the household,' 'the bread winner' and the 'lord and master' of all. Women are to be submissive, quiet and obedient. Assertiveness is equated with selfishness ... [Women] spend most of their lives under strict supervision of the family, in order to acquire 'gender specific' behaviour. (George, n.d., n.p.)

A report by the South East Asian Services Centre is more ambivalent:

The Vietnamese family structure is patriarchal in nature. The observance of strict obedience, filial piety, and loyalty within the family, could be seen as a form of social and political control; however, one can also see it as a kind of bargain [between the husband and wife] to secure the basic provision for living. (South East Asian Services Centre 1992, 10)

Sometimes reports note how the exigencies of adapting and settling in Canada may lead to some modification in gender roles. Women, for example, may work outside the home for the first time in Canada (Chinese Family Life Services 1989; Papp 1995). Other problems can become aggravated if the wife can find employment (even menial work at minimum wage) and the husband cannot (South East Asian Services Centre 1992). A report by the Chinese Family Life Services says that such changes can provoke violence in the husband:

To most immigrants, underemployment and occupational changes are ego shattering and depressive realities. When traditional men find themselves having to share power and status with their wives, they may resort to further asserting their authority over their wives ... losing control over their families is especially unbearable. To Chinese Canadians, the redistribution of power in the family acts as a threat to their concept of manhood and husbandhood. In order to restore familiarity and equilibrium within themselves and in the family, some traditional men resort to violence to regain control and to reduce their pain and hurt. (Chinese Family Life Services 1989, 2)

Almost all the reports say that migration has cut the women off from their network of relatives and friends and consequently isolated them in Canada.[5] An abused woman cannot always count on her family or the immigrant ethnic and racial communities for help (Papp 1990, 39–40, 61–2). One South Asian woman who has documented her history of abuse in Canada reported:

> I know my parents loved me and did not want me to be beaten, but every time I told them about the abuse my mother would cry and say, 'We have to find a way of helping your husband. He must find a job that suits him well. He needs to build up his confidence and you must be brave and help him. You must keep the family together.'
>
> My father's inability to help me and my husband made him angry and he would yell at me ... I would go back home to the same situation. No one in my family felt they could tell my husband that he had a problem he needed to deal with [because] if my husband became offended, as he was likely to do, he might walk out and leave me. This too would cause shame for the family ... My family tried to console me and suggest ways that I could make things better for my husband and myself. (Papp 1995, 19)

Sometimes communities may be unsympathetic to a woman who reports abuse, and the threat of being ostracized by the community heightens a woman's sense of isolation and loss (Pinedo and Santinoli 1991, 67). The woman may be afraid that if she reveals her situation she will be 'looked down upon,' that she will besmirch the family's honour, or cause 'a loss of face' for the family. A report by the Korean-Canadian Women's Association states:

> ... the women are isolated from the community because of shame and embarrassment ... They are ostracized by the community because they decided to break free from the violence. They are labelled as radical women and bad wives/unfit mothers because they had the courage to seek dignity for themselves and their children as

equal human beings with rights to safety, security, love and peace in
the home ... [A]nd because they wanted to help other women in violent situations from isolation and fears of abuse and perhaps death.
(Korean-Canadian Women's Association 1992b, n.p.)

The threat against their position within the community is compounded by fears about the attitude of the police towards them if
they report abuse. Whether women perceive the police as helpful
or oppressive is to some extent determined by their experiences in
their country of birth. The South East Asian Services Centre
argues that the history of Vietnam makes many women fear state
personnel as 'agents of oppression, autocracy, corruption, and
exploitation.' They are therefore wary of asking the police to protect them from the violence of their spouses. A Vietnamese
woman, the Centre says, would rather 'sacrifice her well being than
be involved with the police ... unless it becomes an issue of life and
death' (1992, 17–18).[6]

The interaction between black Canadians and the police has
been particularly tense and problematic. Police in Toronto have
been accused of racism. Black women are apprehensive that seeking help from the police would only reinforce stereotypes that 'violence is normal in black families' (Musisi and Muktar 1992, 161).
An abused black woman may also fear that the community will say
she used a 'repressive institution to inflict more pain on "the poor
man"' (Pinedo and Santinoli 1991, 67). If the man is found guilty
and sent to jail, the economic survival of the family will be jeopardized, condemning the family to 'perpetual poverty and membership in the underclass' (Musisi and Muktar 1992, 164).[7]

The reports note that abused immigrant women are unfamiliar
with the concept of social services and the code of confidentiality,
so that they may be reluctant to seek the intervention of service
providers. The reports do not explain, however, whether this unfamiliarity is shared by both middle-class and working-class women
or by both rural and urban women. They assert that there is a
demand for professional social services within their communities,
particularly since immigration has deprived the women of the support of their relatives, and they argue that the problem is not so

much the abused women's reluctance in using their services but their lack of information about them. Consequently, they recommend that more information be made available about their services in Canada.

Community-based Groups versus Mainstream Social Service Agencies

Community-based groups argue that working-class, non–English-speaking women are alienated by Eurocentric norms in mainstream social service agencies and are discriminated against by service providers in them. The groups' familiarity with the cultures of the women and their ability to communicate with them in their mother tongues make them better able to meet their needs. These claims are frequently accepted at face value by government agencies, although there are some problems with the arguments.

Community-based groups are critical of the initiatives taken by mainstream social service agencies to introduce antiracist policies and practices within their organizations, as well as their attempts to hire women from Asia, Africa, and the Caribbean. They defend their own organizations by arguing that they offer antiracist social services not available elsewhere, that the service providers in their agencies have good academic credentials, and that they deliver services in a professional manner.

Community-based organizations that provide services to women who are victims of violence offer what they call 'holistic services' on a one-to-one basis in small groups. They help victims of abuse by intervening on their behalf during crises and by counselling them. They escort women to places which would otherwise be intimidating for them, such as courts, lawyers' offices, and police stations. Service providers help them to fill out forms for housing and welfare. In addition, they organize support groups for victims of abuse to help them make the transition to living on their own. Some provide English-language classes, or help women enrol in skill-development courses, or guide them in résumé writing and finding jobs.

For example, the objectives of the Korean-Canadian Women's Association, as explained in its brochures, are 'to provide culturally sensitive and linguistically appropriate family and social services, educational programs, and to assist and encourage Korean-Canadian women and their families to better integrate and actively participate in the Canadian society.' Its director describes the social services that are offered by the Korean-Canadian Women's Association as follows:

> We provide social services, counselling for abused women, and educational programs to Korean women, [regardless of] their immigration status. We [occasionally organize] educational programs and seminars on racism, family violence, and wife assault. Once we even had a group for alcohol addiction. We have workgroups on anything that promotes the well-being of the community. This year we [publicized the plight of] Korean women who were abused by Japanese and other soldiers during the Second World War.
>
> We deal a lot with women who are abused by their husbands and in-laws. We provide counselling to them, [give them] information, and refer them to lawyers. When they go to see lawyers, we provide interpreters for them. If there is a court hearing, one of our staff will go with the women to the court for [emotional] support. We help [them apply for] legal aid, housing, and welfare.
>
> We have classes for women who need to learn the English language. Nowadays we have three LINC [Language Instruction for Newcomers] classes. Most of the women are new immigrants. We provide TTC [transit] tokens and arrange childcare for them. Some women were in our wife abuse support group and then they went into the language classes. But they felt uncomfortable. [In the classes, women are frequently asked] to introduce themselves, talk about their family, but the women did not want to lie. They felt bad, so they don't go. (Interview, 28 June 1993)

The director of the South East Asian Legal Aid Clinic explained:

> We also serve victims of wife abuse. We give them legal advice and provide referral to counsellors. When people call us, they do not tell

us that this is a wife abuse situation; they only tell us that they want to leave their husbands. So we will give them advice. We tell them that they can apply for welfare if they don't have money. Sometimes [we have to] negotiate with the police, because even now they may be unwilling to lay charges. (Interview, 18 June 1993)

A counsellor at the South Asian Women's Group noted:

We offer information, referral, and supportive counselling. In most cases, immigrant women who cannot speak the language come in because they need forms filled out or they need language training. For example, if a woman needs some financial assistance, we help her fill out forms. We find out what kind of services are free and [give] this information to the women.

  We refer women to different services, depending on their needs. We facilitate their [getting in touch] with lawyers. We have a list of lawyers that have good track records, take legal-aid cases, and are sympathetic. Sometimes we take a woman to a shelter. (Interview, 3 March 1994)

One of the primary arguments of community-based groups is that they provide services to women in their own language. They argue that although the 1991 Canadian Census indicates that there are 191,175 immigrant women who do not speak English or French (MacLeod and Shin 1993, 4), 'services are designed and delivered as if everyone speaks English fluently, subscribes to the same cultural values, and knows where to find the family services they need' (Multicultural Coalition for Access to Family Services 1991, 1). Abused women who do not speak English are at a particular disadvantage:

These women often become the brunt of negative stereotypes and myths. They are silently dismissed too often as being less deserving of special services or programs to help them with their abuse, because 'they are too lazy to learn to speak English or French,' or because 'they accept the abuse ... it's part of their culture.' They are dismissed because they have been in Canada for many years,

but have not become part of the mainstream. (MacLeod and Shin
1993, 2)

However, community-based groups cannot provide services in all
the different languages or dialects of their ethnic group. They are
usually familiar with the most common ones, but many others are
not spoken by any of their staff members.

Service providers in community-based groups act, whenever possible, as cultural and linguistic interpreters for women who are in
shelters or hospitals or have been taken to a mainstream social service agency by the police. Mainstream agencies can seek the help
of societies like the Barbara Schlifer Clinic that locate interpreters
in many different languages. Community-based groups point out,
however, that mainstream agencies often select inappropriate individuals for interpreting (family members or children), and argue
that most interpreters are not trained to work with abused women
(Toronto Advisory Committee 1992, 13). They point to surveys
that show that 'respondents overwhelming[ly] wanted counselling
services, hotlines, and support groups to be conducted in their
own language and by women from their own communities' (Toronto Advisory Committee 1992, 10).

Community-based groups argue that mainstream social service
agencies, the police, the justice system, and shelters are racist.
Mainstream social service agencies often exhibit ethnocentrism,
lack of sensitivity, and unfamiliarity with the cultural mores of
women from Asia, Africa, and the Caribbean. A report on non–
English-speaking and non–French-speaking women who are victims of abuse is critical of the value system implicit in the social services provided by mainstream agencies:

Many of the women interviewed find that existing services, with
their emphasis on individualism and centred on North American
culture and values, do not validate nor recognize their cultures and
value systems. Similarly, many of the women, even some of those
who want their husbands punished for their abusive behaviour, do
not understand a model of help which offers women support as individuals, but offers nothing to help their children and their hus-

bands. In their eyes, all members of the family are suffering and therefore all members of the family should be offered help. (MacLeod and Shin 1993, iii)

A report by the South East Asian Service Centre recommends changes in its own agency:

In a few cases, we were told that front line workers did not respond to the Vietnamese women's indirect messages asking for help or perhaps did not appreciate the clients' dire predicament sometimes because of the timidity of help seeking behaviours, i.e., their help seeking behaviour can be very different from what the workers usually come across. The fact is that *the unfortunate victims who genuinely need help are so affected by traditional beliefs and the restrictions these place upon them* that they find it all the more difficult to extricate themselves when they came to a foreign land. For this reason, we believe it is time to co-ordinate various programs to heighten the community's recognition that wife abuse should not be tolerated and, equally important, to sensitize the front line workers' awareness of the concerns of the Vietnamese women with respect to the wife abuse issue. (South East Asian Services Centre 1992, 2)

Women from Asia, Africa, and the Caribbean encounter difficulties when they live in shelters (which provide for a communal form of living). There are no shelters for any specific ethnic group in Toronto but the Shirley Samaroo House (which closed in 1995) was for immigrant women. An annual report of the Shirley Samaroo House argues that immigrant women have 'special needs because of the difficulties in confronting the barriers imposed by race, class position, language and the pressure to assimilate into mainstream society' (Shirley Samaroo House 1988, 4). Reports of several organizations reiterate that non–English-speaking women from their groups encounter difficulties when they live in shelters because they cannot communicate with the staff and other residents, or because they have different food requirements, or because their cultural mores are misunderstood (Korean-Canadian Women's Association 1992a).

Reports by community-based groups invariably note the racism of staff members at shelters and of other (white) residents (Kohli 1991a, 1993; Korean-Canadian Women's Association 1992b).[8] Rita Kohli, a South Asian who worked for several years at shelters for women, is particularly bitter about the racism that she encountered at the shelters from white service providers and white residents (Kohli 1993). One South Asian counsellor described her own and other women's experiences of racism at the Shirley Samaroo House:

White women [residents in the shelters] were racist towards me because of my [South Asian] dress. But it's not just the dress – it's how they think about people who dress like that. The legitimacy [or credibility], you know, just goes. The fact that I could speak fluent English – or speak English at all, for that matter – that was very difficult for the residents. [In addition], I was the counsellor and she the client. I had to incorporate [antiracism education] in my counselling.

There were times when we also had to deal with racism from white women against women of other cultures. It was problematic – because we are a crisis shelter dealing with violence [against women]. [We know that] a woman is in pain when she leaves her home, [but] we had to start a process of [antiracist] education for her. If we don't start a process of education for her, what are we going to do in terms of the empowerment of the other women that are experiencing racism? We had to grapple with and come to terms with the fact that, yes, a [white woman] is in crisis, but that doesn't give her the right to oppress other people because of that crisis. We had to support her, at the same time saying to her, 'No – it's not okay to be racist.' It was a very very hard thing to do.

We went through various ways of looking at it and how it would affect our service delivery. I mean, would we give her a warning, would we send her away? Obviously we can't send her away, [but] what do you do? Some women took a very political position of associating racism with violence, you know, and [with] letting women do violence to other women. [They objected] to imposing that kind of violence on the [racialized] women using the services. At Shirley

Samaroo House we could not [overlook] racism – as some other shelters [might] gloss over it. At Shirley Samaroo House we would make it an occasion for conflict mediation or conflict resolution. We would state in very clear terms the unacceptability of her [the white woman's] position. It could not be tolerated and if she continues to [be racist], she would be asked to leave. (Interview, 6 Oct. 1992)

Community-based groups point out that although they are not funded for counselling women at shelters, they nevertheless have to keep in touch with women from their communities who are living in shelters and mediate on their behalf with white service providers there (Korean-Canadian Women's Association 1992b; Musisi and Muktar 1992; Chinese Family Life Services 1989).

Many women are reluctant to go to live at shelters. The report by the Chinese Family Life Services of Metro Toronto explains (1989, 27):

Most Chinese-Canadian women we counselled reacted with a feeling of abhorrence to the idea of going to a shelter. Although these women realized that shelters were safe places and our staff would continue to counsel them, they attached a feeling of homelessness and hopelessness to shelter accommodation. Some women felt that their marriages would dissolve once they left home. Others perceived shelters to be a last resort ... In order to reduce these women's anxieties about shelter living, we often had to escort them to shelters and telephone them the next day to inquire about their well-being.

A report by the South East Asian Services Centre argues that most Vietnamese victims of abuse hope to improve their family situation, so that if 'it means choosing between being abused by women of other races/ethnic groups ... and being abused by their husbands, Vietnamese and Chinese-speaking Vietnamese women would rather return to their own homes' (South East Asian Services Centre 1992, 27).

Social service agencies generally lack personnel from many ethnic and racial groups. The reports argue that since the qualifications obtained by women in Third World countries are devalued, they are excluded from employment opportunities with main-stream social service agencies. The reports recommend instituting policies which would encourage the hiring of minorities and show the 'commitment [of mainstream social service agencies] to address the needs of diverse ethnocultural and racial communities' (Multicultural Coalition for Access to Family Services 1991, 40).

The complaints about cultural insensitivity and racism made by community-based groups have led to the introduction of new pro-grams in government agencies. For example, the Ministry of Citi-zenship funded the Cultural Interpreters Training Project, the Cross-Cultural Training and Resource Development Programs, and Information and Education Programs and Resources for non–English-speaking women (Ontario Immigrant and Visible-Minority Women's Organization 1991, 19–21). Mainstream social service agencies have hired more personnel from ethnic and racial groups and instituted cross-cultural training for their staff. Some consult-ants have proposed antiracist models of delivering social services that would enable organizations to 'survive and thrive' (Minors 1996, 196).

However, Carol Tator, president and acting executive director of the Urban Alliance on Race Relations for several years, expresses grave doubts about the changes made in mainstream social service agencies:

> In many cases, the nature of the change has been cosmetic rather than substantive; ad hoc and isolated rather than integrated and sys-temic; involving short-term interventions rather than long-term strategies. Organizational policies have been developed, but not in the context of anti-racist organizational change; community out-reach has been initiated, but power has not been shared; recruit-ment of board members and volunteers from minority communities has increased, but in largely token numbers. Thus, racial and cul-tural barriers to access and equity for people of colour continue to operate within most human service organizations. (Tator 1996, 169)

Similarly, the Ontario Council of Agencies Serving Immigrants (OCASI) feels that the changes are inadequate:

Some mainstream organizations have made token gestures such as providing cross-cultural sensitization training to staff or hiring one racial minority staff. Without fundamental changes such as having immigrants and refugees represented on Boards of Directors, eliminating racist policies and practices and adopting explicitly anti-racist ones (such as offering services in the languages of immigrants and refugees, adopting employment equity policies and practices, and ensuring community participation in strategic planning, needs assessment, program planning and evaluation) changes made can only be cosmetic. (OCASI 1993, 9)

Community-based groups argue that their services are critically significant in enabling immigrant women to gain access to social services, but funding agencies think of them as providing mainly 'menial referral work, translation, and interpretation services' (OCASI 1990, 61). They point to the cost effectiveness of the programs offered by community-based groups, the professional nature of their services, and the unique (rather than 'parallel' or 'duplicate') services which are specifically geared to the needs of their immigrant clientele (Multicultural Coalition for Access to Family Services 1991; OCASI 1993). They add that allocating resources to them has other secondary benefits, such as creating jobs within community-based organizations and developing community leaders within the boards of directors of these agencies (OCASI 1993, 16).

The tensions between community-based agencies and mainstream social service agencies suggest that there is competition between them, although their rhetoric refers to collaboration, cooperation, and the need to share information. Sometimes providing services requires collaboration. For example, the Witness Protection Program may look to community-based groups for some direction in interpreting the cultural issues of an abused woman's case and may refer clients to them for services (language classes and support groups); or personnel from mainstream agencies may volunteer to sit on the boards of community-based agencies and participate in their workshops and conferences on wife abuse. Nonetheless, despite such collaboration and cooperation, there is an undercurrent of tension. Community-based groups question the distribution of funds between themselves and mainstream agencies, and argue that it is unfair that, despite their larger clientele, they receive fewer funds (Multicultural Coalition for Access to Family Services 1991). At other times, counsellors in community-based agencies complain about the disparities between their wages and benefits and those of personnel in mainstream agencies.

Conclusion

The documentation of wife abuse by community-based organizations has been supported by government agencies. Such documentation by women from Asia, Africa, and the Caribbean has avoided the problem of racist or ethnocentric interpretations of their cultures and of the difficulties experienced by women in their communities. The *raison d'être* of these reports is to make a case for services under the auspices of the group. Therefore, the reports focus on the difficulties the women encounter in gaining access to social services. The reports identify patriarchy as the cause of abuse, but they seldom discuss how patriarchy is experienced within their respective cultures or criticize the socialization of the abused women which makes them reluctant to acknowledge abuse. Despite such problems, the reports have facilitated the provision of social services, and information about legislation and social assistance has made some choices and alternatives available to abused working-class women from Asia, Africa, and the Caribbean if they desire to leave their abusive spouses. One Muslim South Asian counsellor said:

> The law empowers women. [Before the law about wife abuse was introduced] the woman was not in a position to negotiate with her husband about his violent behaviour. But nowadays things have changed. Now they don't have to go through the abuse. Now she can say, 'If you beat me and the kids, I will use this option of calling the police' ... Women have a greater opportunity and freedom to truly

achieve equality when it comes to their relationships with their husbands and family. In Canada, [South Asian] women are provided with facilities and resources [from the state]. In Canada, even if a woman has no education, no skills, she can do something. She can learn English. She can start off by working in a factory. If a woman gets a job, she can become more independent.

When I speak to the women, they say, 'I took [the abuse] for ten years but no more. I want separation. I want divorce.' Not every woman is saying, 'I really would like this marriage to work.' Women are changing their values. They are saying, 'I have had it. This is it.' This is quite amazing. (Interview, 1 May 1992)

FIVE

Counsellors and Their Work

Although recent feminist theory acknowledges the integrated nature of race, class, and gender oppression, feminist practice often treats gender inequality as the primary causal factor in wife abuse. Gender inequality tends to be the primary concern of social workers, too, most of whom are white and middle-class (as are most Western feminists). In contrast, counsellors and social workers who are cognizant of how the racism and classism of the larger society limit the choices of abused women from Asia, Africa, and the Caribbean tend to devote their writing to documenting experiences of racism and classism and to explaining their cultures to members of the dominant society.

Handbooks on wife abuse that have been produced by community-based groups and by social workers generally reflect the mainstream feminist emphasis on gender inequality and oppression. This literature tends to describe both abused women and counsellors in generic terms, thereby rendering invisible the race, class, and gender oppression experienced by immigrant women from Asia, Africa, and the Caribbean. Handbooks that discuss counselling abused women from Asia, Africa, and the Caribbean advise counsellors to be courteous and to show respect for the culture of other women, but they do not analyse the impact of racial inequality on abused women or on the relationships between white counsellors and these women.

Community-based agencies do not fit feminist models of organization, and their work does not always conform to feminist ideals.

Feminists have often criticized the conventional norms promoted by many social workers, but the practices of community-based groups still incorporate some of these norms. They often must make compromises with feminist theory in coping with the practical, everyday challenges of women struggling to survive in a racist and sexist society. Community-based groups do fight gender oppression by providing services to victims of wife abuse. However, the difficult processes of obtaining resources and designing programs and services to meet both the needs of their clients and the desires of the state agencies that fund them force them to focus on providing services for which resources are available (e.g., settlement and adaptation services) rather than on, for example, meeting with abused women for counselling as often as they would prefer.

This chapter examines some of the tensions and contradictions experienced by community-based agencies that provide services to abused women. The first section discusses the current debate over the professionalization of counselling services; the second analyses feminist ideals underlying the instructional literature on counselling abused women; and the third explores some implications of the idea of racially neutral counselling.

Counsellors and Their Expertise

The work of counsellors is much like that of social workers and therapists, but social workers and therapists have academic credentials which make them professionals, while counsellors may not have such academic qualifications. Feminists are wary of the power and authority that have been exercised by professionals (Brown 1994, 96); but counsellors may still be perceived as authorities by abused women, and counsellors working at community-based groups show ambivalent attitudes towards the exercise of power and authority in their own work.

Counsellors frequently think of themselves as 'front-line' workers who are called upon to find solutions to complex personal, social, and political problems confronted by abused women. If a community-based group has sufficient funds, it hires a counsellor specifically to help abused women. Otherwise, all its counsellors are expected to help them, whether they are seeking settlement and adaptation services, English-language classes, or solutions to personal problems.

The counsellors specially trained to help abused women may have acquired what feminist theoreticians would describe as 'professional knowledge.' Feminists object to 'professional knowledge' because established professions such as psychiatry and social work have tended to perpetuate patriarchal (and racist and classist) norms (Dominelli 1988; Lloyd 1995; Greene 1995; Brown 1994). Prior to the pioneering work of Erin Pizzy with battered women in the United Kingdom, male discourse on abused women often attributed the violence perpetrated against them to their own behaviour, attitudes, or temperament. It attached little significance to the socio-economic or political contexts in which violence was perpetrated (Tifft 1993; Dobash and Dobash 1992; Johnson 1995, 14–18).

Professionals also exercise power through their ability to define issues and problems. Feminists have argued that 'androcentric knowledge' (based on male interpretations and perspectives) encourages professionals to attach less significance to women's particular experiences of oppression – for instance, when that oppression might involve racism. Women from Asia, Africa, and the Caribbean encounter racism while seeking employment, but their failure to secure work and their consequent dependence on public resources (or social assistance) may be construed by social workers as signs of personal inadequacy or lack of motivation.

Beverly Greene argues that the aim of many social workers is to encourage their clients to behave 'appropriately' and to 'conform or fit into the prevailing social order, regardless of its suitability for them ... The tendency to stigmatize cultural norms and practices that deviate from white, Anglo-Saxon, Protestant, and middle-class norms reflects the use of the dominant culture as the standard or norm, against which all others are deemed either similar and normative or different and therefore deficient' (Greene 1994, 334). In

Canada the assimilationist philosophy prevalent until the 1960s encouraged service providers to 'Canadianize' new women immigrants by imposing white, middle-class, and Anglo-Saxon norms on them (Iacovetta 1995).

Racialized people are frequently 'singled out by the media as "having problems" that require a disproportionate amount of political attention or public resources to solve'; or they are seen as 'creating problems' that threaten the political, social, or moral order of society (Henry et al. 1995, 235). When visible minorities appear in Canadian newspapers or on television, they are often presented 'as troubled immigrants in a dazzling array of trouble spots; hassling police, stumping immigration authorities, cheating on welfare, or battling among themselves or with their own families' (Siddiqui 1993, quoted in Henry et al. 1995, 235).

Immigrant clients are often assumed to conform to stereotypes associated with their ethnic group. Social workers may try to overcome these stereotypes by counselling racialized clients as if they were no different from non-racialized people (except for having *more* of the problems everyone has). But the attempt by professionals to treat racialized women in a 'colour-blind' fashion decontextualizes race and obscures the 'power differential and privileges accessible to white professionals but not black clients' (Dominelli 1988, 32–44). Lauren Brown argues that inattention to racism by a white therapist helping a racialized client 'serves to perpetuate unspoken power imbalances' between them:

> The silence of the white feminist therapist communicates that the experiences of being the target of racism in the life of her client of color, and in the therapy room, are unimportant. The white woman will have, without speaking, imposed her unexamined values on her client of color. The effects of racism are such that unless white women take the initiative to acknowledge racism as an issue for ourselves, women of color will be excluded or will choose to absent themselves from the precincts of feminist therapy because white people will have taken the power to define the 'legitimate' terms of discourse. (Brown 1995, 141)

In contrast, feminists hold that the task of a social worker, thera-pist, or counsellor is not 'to make the clients fit into oppressive, and by definition, unhealthy circumstances; rather, it is to assist cli-ents in using their personal resources to challenge and alter their circumstances in ways that are consistent with their values' (Greene 1994, 335; see also Christensen 1995). Feminists advocate relying more on women's experience to guide them in identifying what oppresses them and in determining how to combat it. They argue that clients have the 'authority of experience' and are the 'experts' on their own situation. Instead of decontextualizing the experiences of their clients and attributing their problems to cir-cumstances in their backgrounds, and instead of imposing middle-class norms as models for their behaviour, feminists encourage therapists and social workers to analyse their own values and to incorporate antiracist strategies in their work (Adleman and Enguidanos 1995; see also Paquet-Deehy, Rinfret-Raynor, and Larouche 1992). Feminists emphasize developing the women's own capabilities, while recognizing the enormous problems they confront in a race- and gender-biased society.

However, the non-professional 'facilitation' advocated by femi-nists may raise questions about 'lack of standards,' as well as doubts about the expertise of counsellors who engage in it (Minicucci 1994). Also, both community-based groups and professionals point out that their clients usually have a more pressing need for imme-diate social services than for strategies of social change.

Most community-based groups that offer services to abused women aim at achieving professionalism in their practical work, although they maintain that they are feminist in their theoretical orientation. They try to retain what is valuable in professional social work while rejecting those features of which feminists are most critical. Terry Gillespie, a sociologist, endorses this approach: 'it is possible to assume the more positive attributes associated with professionalism – for example, established exper-tise, specialist service provision, consultative work, extensive and ongoing training – while rejecting the more negative aspects com-monly identified, such as authoritarianism, male-dominated hier-archies, power structures, "masculinist" service philosophies and provision implicit in, for example, the medicalisation and patholo-gisation of rape' (Gillespie 1994, 22).

Counsellors in these organizations invariably indicated in inter-views that they accepted feminist explanations of wife abuse, which emphasize power relations within the family and gender inequali-ties that keep women trapped in abusive homes. The counsellors did not see themselves as 'neutral' or 'objective' observers but as advocates of abused women in their communities. They were also critical of the ethnocentric practices of white social workers in mainstream agencies, arguing that abuse of women from their communities had to be understood in culturally specific ways and that their needs for services were different from those of white women. However, several counsellors followed the standard social-work practices, such as maintaining case histories, although these tend to abstract the individual from her social context.

Many community-based groups make a point of emphasizing the professional nature of the services they offer, especially when they are applying for funding or participating in workshops and conferences with social workers from mainstream agencies. A report by the Chinese Family Life Services argued that 'funders ought to recognize that the Chinese-Canadian community has the human resources to deliver quality professional services to wife assault clients and their families' (1989, ii). The Korean-Canadian Women's Association asserted that its counsellors were 'profes-sionally trained people,' and it invited Korean-Canadian psychia-trists, social workers, and professors to lead discussions at its workshops on violence in the family (1988, 27).

The Ontario Council of Agencies Serving Immigrants (OCASI) objected to the stereotype that its agencies were 'amateur, unpro-fessional organizations, providing assistance mainly on a volunteer basis.' The truth, it said, was that 'the staff and management are not lacking for educational degrees' (1993, 14–15). OCASI advocates training and 'professional development' for women who work in community-based organizations with abused women. The training ranges from learning to be culturally sensitive to learning how to mobilize immigrant women for political action (1990, 64–5).

OCASI asserts the equality of community-based agencies with

mainstream social service agencies. It sees this strategy as a way of fighting racism in social services and making them more responsive to the diverse cultural and social needs of the population. At the same time, it provides arguments for equalizing employment-related benefits in both sets of organizations. Most community-based groups, in making pay-equity calculations, use a state agency as a model for determining wages and benefits. This sometimes enables community-based groups to claim retroactive wage increments under pay-equity legislation and to add these increments to projected budgets for ongoing programs. Equalizing wages and benefits between mainstream agencies (which are dominated by white middle-class women) and community-based agencies (which are dominated by women from Asia, Africa, and the Caribbean) goes some way towards overcoming systemic racism.

Some organizations seek professional expertise by hiring women with strong academic credentials (although not necessarily in social work) and by encouraging other staff members to acquire professional training by attending courses in community colleges (e.g., courses on working with abused women or in social work). Others give priority to work experience, personal experience of abuse, or interpersonal skills.[1]

Feminists support organizational structures which promote equality between the service providers and the women they serve. They favour collectives, in which all women participate in decision-making and all jobs are rotated among the staff. Since educational qualifications often form the basis of hierarchies in organizations, collectives place greater significance on the experience of women than on their educational qualifications: 'The ideal is that responsibility, knowledge, and accountability will be shared equally by all members. No one is placed in the position of being expert, and everyone is assumed to want to engage in all of the tasks equally' (Ristock 1991, 53; see also Ontario Association of Interval and Transition Houses 1991b, 52–8).

Collectives are strongly opposed to any exercise of power which they perceive as 'negative, hurtful, and oppressive' (Ristock 1991, 46). They are committed to sharing authority equally, engaging in decision-making by consensus, and empowering women for whom they provide services. The ideal is to reduce the differences between the 'experts' and their clients, but, in practice, workers in collectives still exercise some power over the women for whom they provide services, and some staff members exercise power over others.

Some organizations establish job hierarchies with well-defined lines of authority and responsibility, arguing that these structures help provide efficient services. Others describe themselves as collectives and aim at eliminating status distinctions based on educational qualifications or job descriptions. In either case, the ways in which decisions are made in the organizations change over time with changes in their boards or executive directors.

Community-based groups engaged in working with abused women agree that abuse is an exercise of power but differ among themselves in determining how women experience men's exercise of power and domination. Linda MacLeod surveyed twenty-nine projects funded by the Family Violence Prevention Division of Health Canada and found that, while all the projects saw abuse as a means of exercising power and domination, only some of them used broad definitions which included spiritual and financial abuse. All the projects saw abuse as including 'structural and institutional violence as well as violence among individuals' (1994, 30), and some felt that even 'insufficient staff, or intervention by untrained staff in violent situations,' constitutes an exercise of power 'to keep people insecure and unequal.' The National Organization for Immigrant and Visible-Minority Women argued that power can be exercised by 'stressing the differences rather than the commonalities among people; preventing people from thinking of the complexity of life problems so that they will not be able to come up with effective solutions; blaming and ridiculing women for not learning English; keeping women as marginal employees; and giving social assistance intended for the whole family to the man' (MacLeod 1994, 31–2).

Counsellors at community-based organizations come from diverse backgrounds. Some have professional social-work qualifications; others do not. Some have undergraduate or graduate degrees in various disciplines. Some are enrolled in social-work courses offered by universities and community colleges. Others rely on opportunities for professional development offered by various conferences and workshops hosted by community-based groups.

Even though counsellors in community-based groups have a wide range of work experience in their countries of origin (they include former university teachers, accountants, travel agents, and business executives), as recent immigrants they can gain valuable Canadian experience by working with community-based organizations. However, women who have been in Canada for several years and second-generation immigrants may feel ghettoized and marginalized by practices which attach importance only to their ethnic identity. When community-based groups or mainstream social service agencies attach significance only to women's knowledge of their own culture or to their ability to speak different languages, rather than to their educational qualifications and professional expertise, they erode the sense of accomplishment of those women who have professional qualifications. Moreover, while feminist theory attacks the power implicit in professional expertise, many women from Asia, Africa, and the Caribbean want to be considered professionals, and they obtain satisfaction from this status. Valuing their experience over their educational qualifications and professional expertise strikes them as another manifestation of racism.

Some women from Asia, Africa, and the Caribbean argue that they have been trained in the patriarchal values of their professions and must struggle to replace them with counselling paradigms developed from their own experience of race, class, and gender oppression (Chaudhry 1992; see also Wang 1995). Even so, it is difficult to combine the approaches, and counsellors are wary of 'unprofessional' feminist therapy:

> The places that are available to us are the very institutions whose structure and philosophies are antithetical to feminist principles. Some of us think that after going through such curriculums, we can integrate our feminism with our training. In retrospect, this has not proven a viable option without massive 'unlearning.' There are others who try to circumvent attending mainstream institutions and

undertake the work based on their passion for change and [commit-
ment] to feminist principles. Often, unfortunately, this route pro-
duces a different set of problems when [counselling] is so totally
devoid of professional standards. (Minicucci 1995, 62)

Despite their desire to provide feminist counselling outside the
paradigms of traditional professional social work, the community-
based groups emphasize their ability to provide professional
counselling to abused women living in their communities. The
attractions of professionalism are evident in a Filipino-Canadian
manual's claim that abused women express 'the need to have professional, skilled, informed, trusted and non-judgemental persons within the community who can be available to assist women
in violent situations' (Ocampo and Villasin 1993, 49).

Counsellors in community-based organizations are sensitive to
the systemic sexism and racism of professional social-work paradigms and institutions, but during my interviews, counsellors usually limited themselves to describing ways of avoiding sexism or
racism in counselling (showing respect for the culture of other
women, creating an informal environment in which the abused
woman could feel at ease) or simply to asserting the racism of
white social workers in mainstream social service agencies.

Racism in employment has been one of the worst problems for
immigrants from Asia, Africa, and the Caribbean. Their complaints about systemic racism centre around three issues. First,
educational qualifications and work experience obtained in Third
World countries are devalued by Canadian employers. Second,
immigrants from Asia, Africa, and the Caribbean experience race
and gender discrimination in hiring practices. Third, when these
immigrants are hired, they are concentrated in entry-level jobs or
in contract positions. One study in Nova Scotia reported:

Black social work graduates from the Maritime School of Social
Work found less desirable jobs than others, including limited or
term positions and more part-time jobs. Moreover, once they
obtained work, they found that their opportunities for advancement
were relatively limited and salary levels low ... Black social workers

had been less successful than the majority group in accessing the more prestigious social work jobs, including family counselling, hospital social work, and administrative or supervisory positions. (Henry et al. 1995, 156)

Community-based agencies have argued that the lack of personnel from Asia, Africa, and the Caribbean in mainstream social service agencies perpetuates ethnocentrism and denies equal access to services for women from their communities (OCASI 1993; Mederios 1991; Agard 1987).

Counsellors in community-based groups insist that they have a greater understanding of the cultures of abused clients from Asia, Africa, and the Caribbean than white middle-class counsellors in mainstream social service agencies (Rafiq 1991; Kohli 1991a; Pinedo and Santinoli 1991). However, they often describe diverse clients as belonging to a single culture. For example, the Chinese Family Life Services does not distinguish between the classes or countries of origin of its Chinese clientele. It often generalizes, saying, for example, that 'since Chinese-Canadians are very much influenced by traditional values which stress harmony, selflessness and interdependence, counselling techniques were channelled toward acknowledging and fostering these values in a constructive manner' (1989, 24).

One South Asian respondent emphasized the advantages enjoyed by counsellors and clients when they share similar cultural backgrounds (though she also acknowledged that differences of class, language, and religion exist among South Asian women which can create barriers between South Asian counsellors and South Asian clients):

When a woman comes into [the office] and she sees me dressed in South Asian clothes, you know something automatically happens. There is an understanding of where I'm coming from, the language that I speak, [and] how I speak it.

What is meaningful in a culture gets translated in the way you interact with the person you're counselling. When people are in crisis, their reserves of strength are already being used up – they need familiarity, they need to be reached out [to]. So for a [woman from an ethnic or racial group] to have to deal with an agency with a language and a way of looking at things that are very different from [hers] is an extra burden. (Interview, 6 Oct. 1992)

The feminist principle adopted by some community-based groups of assigning value to the experience of the women they serve has helped women from Asia, Africa, and the Caribbean to gain recognition for educational credentials and work experience from their countries of origin when they are seeking paid work. Some of these women have been hired by community-based groups because they bring understanding of the culture of the groups' clientele and knowledge of the language spoken by the women who come to them for services. (Similarly, women who have left abusive relationships have taken up volunteer and paid work in community-based organizations.) Their knowledge and experience establish empathy with the women whom they serve and provide insight into their lives. Counsellors at community-based organizations express satisfaction with working with women from their own racial and ethnic communities, but there is not always a perfect fit between feminist principles and counselling practices or between an organization's ideals and its day-to-day reality.

Handbooks and Manuals for Counsellors Working with Abused Women

Research on counselling and handbooks on counselling have been funded by the Ontario Ministry of Community and Social Services, Family Division Program; the National Clearinghouse on Family Violence, Health and Welfare Canada; and the Ministry of Citizenship. References to two handbooks on counselling abused women appear often in the available literature on wife abuse. One of these books, *Understanding Wife Assault: A Training Manual for Counsellors and Advocates* (1985), was written by a social worker, Deborah Sinclair; the other, *Working with Assaulted Immigrant Women: A Hand-*

book for Lay Counsellors (1985),[2] was written by two counsellors, Monica Riutort and Shirley Small. Both manuals identify gender inequality as the primary cause of abuse. Riutort and Small instruct counsellors on the rights of immigrant women to social assistance and explain how they can be helped to access it. However, neither book addresses the racism that oppresses many women and makes it particularly difficult for them to leave abusive homes.

Linda MacLeod, a freelance journalist who has written extensively on violence against women, has surveyed some current counselling strategies in *Counselling for Change: Evolutionary Trends in Counselling Services for Women Who Are Abused and for Their Children in Canada* (1990). MacLeod, like Sinclair and Riutort and Small, focuses primarily on gender oppression in this book, though in some of her other writings on abuse she addresses the cultural differences among women. She nevertheless uses an 'additive analysis,' according to which women from Asia, Africa, and the Caribbean are oppressed by gender, race, and class, but experience them separately rather than as interrelated. Feminists from Asia, Africa, and the Caribbean have argued that they experience sexism in different ways from white women and that their multiple oppressions cannot be reduced to 'mere arithmetic' since 'how one form of oppression is experienced is influenced by and influences how another form is experienced' (Spelman 1988, 123). One of the few studies on counselling abused women that does not use an additive analysis is an article by Barbara Pressman, a family therapist in private practice: 'Violence against Women: Ramifications of Gender, Class, and Race Inequality' (1994).

Community-based groups have also produced their own handbooks. For example, COSTI has prepared a handbook for its counsellors entitled *Wife Assault / Woman Abuse* (1993). It, too, focuses on gender oppression and makes very few references to the experiences of immigrant women. Some articles written by activist women from Asia, Africa, and the Caribbean appear in Fauzia Rafiq's *Towards Equal Access: A Handbook for Service Providers* (1991). They explain the gender values and norms of various groups and give some suggestions about how counsellors can become culturally sensitive (see also Kohli 1993). The assumption is that counsellors should fill in the gaps in their understanding of the different cultures of women but not necessarily learn how their clients experience power and privilege.

Counselling tends to be defined fairly broadly in the literature on abused women. For Linda MacLeod, for instance, it 'encompasses anything that can help strengthen and empower women' (MacLeod 1990, 8). Counselling may be one-to-one or in a group led by a counsellor or facilitator. Sometimes counselling begins as crisis intervention when a woman comes to a community-based organization or a shelter and then continues over a period of several months (Kohli 1991a). Abused women are counselled on a range of issues – from coping with psychological and emotional trauma to working out the practical details of leaving an abusive spouse (which may include laying charges, establishing a new home, and finding a job).

The manuals and handbooks, mostly written by white middle-class women, provide advice to counsellors on how to help abused women move from the position of a 'victim' to that of a 'victor over violence' (Sinclair 1985, 65). They describe how counsellors should interact with victims of wife abuse; for example, how to pace questions and whether to probe for details about the abuse. Some manuals explain Canadian law on sexual assault, immigration and sponsorship, and regulations for social assistance (Sinclair 1985, Riutort and Small 1985, MacLeod 1990, COSTI 1993); however, they address very few of the problems faced by poor or working-class abused women, and they rarely include any discussion of racism.

The challenge of counselling an abused woman can be daunting to a counsellor. Some abused women face critical issues of life and death, and counsellors must sometimes guess the extent of violence with which an abused woman is confronted if she does not reveal it immediately or is not aware of its seriousness (COSTI 1993). Since a woman who goes back to a violent home may be killed, counsellors feel responsible for the woman's physical safety. Guides and manuals seek to reassure the counsellors:

Wife assault is not an easy subject to deal with. It hurts. It is scary. We were seldom trained to think about it, let alone counsel real, live victims. Some of us hide behind our professional masks, desperately trying to sound knowledgeable and to make sense of it, but inside we tremble. It makes us sick and we feel inadequate, embarrassed, frustrated. (Sinclair 1985, 11)

The handbooks advise counsellors to focus on the 'social context' to help a woman move from 'passive dependency to self-determination and autonomy,' or from 'debilitating fear to energizing affirmative anger' (Riutort and Small 1985, 17). They contrast their feminist analyses of abuse to the more traditional view which treats it as the result of 'interaction gone wrong' or of poorly developed 'communication skills' (ibid., 5).

One feminist handbook identifies several goals for counselling sessions:

(a) to make the women aware of their specific condition and the factors which perpetuate their oppression; (b) to help them regain power over their lives, their environment and their bodies by becoming more autonomous and affirmative; (c) to help them develop a sense of personal identity; (d) to increase and restore self-esteem; (e) eventually to promote social change. (Poirer, Paquet-Deehy and Legault 1985, quoted in Paquet-Deehy, Rinfret-Raynor, and Larouche 1992, 4)

Monica Riutort and Shirley Small describe the goals of counselling in terms of a series of stages in which 'consciousness-raising (in counselling and in groups)' leads to 'awareness of [the] status of women as second-class citizens,' which in turn leads to awareness 'that control is in the system' and the 'system is to blame,' and eventually to 'affirmative anger' which will prompt constructive action (Riutort and Small 1985, 17). Deborah Sinclair tells counsellors that an abused woman may undergo 'anger, ambivalence and mourning before she develops a sense of self-worth, an ability to be assertive and [have] a renewed sense of trust in her judgement' (1985, 65). She guides counsellors with a summary of 'short-term counselling issues':

1. Dealing with her safety and ongoing protection issues.
2. Broadening her support system, decreasing her isolation.
3. Dealing realistically with her fear by providing her with accurate information, facilitating her access to needed resources and outlining her alternatives.
4. Increasing her awareness of her rights and responsibilities, such as legal rights.
5. Helping her understand the impact of violence on her children.
6. Educating her on the characteristics of the offender so she will be better informed about the dynamics of violence. This will enable her to clearly separate out his responsibilities (such as control of his violent behaviour) and her responsibilities (such as protecting herself).
7. Mobilizing her anger in a constructive, energy-producing way.
8. Increas[ing] her sense of control over her environment.
9. Changing any of her beliefs that may contribute to her victimization, such as staying for the sake of the children.
10. Increasing her economic independence by exploring her opportunities for advancement, such as job-training.
11. Dealing with her movement from the victim position to that of personal empowerment. The transition period is often painful. It brings with it a number of feelings to sort out, such as anger, ambivalence, guilt, sadness. It may also bring a number of concrete changes that are stressful, such as locating housing and day care, returning to the workforce, coping as a single parent, loss in standard of living. (Sinclair 1985, 64)

Most of the manuals recommend that counsellors discard the values of professional objectivity and neutrality in their work with abused women and take on the role of advocates for abused women. Counsellors are advised to tell their clients that abuse is a crime and is not to be tolerated. They are urged to help their clients to 'decrease victim behaviour and develop an awareness of the socio-political context of the violence' (Paquet-Deehy, Rinfret-Raynor, and Larouche 1992, 4).

The manuals are written from a feminist perspective, but MacLeod reports that in practice counsellors tend to focus on the whole family of the abused woman rather than primarily or solely on the woman herself (MacLeod 1990, 11). Some counsellors describe their own personal experiences when speaking with clients, to show them that their experiences are widely shared and to reduce the social distance between themselves and their clients. They try to make their remarks 'non-competitive, non-controlling, and non-interruptive,' and they try to avoid presenting themselves as authorities. They also try especially not to make decisions for their clients. One counsellor remarked:

> We do not stress that they should leave home. We don't press women or children to talk about the violence until they are ready to talk about it. We feel that the way they have learned to talk about their experiences and the way they deal with the violence is part of their survival skill package. We respect that learning, and help women and children extend it to reduce the violence in their lives. (Quoted in MacLeod 1990, 9)

The manuals do not provide much guidance on measuring the success of their counselling. Instead they rearticulate long-term goals of transforming gender relations. The goal of preventing violence against women is described as the result of a 'positive movement' towards removing race, class, and gender inequalities, increasing participation of oppressed groups in decision-making, and empowering all 'individuals and groups' (MacLeod 1994, 16). However, counsellors must reconcile the need to help women resolve practical difficulties with the desire to advocate social and structural change.

The need for counselling across lines of race and class makes it imperative to resolve differences of power and privilege between counsellors and abused women, particularly when counsellor and client differ in race and class. In mainstream agencies, often the counsellor is a white middle-class woman, and the client is a working-class woman from Asia, Africa, and the Caribbean or a new immigrant from a stigmatized ethnic group (e.g., Southern Europeans), or the counsellor and the client are both women from Asia, Africa, or the Caribbean but differ from each other in class (and in religion, language, and culture). The literature by white middle-class women does not address differences like these (Sinclair 1985; Riutort and Small 1985; MacLeod 1990; Paquet-Deehy, Rinfret-Raynor, and Larouche 1992; Janz 1993); and the literature by women from Asia, Africa, and the Caribbean tends to assume that counsellors and clients in community-based organizations belong to a homogeneous ethnic group and share similar cultural values (Rafiq 1991; Kohli 1991a; Chinese Family Life Services 1989).[3]

The manuals do not refer to the race, class, or ethnic identity of either the counsellor or the client. The handbook by COSTI does not discuss the difficulties of a non–English-speaking abused woman (1993), and MacLeod's handbook (which seems to use 'generic' models of counsellors and clients of no particular race and class) does not discuss the problems of resolving differences in race, ethnicity, or class in counselling sessions (1990).

A feminist project on 'conjugal violence' in Quebec described as 'action research' (it combined training of social workers with collecting data) does not even distinguish between French and English Canadians (Paquet-Deehy, Rinfret-Raynor, and Larouche 1992). It simply assumes that counselling occurs between women who speak the same language. Although it documents the institutional biases of mainstream social-work agencies (for example, their reluctance to allow social workers to participate in the training sessions or to support their adoption of feminist counselling techniques), it does not mention counselling immigrant women from Asia, Africa, and the Caribbean.

Counselling itself assumes some inequality between counsellor and client. The counsellor has access to information that is needed by the abused woman and knowledge of how the system works, and she may also have professional credentials. The abused woman is dependent on the counsellor to help her through her crisis. In addition, the counsellor and the client bring with them some stereotypical beliefs about the racial, class, and ethnic identity of each other, about women who experience domestic violence, and about its causes (Lloyd 1995, 159). Even when counsellor and client have the same ethnicity, the counsellor may be an assimilated immigrant who shares many of the values of middle-class white Canadian society, and the client may be a working-class woman who retains many of the values of her ethnic group. The process of negotiating such differences can be emotionally difficult for both women. However, the literature on counselling abused women largely ignores these aspects of the counselling experience. Handbooks and manuals advise counsellors to be 'sensitive' to cultural differences, but they do not examine the ways in which power, privilege, or even racism may be manifested by a white counsellor working with abused women from Asia, Africa, and the Caribbean or the ways in which racism in Canadian society limits the choices that such an abused woman has if she decides to leave an abusive relationship.

Feminist handbooks and manuals give some general advice about avoiding power relationships. MacLeod reports that counsellors described their role as 'helping women to recognize their own strengths, to trust their own feelings and to take some responsibility for self-protection.' They said that they were helping women to realize greater 'self-esteem and autonomy' and to augment their strengths (1990). Sinclair advises that counsellors should allow assaulted women to make their own decisions and says that by 'respecting those decisions even when they are not the ones counsellors would make for themselves, counsellors can ... indicate their belief in the woman's strength' (Sinclair 1985, 48). However, the handbooks do not elaborate these points in the context of cross-race or cross-class counselling, and they do not address the specific challenge of relinquishing authority based on race or class privilege.

Counselling is a two-way street, despite the situational inequality. Counselling an abused woman sometimes leads the counsellor to acknowledge her own oppression, to confront her own fears and anxieties, and to reassess her own ways of dealing with them (Siegel 1990, 330). Laura Brown recommends that counsellors 'unpack' their assumptions about categories such as 'male' and 'female' and question their beliefs about what is 'normal,' 'natural,' and 'to be expected' (Brown 1994, 99). 'Inquiry and disruption' of this sort can help the counsellor to become conscious of her own race or class privilege, to discover the biases and assumptions underlying many of her counselling techniques, and to see what meaning her identity has for her client. The reluctance of a woman from Asia, Africa, or the Caribbean to disclose information about her situation may not be a sign of 'resistance' but may point to fear, distrust, and the need to protect herself until some trust has been established between her and the counsellor (Pressman 1994, 381).

Riutort and Small report that when they first started counselling assaulted women, they only considered how they could change 'their' thinking and help 'them' feel less inadequate. 'Before long we came to realize – painfully – how much "they" were changing "our" thinking, helping "us" to shed false feelings of inadequacy' (1985, 1). The mutuality of the counselling process is also recognized by a South Asian counsellor, who says that 'working out the puzzles of their lives helped me to understand my own dilemmas. I drew strength from those who were beaten and abused ... I fought their battles and won my own wars' (Papp 1995, 120).

The 'action research' in Quebec provided social workers with an opportunity for reflecting on their lives and on the values of the institutions in which they work. Although they found it difficult to overcome the patriarchal biases embedded in the culture of social work, they said that counselling helped them to overcome 'feminine conditioning' and reduced their anxiety over their professional performance. They learned to overcome the desire to be 'maternal' or to take charge of their clients' lives, which had made them feel that they never did enough or were not professional enough. Paquet-Deehy, Rinfret-Raynor, and Larouche found that the 'closer the material presented by the clients was to their own vulnerabilities as women, as well as their own fears (the fear of rape for example),' the greater their anxiety was about being able to help them (1992, 15). Counselling victims of abuse helped them become assertive and 'gain power' over their own lives (ibid., 13–17).

Racial differences between counsellors and their clients can cause additional anxieties. One Jewish-American woman imagined how she might articulate her fears to a racialized woman she was counselling:

> When I realize that I have been inattentive to the ways in which I contribute to your oppression, I feel a deep sense of inadequacy, combined with the full weight of my privileged status. I feel angry at you and at myself for uncovering my insensitivities. I also feel angry and wish to withdraw from you when you have been unaware of how you have contributed to my oppression, or when you persist in denying my pain. The barriers go up. This shame and this anger get in our way and would keep us divided ... The effort to move from anger to empathy is painful and difficult; when it does happen, the rewards are joyful and invigorating. (Siegel 1990, 332–3)

COSTI recommends that counsellors be sensitive to the cultural differences between themselves and the abused woman. They should become 'clear' about their own 'biases and prejudices,' remember that abused women come from all classes and cultures, and recognize that each individual is 'unique' and brings her 'own personal history and experience to each situation' (1993). Manuals generally advise counsellors to be considerate and show respect. Sinclair says that 'counsellors and advocates must first examine their own values and beliefs' and then present themselves as 'role models of competent, successful, and assertive women' (Sinclair 1985, 48).

In contrast, Brown argues that there is always an essential asymmetry in the relationship between client and counsellor, and the aim of establishing an egalitarian relationship between the two is not achieved by denying the counsellor's power but by achieving 'thorough, thoughtful, and complex understanding and acceptance of her power' (1994, 105). A counsellor's denial of her power does not make it disappear. It may even disempower the client by denying the reality of how she experiences her relationship with the counsellor. However, acknowledging race privilege is fraught with tensions and difficulties for white feminists. Accustomed to thinking of themselves as outsiders, white feminists sometimes have difficulty identifying themselves as insiders. They may think that

> after all, when we have experienced being non-privileged, how can we possibly be contributing to remaining privileges? We can partially identify and empathize with women of colour because of our own experiences with the 'isms' that have oppressed or limited us. What is excruciatingly difficult for many White feminists to comprehend is how we might be the perpetrators, the enforcers, the reinforcers of White Privilege. (Rave 1990, 320)

Counsellors 'cannot help [an abused woman] develop strategies for dealing with reality if they engage in the defensive flight and avoidance of an anxiety-provoking issue' (Greene 1986, 53). Acknowledging racial privilege and oppression can bring relief and precipitate 'the healing when the client feels validated and understood' (Siegel 1990, 330). The colour-blind advice in the handbooks and manuals does not acknowledge these anxieties and tensions.

Implications of Class- and Colour-Blind Counselling

The manuals on counselling victims of wife abuse emphasize the need to focus on the 'social context' of abuse, but they restrict themselves to gender relations. Many regard gender as sufficient to create a sense of commonality and solidarity among the women. They do not discuss the social, political, and economic contexts in which violence is perpetrated or in which counselling services are made available to abused women. They fail to acknowledge the ways power and privilege are manifested between white counsellors and abused women from Asia, Africa, and the Caribbean or the ways in which racism limits the choices available to an abused woman. The manuals give little direction to counsellors who want to come to terms with the abused woman's experience of racism in Canadian society.

A white middle-class feminist bias pervades the manuals on wife abuse. They seem to assume that women, regardless of their race and class, subscribe to feminist values. A woman who is seeking to escape abuse is assumed to be dissatisfied with gender roles and to share the feminist desire to bring about social change. However, although abused women want to stop the violence that is being inflicted upon them, they may not object to their traditional gender roles as wives and mothers and may have little desire to critique their cultural or political ideologies.

In advocating their broad ideals and goals, the manuals do not exhibit much appreciation of the reasons many women may have for being reluctant to become 'independent and autonomous' persons. Nor do they address the problems faced by women who *are* prepared to reject the values and norms of their culture or community. These women risk rejection by their immediate families, other relatives, and the members of their communities.

Feminists from Asia, Africa, and the Caribbean have sometimes defended the family against white middle-class feminists who identify it as a primary site of women's oppression (Barrett and McIntosh 1985). Their defence of the family does not deny the gender inequalities within the family but rather argues that many women need the support available to them from their families to survive in a racist society. For immigrants, families can serve as a source of psychological and emotional comfort and a haven in a racist society. Moreover, women and men from Asia, Africa, and the Caribbean experience solidarity with each other in their struggle to resist and overcome racism (Davis 1983; hooks 1984, 1988; Carby 1982; Ramazanoglu 1989, 148–9, 183; Bhatti-Sinclair 1994). Counsellors discover that abused women from Asia, Africa, and the Caribbean may not want to leave an abusive partner: '[B]lack women's ambivalence and their gnawing recognition of all the outrages and injustices against their partners are powerful forces to generate defensiveness, support, and protection rather than condemnation or even questioning of the partner's behaviour' (Pressman 1994, 368–9). If they leave, they may lose the support of their extended family. Their lack of power is accentuated and they are further marginalized.

Immigrant families from Asia, Africa, and the Caribbean have been partly constructed by the racist discourse and practices of the larger society (Javed 1995). When abuse occurs in Asian or black families, racial stereotypes further oppress women. South Asian women, for example, are sometimes perceived as passive victims of arranged marriages (Agnew 1993b). White service providers sometimes do not seriously explore alternatives with South Asian women because they believe mistakenly that as 'traditional women' they will soon return to their abusive homes (interview, 28 April 1992).

Patriarchal values may limit the willingness of an ethnic or racial community to help an abused woman. The community may be critical of a woman who reveals her situation to white Canadian society, for fear of further reinforcing the negative stereotypes of the larger society.

Working-class women from Asia, Africa, and the Caribbean may be reluctant to charge their spouses with abuse and take on responsibility for providing for themselves and their children. Lack of skills and education may force women into a lower standard of living. Although an abused woman may have access to social assistance, the road to 'empowerment' and 'independence' may be very long and hard, intimidating many working-class women, particularly if they do not speak English. The manuals are short on advice for these women.

Scholars disagree on how to conceptualize the relationship between race and class (Satzewich 1991). Racism has sometimes been analyzed solely in terms of the economics of class and production relations. Daiva Stasiulis argues, however, that '"racial" and "ethnic" divisions cannot be reduced to or seen as completely determined by the structural contradictions of capitalist societies.' Race and racism are not epiphenomenal to class; they have 'their own complex and historically specific modes' (Stasiulis 1990, 279). Class alone does not determine social position. 'Class position signals certain commonalities of location within the social structure but class articulates with other axes of differentiation such as racism in ... delineating the precise social position of specific categories of women' (Brah 1992, 131). Gender also plays a role, but most theories of race and class have not integrated gender into their analysis (Stasiulis 1990, 280).

Patriarchal capitalism exploits women, but the nature and extent of this exploitation varies according to their class, race, and country of origin. The expansion of capitalism has been accompanied by underdevelopment in Third World countries, and women's struggle for economic survival has sometimes compelled them to emigrate. Domestic workers from the Caribbean have come to Canada, but restrictive immigration policies have led to their economic and sexual exploitation here (Calliste 1989; Daenzer 1993). Young Filipino women have been driven by poverty to come to Canada as mail-order brides of much older men and have sometimes subsequently been abused by their spouses (interview, 10 Sept. 1995). Patriarchal immigration policies have in the recent past designated all women as 'dependants' of male immigrants, denied them language training, and consequently forced them into unskilled, low-paid manual work (Boyd 1991).

The class location of women from Asia, Africa, and the Caribbean in Canada is partly determined by the international gendered division of labour that has displaced and exploited women in their own countries, created divisions between women living in Third World and developed countries, and made it difficult for them to have solidarity with each other. The use by multinational corporations of the cheap labour of Third World women has adversely affected the employment of women at the lower rung of the labour force in developed countries. Jobs that are labour-intensive or require limited and easily learned skills get exported to Third World countries. The 'reserve army of labour' in Third World countries depresses wages in developed countries and creates conditions for the further exploitation of non–English-speaking, working-class immigrant women, some of whom are compelled to accept part-time, casual work or to become homeworkers to earn a wage (Mitter 1986; Rowbotham and Mitter 1994; Mies 1986).

Janine Brodie argues that in the structural adjustment occurring in the Canadian economy in the 1990s, the 'burden of adjustment has largely been carried by working-class, less educated, and immigrant women' (Brodie 1994, 51). In the first three years of the Free Trade Agreement between Canada and the United States, women's employment decreased by 11 per cent, or 66,400 jobs. Most of these jobs were in clothing manufacturing, where 19,000 of the jobs were lost (a 20 per cent decline), followed by electrical-products manufacturing, where 10,300 of jobs were lost (a 17 per cent decline) (Cohen 1994, 109).

Garment-manufacturing plants in Canada have closed in increasing numbers and moved to Pacific Rim countries. These manufacturing facilities have been replaced by thousands of women working from their homes, combining their household work and care of small children with paid work. Research by the International Ladies Garment Workers' Union shows that 'homeworkers are mainly immigrant women, paid as little as $1.00 an hour and rarely more that $4.50' (Yalnizyan 1993, 289). Women stay in abusive relations because so few choices or alternatives are available to them (Lloyd 1995, 158).

There is some discussion in the manuals of how to access social assistance and some analysis of immigration policy. This information enables abused women to make short-term plans and is most helpful to those women whose physical safety is immediately threatened. However, abused women who are confronted with a long-term threat of physical injury need information on resources that would enable them to become economically self-sufficient and to support themselves and their children. When the abused woman is a non–English-speaking woman from Asia, Africa, or the Caribbean, she needs information on how to access English-language classes and training opportunities that are available to her, given her education, level of skills, and work experience. She needs to know what job opportunities are available to her. The manuals do not address these issues.

Conclusion

Feminist theory recognizes the integrated nature of race, class, and gender oppression, but feminist practice continues to give priority to gender oppression. Consequently, the everyday realities of abused women's lives remain shadowed by racist stereotypes. Women from Asia, Africa, and the Caribbean are sometimes reluctant to adopt feminist ideals of 'empowerment' and 'autonomy,' not because they lack consciousness of their own oppression and exploitation, but because a realistic assessment of their situation reveals the need to adopt immediate practical strategies to ensure their survival.

Women from Asia, Africa, and the Caribbean need to struggle against both the sexism of their community and the racism of the larger society. Socialist feminists argue that since all forms of oppression – class, gender, and race – are intertwined, overthrowing one system of domination requires overthrowing all of them. In practice, however, women from Asia, Africa, and the Caribbean are sometimes compelled to choose between participating actively in antiracism struggles or participating in feminist struggles. Community-based groups of these women frequently support other women's groups (dominated by white women) in struggling for specific reforms (e.g., more stringent penalties for perpetrators of wife abuse), but the alliances rarely combine attacks on race and gender oppression. The tendency to separate issues of gender from issues of race or class is also manifested in the work of counsellors helping abused women from Asia, Africa, and the Caribbean.

SIX

Interviews with Counsellors

Counsellors at community-based groups and the women whom they help are frequently from the same ethnic background. As 'cultural insiders,' the counsellors have a familiarity with the culture and values of their ethnic or racial group that helps them to narrow the distance between themselves and their clients. This eliminates some of the problems that may arise when counsellor and client are from different cultural backgrounds. Common experiences of racism also create empathy between the women and help the counsellors to understand the sources of some of the difficulties that their clients are experiencing. However, differences between the counsellors and the clients – for example, class, religion, and political ideology – are seldom discussed in the literature on abused women by community-based groups, and counsellors tend to emphasize the similarities between themselves and the women they are helping, seldom making any reference to conflicts and tensions that may occur between them. The interviews that follow address some of the challenges that the counsellors face in trying to help abused women from Asia, Africa, and the Caribbean.

The measured tone of the interviewees and their moderate views reflect the perspectives of most counsellors in the community-based organizations. However, the counsellors are not a homogeneous group, with identical beliefs and values. Some women in the organizations are militant proponents of feminism and antiracism, and they are not reluctant to identify issues, to point fingers, and to demand changes. Nevertheless, they have been marginalized by the move towards providing social services to abused women.

Community-based groups and shelters that depend on funds from governments perceive feminist and antiracist activists as creating conflict. Many of the jobs in community-based groups are contract positions ranging from a few months to a year, depending on the kind of funding the program has secured, and women who are militant and articulate are not often rehired in those positions. One lesbian South Asian woman who speaks fluent English and has a master's degree in sociology spoke of being 'punished' for identifying racist practices by shelter staff and residents. She had pressured the board and staff to initiate discussions on homophobia with residents and their children. She lost her job at that shelter and was subsequently unable to find even a part-time job in any other community-based organization (interview, 8 July 1993). Counsellors who are moderate are favoured by personnel in government agencies, and they are successful in obtaining funds for the organization. It is they who are represented in these interviews.

The counsellors whose interviews are presented here focus on providing services that will facilitate a woman's social and economic independence. They downplay other issues in the woman's life or tensions between themselves and their clients. The underlying rationale for the many programs that they administer is to enhance the access of working-class, non–English-speaking women from Asia, Africa, and the Caribbean to social services. Their emphasis on social services is a pragmatic response to the trauma experienced by many of the women who come to them for help.

Counsellors at community-based groups empower abused women from Asia, Africa, and the Caribbean by making resources and information available to them. They help women sort through the options available to them and help them in accessing resources. For example, a woman who is thinking of leaving an abusive spouse may be encouraged to join an English-language class, enrol in a vocational training course, or join a support group. These strategies help abused women to see that there are other women who are faced with similar difficulties. They can draw some strength from numbers and reinforce their determination to continue their struggle against the oppression and violence of their spouses (Dutton-Douglas and Dionne 1992, 115–17).

Counsellors validate an abused woman's feelings of outrage and provide a safe space where she can express her anger and pain, sometimes for the first time. Counselling provides an opportunity for the woman to recover from abuse and to rebuild her self-esteem, to see herself as a survivor rather than a victim (Dutton-Douglas and Dionne 1992, 118).

The community-based groups say that a counsellor who is familiar with the culture of an abused woman can help her understand the emotional, psychological, and cultural barriers that make it difficult for her to leave an abusive home. For example, many women from traditional Chinese families value interdependence, harmonious relationships, and reciprocal obligations (Lau 1995, 121–2). An abused woman who wished to leave her spouse would be contravening some of the basic values of her culture – to 'persevere, keep peace, and care for the home and husband under any circumstances' (Ho 1990, 143). Even the decision to seek outside help threatens shame and loss of face for the entire family. The community-based organizations argue that a Chinese counsellor better understands her difficulties in deciding to leave or to stay in the abusive family than a counsellor from a Western culture, who might regard her as merely indecisive.

Middle-class counsellors have positioned themselves as mediators between working-class women from Asia, Africa, and the Caribbean and government agencies, and they have advocated for access to social services on their behalf. Sometimes counsellors are motivated by personal experience of racism to work in community-based groups to provide services to abused women from their own communities. Race, ethnicity, and the experience of being an immigrant create solidarity and empathy between the counsellors and their clients, even though differences remain. In the interviews, the counsellors do not address differences in class or in political ideology which may create social distance between them and their clients.

In the community-based organizations, feminist beliefs and values coexist alongside traditional ideas about gender relations.

Sometimes the latter can be used to give support to an abused woman. Some Asian cultures give priority to the well-being of the family and consider pursuing individual happiness as selfish (Lau 1995; Ho 1990). Consequently, the Chinese Family Life Services recommends that counsellors advise a woman that leaving home could prevent 'worse things happening to the husband and children,' and they use traditional metaphors to help a woman resist further abuse (1989, 24). Although abuse is tolerated by many traditional cultures as an expression of patriarchal power and authority, almost all cultures have ways of sanctioning the more extreme expressions of abuse. It is possible to 'mobilize positive values of respect, responsibility, caring, and interdependence that are the strengths of the community' on behalf of the woman (Ratna and Wheeler 1995, 143). Elders or respected community members can help loosen the hold of a woman's loyalty to her husband by giving her permission to escape dangerous situations (Ho 1990, 146); and the threat of losing face or bringing shame upon the family can sometimes deter the man from additional acts of violence (Lau 1995).

The interviews suggest the need for more specific and detailed studies of immigrant groups from Asia, Africa, and the Caribbean. Some interesting questions emerge. Do abused women's expectations of the kind of help they can receive from counsellors differ according to their ethnic and racial groups (Campbell 1993)? Does cultural sensitivity eliminate the biases that women from Asia, Africa, and the Caribbean would encounter in seeking help from mainstream social service agencies? Should the community-based groups also strive to overcome ideological and class differences between counsellors and clients? And, most important, does the work of the groups demonstrably reduce violence in the lives of their clients?

While this study focuses on community-based groups and service providers, issues of confidentiality make it difficult to identify and interview abused women who are receiving services. Nonetheless, research needs to be done to measure the effectiveness of the services provided by community-based groups, especially from the perspective of those who are receiving help.

First Interview

In an interview on 28 June 1993, Tiffany (a pseudonym), the executive director of the Korean-Canadian Women's Association, described growing up in Toronto and the cultural conflicts she experienced. She explained how her work with the Women's Association has helped her to understand and appreciate Korean values and norms, and to develop a strong sense of cultural identity:

I came to Canada when I was fourteen years old. I started school in grade 8. During the 1970s there were not that many Koreans in Toronto. Many of my high-school [friends] didn't know where Korea was! It is only after the Olympics that people came to know about Korea widely.

In Korea my dad was a social worker and my mom a pharmacist, but when they came here they could not do those jobs. My mom started to work in a factory on a night shift. [Soon after that], they started a small business – a variety store. But they didn't like that. They wanted to be professionals and they wanted their children to be professionals. So they pushed us to integrate with the mainstream. We were told not to speak Korean but to speak English – even at home. They wanted me to become a lawyer or a doctor, i.e., jobs [in which] you could be independent. But I went on to study theology in university.

In high school I didn't want to hang out with the Koreans because I was ashamed. I wanted to be white. Many of us were lonely. But the new generation is different. The Koreans are well settled now. Young Koreans are now proud of being Korean and they hang out with other Koreans.

I constantly struggle with Korean cultural values about women. Korean [culture requires that a] woman should be married, have a family, and a husband. To be a full woman you need to be a mother and a wife. [These values were a source of] personal struggle for me. Rejecting or devaluing the role of wife and mother is not good for women. But when the focus is only on those roles, then it is problematic. For instance, I will be thirty in August but I am not married. I feel the pressure [from my parents] to be married. I want them to be happy.

Working with [the Korean-Canadian Women's Association] has helped me to understand Korean culture. I have learned about Korean people, their cultural values – to appreciate their social norms. It has given me a clear identity. I am not fully a Korean or a Canadian, but I am a Korean Canadian.

Some women who work with community-based organizations first came to them as clients for the social services they offer. Other women from the community began working for the organizations as volunteers and later became paid workers:

I used to work with Hugh Centre, a residential house for teenage girls. A friend of mine [spoke] about me to the coordinator of the Korean-Canadian Women's Association, and she called me and asked me if I was interested in doing some interpreting for Korean women who came to the shelters. I started doing that. Then the Korean-Canadian Women's Association wanted to hire a part-time worker, and I started working there. Within two or three months, they needed a full-time worker.

[At present] we have two [other] full-time counsellors. None of us have a degree in counselling. But a new counsellor [who is joining us soon] has a master's degree in social work from Korea and about twenty years of work experience there.

In the following, Tiffany described some of the socio-economic characteristics of the women who come to the organization:

Women who come to our organization range from eighteen to seventy years. A lot of women have landed immigrant status before they come to Canada, and most have come as sponsored wives. But if a woman comes [as a fiancée], it becomes another power issue. In one case, a woman has been here for three years and the man has not married her yet. So she is illegal. A woman puts all her trust in the man [and he betrays her].

The women who come to our organization may be coming from a middle-class background, but by themselves they are very poor. They have no independent cash or income. When they separated from their husbands, they had nothing. A large percentage of Koreans run small businesses like variety stores, corner grocery stores, fruit and vegetable markets, and nowadays doughnut shops. These are family-run businesses; women also work in them. When the [couple] gets divorced, women can get half the family business, but the business is all mortgaged. Or the variety stores may not be doing well. There is nothing to get. Other women started working in factories within a month of coming to Canada. They may not even have ever gone to English classes [so that they speak little or no English].

Some Korean wives have endured abuse. Korean women, like South Asian women, do not necessarily want to end their marriages when they come to the Korean-Canadian Women's Association for help, but are only seeking escape from the violence in their families:

The Korean-Canadian Women's Association is now known in the community, so the women may contact us directly. The women never give out their names. When women call, they want to know: how do I get divorced, do I need a lawyer? [And they ask questions] about family law. We ask them if there is violence at home or if [the spouse has been] abusive. Almost 80 per cent of the time, the women say, 'Oh yes, he used to hit me, but that's OK. I could take that, because physical wounds heal, but I cannot take psychological and emotional abuse.'

Emotional abuse may involve swearing. In Korea, when someone swears at you, it is like he is cursing you. The emotional impact [of the verbal abuse] is much greater than in the English language. A lot of women complain about how abusive language makes them feel dirty and stupid. In the Korean language, some of the swear words really degrade you as a human being and as a woman.

A form of emotional abuse is confining the women to the home and not letting them go out – [for example,] to English-language classes or to visit friends. Another common form of emotional abuse is when the in-laws and the husband treat the wife as a housemaid. The man sides with his father and mother, and they may constantly rebuke the woman for not being a good daughter-in-law. One woman said that her mother-in-law used to complain to her husband about her when he came home. Then the mother and husband would sit on a couch and make the woman kneel on the floor in front of them and beg their forgiveness. That kind of humiliation and degradation the woman [resents]. A lot of women felt betrayed by their husbands. A lot of women have no relatives of their own in Canada. The women feel devastated.

It is not that physical abuse is not common in our culture. There is a lot of hitting with fists and kicking, but the women minimize that kind of abuse. But when it [becomes] severe, it is problematic. One woman was changing her baby's diaper, and the husband, [who had been] drinking, came behind the woman with a frying pan and hit her head, then went to another room and went to bed. She started to bleed. Previously, when this man had hit her with a broken bottle or kicked her, she had never called the police. But he had once told her to call 911 if something happened to the children. She remembered that. Since she was losing a lot of blood and was starting to lose consciousness, she called 911. The ambulance and the police came, and they charged the man. [In another case] a man sits playing with the Exacto knife all night long and at times holds it to the woman's neck threateningly.

The Korean women just want their husbands to stop beating them. They do not want to charge their husbands or break up their family. They feel, if they charge the husband, it will end their marriage. Some men may be willing to try it again, but others will say, 'How dare you report me to the police?' and 'How can I trust you as a wife?'

Women also don't want to charge [their husbands] if they have children [because they think] it will bring shame on the children. The culture values having a family and devalues divorce and a broken family. [They believe] that a child should feel he has a mom and dad. They don't think that a child who is living in [an abusive home] is harmed. From outside, everything should look fine. That's what counts for them.

In Korea women do not even think of calling the police. In Canada some women do call the police but only in the most desperate situation, [such as] when she fears for her life. [Often] the women regret calling the police [because they are not always sensitive to the needs of non-English-speaking women]. One woman had bruises on her body. The woman said to the police, 'I don't speak English,' but the police said, 'You speak English fine. You don't need an interpreter.' There are all kinds of horrible stories.

Almost all community-based groups keenly advocate the use of support groups for abused women. The term 'support group' is used extensively in the literature of community-based groups to refer to any meeting among women which emphasizes peer support (Moussa 1994; Sinclair 1985). Support groups bring together women who share similar concerns and social positions (e.g., abused women, immigrant and refugee women), share a common ethnic or racial background (e.g., the Somalian women's group), or speak the same language. However, explicitly identifying a group's members as abused women discourages attendance. A woman may resist describing herself as abused, or she may be reluctant to disclose her situation to other women. Abused women may also be prevented from attending support groups by their spouses. Helene Moussa, a political activist, recommends that support groups for abused women adopt some innocuous name such as 'cultural group' or 'resource centre' to overcome women's reluctance to join them (1994, 49–51).

Support groups can be organized around any number of goals and objectives. Moussa identifies four types of support groups for immigrant and refugee women: those that teach 'life skills' in Canada; those that provide information on how to access social and legal services; those that focus on the 'politics of violence against women'; and those that focus on recreational and social activities. She recommends that support groups that address the 'politics of violence against women' should discuss some of the following themes: gender relations; violence against women in the countries of origin and in Canada; and how 'racism and class/caste structures' affect refugee and immigrant families. The groups should also seek to teach non-violent conflict resolution, develop safety plans for each woman, and instruct them in Wendo as a 'self-empowering skill' (1994, 56–7).

Support groups resemble the consciousness-raising sessions popular among feminists during the 1970s. Small informal groups of women would meet and discuss their experiences of oppression and their feelings of resentment and unhappiness. These discussions enabled women to see the common patterns in their experiences and to realize that their problems were not a result of individual failing but were systemic to gender relations. The support groups organized by community-based organizations share some of the aims of the feminist groups of the 1970s – sharing experiences, breaking out of the isolation of nuclear families, discussing alternative explanations of why abuse occurs, and empowering or helping women 'gain more control over their lives' (Riutort and Small 1985; Women's Support Group Committee 1990). However, since support groups are formally organized, funded by government agencies, and led by facilitators (frequently counsellors who work with community-based organizations), they do not necessarily articulate such political goals as transforming gender relations or raising the consciousness of the women (although that may occur). Support groups are mostly intended to provide information or group counselling, and to help women become self-reliant (i.e., reduce their dependence on community-based groups or other social service agencies) by forming networks with other women (Women's Support Group Committee 1990). Even so, as Tiffany explained, it is not always easy to persuade women to join these groups:

We have support groups for single mothers, seniors, and an interracial married women's group. There is also a young women's group. Each support group is different.

   We started a support group for women who are abused because a number of women were asking for this sort of [opportunity] to come together and talk. I planned for the group to meet once a week. [All the women I contacted] had left their abusive situations and were living in Ontario housing. They could come if they wanted to, but were ashamed. That is why it took them a long time [to build up the confidence] to come.

   It was really hard to get women to come to the group. At first I contacted about ten women and they all said they would come, but only two showed up. The next week, I called again. They all again said they were coming, but this time only one woman showed up. [Despite the poor attendance] I was quite diligent and continued to call them every week. They all wanted to come. They shared common experiences of abuse, but they didn't want to admit that to the other women. But some women had [other difficulties. Some had] children and they were too tired to come. Others had started to work and they had no time to come.

   We continued with the support group. Sometimes three women came. Some came and then left. Eventually eight women came regularly and were eager to meet other women. We met for about twelve weeks.

The group didn't have a set structure. It was very informal. We had some food. Some [women brought their] children with them. We met [in the main office area], played with the children, and then went to a separate room. Another counsellor co-led the group with me.

In our culture we address women differently according to their age. In Korea a young woman cannot call an older woman by her first name, she has to say Mrs so and so. To break that barrier, we decided to give each person a new name, such as Wind or Sun. That broke the age barrier, and we felt much closer to each other.

The counsellor does not say, 'What do you think is the definition of wife abuse?' or ask, 'What happened, and how did your husband abuse you?' We don't [put them on the spot] that way. But we try to draw out the women indirectly and generate a discussion. In the beginning, the women talked about [innocuous things] such as how their week was. But once they got comfortable, they kept talking about all kinds of personal things.

The counsellors work on the self-esteem of the women. When we do public education programs on wife assault, the women would like to [participate], but they don't because it is a public place. So it is very frustrating. We keep hoping that after some time, they won't feel so ashamed but accept the fact that they were abused and go on with their lives. We hope that they can eventually lead the support group or participate in projects and programs of our agency.

Community-based groups and shelters work together to offer social services to an abused woman. Sometimes, however, there may be disagreements between the staff of a community group and the staff of a shelter over the needs of a particular woman or the division of responsibility between them. Tiffany described some of the difficulties encountered by Korean women in shelters:

[In a case of wife assault], when the police are involved, the officer will take [the woman] to a shelter, and the shelter will call us to interpret. When a woman doesn't speak English at all, we maintain close and regular contact with her while she is living at the shelter. We send someone once a week to [the shelter] to talk to her and find out if she needs anything.

We have had a lot of problems dealing with shelters. I find the shelters have their own philosophy. [Some are] collectives. They have their own way of dealing with the women. They [believe] that the woman in the shelter is their responsibility [and they] are accountable for her. [After] I send a woman to a shelter, I [usually] call the next day to ask how the woman was doing. But the shelter workers would refuse to tell me how they are doing. [Their attitude is], 'Who are you ?' At the same time, the woman would call us once a day to tell us what she needs, if there is a problem with the food, or if [she was] feeling lonely. A lot of misunderstanding occurs because of a lack of language, and sometimes the women feel they were being mistreated by the staff. The Korean women feel so isolated and lonely at a shelter that they don't like to go there.

Sometimes, a woman wants to apply for housing, and days pass and nothing is done [by the shelter staff]. Then I will call and ask what happened with that. Sometimes they are so disorganized! They say, 'Yeah, we are going to do that,' and next day I call and it hasn't been done. I may get another worker, and I have to explain the whole thing again. I feel so frustrated. One woman who keeps going back to [her abusive] home called me late at night, saying that she had left her husband again because he was abusing her and she went to a shelter. She had been there before. It was wintertime, and she knocked on the door and a shelter worker [who answered the door] knew her. She didn't let her inside the shelter because she said her husband knew where the shelter was and he would come there. The woman kept begging, 'I need a place to stay. I have left my husband.' She said all this in her broken English. The shelter worker made her stay outside [while she] called other shelters. The other shelters wouldn't take her also, because she kept returning to her husband. Finally they found a shelter who would take her and they sent her there in a taxi. When I heard this story, I was so amazed that a shelter would [disregard] the safety of this woman. So I called the shelter the next morning and asked for an explanation. They said they would have to take it to the collective. I have talked to about five women at that shelter about it and still have no explanation.

Shelter staff may not get along with Korean women. They [sometimes] think Korean women are passive. Sometimes misunderstanding occurs because the women at the shelter may wish to speak to a Korean woman at the Korean-Canadian Women's Association, [and the staff] are not quite happy about that.

The staff at the shelter has a feminist approach. When a woman comes from an abused situation, they will counsel her to be independent and to leave the spouse. The majority of the Korean women are not intending to separate from the husband, but they are thinking of going back. So they will voluntarily contact the husband. The staff can't understand that. The Korean women in turn feel guilty for calling their husband and not listening to the staff. They start to feel awkward, and a lot of times they just leave the shelter because they can't face the staff.

Second Interview

The Chinese and South East Asian Legal Clinic provides another example of groups from Asia, Africa, and the Caribbean coming together to help disadvantaged members of their own communities. The clinic serves men and women. In an interview on 18 June 1993, Christina (a pseudonym), the executive director (a senior paid administrator), described the services the clinic provides to victims of wife abuse and some of the ways in which it has challenged systemic racial biases in the police force. She began by describing her experiences as a first-generation immigrant from Hong Kong at the University of Waterloo and at the Law School of the University of Toronto:

I came [to Canada] in 1982 and went straight to university. My elder brother came in 1972 and then in 1980 my elder sister came and then I came along with another sister. I spoke almost fluent English when I came to Canada.

My first four years were spent at the University of Waterloo. There most of my friends were foreign students – Chinese from Malaysia, Singapore, and Hong Kong. I didn't feel the school environment was racist and I felt comfortable in being Chinese. After I moved to Toronto I heard more about racism and I started to see it more.

Law school in Toronto was a completely different world. It was really bad. It made me aware as a Chinese Canadian that it was not a place where I could be accepted. In my year there were seven Chinese Canadians and one black student [at the law school]. In the previous year there were two Chinese Canadians. You feel different. I hung out with people who were different or who were Chinese. It made me think how exclusive the society is. [Law school] turned me off. I didn't go to my graduation.

Christina worked with the Legal Education and Action Fund (LEAF), a private foundation which seeks to challenge systemic gender biases in Canadian law:

While I was waiting to write my bar exams, I worked part-time for LEAF. I did some research on the rape shield law and on the language issue. Then they asked me to do a memo [report] on the Persons Day and so I did the research on it. I found out that Persons Day only applies to white women since aboriginal and visible-minority women did not get voting rights till years later. Around that time there was also the issue about the first female lawyer, [who] turned out to be anti-Semitic. [LEAF] acknowledged that the Persons Day was not inclusive, but they didn't change anything. It was disappointing. The organization and the fund-raising committee were dominated by white women at that time. I didn't really expect much.

[Subsequently LEAF launched a Charter challenge against the discrimination experienced by immigrant women in government-sponsored language-learning programs.] But the language issue just died. After we launched the challenge, the government denied funding to everyone. But it was a significant event [because] it was the first time that LEAF worked with visible-minority women. I'll give them some credit for that.

Christina was interested in working with the Chinese community, but she decided to 'check out' a Bay Street law firm before making a final commitment to community-based legal work:

After I graduated from law school, I articled for a Bay Street firm. I joined a big firm with about eighty lawyers. At the law firm, my experiences were atypical. I was the only student who had a senior partner as a mentor. As a senior partner, he was more relaxed, and he recognized that I was very involved with the Chinese community, and he allowed me the freedom to continue with that. There was only one other Chinese lawyer at the firm. There were no South Asians or blacks. I didn't make a great effort to prove that I could fit into the firm or to do any extra work. I wasn't concerned about being hired by them [on a permanent basis].

When I left, I got an $800 donation for the Chinese-Canadian National Council, and the [firm] also bought a table at our banquet.

Middle-class Chinese women, like many other women from Asia, Africa, and the Caribbean, have become more articulate and organized in struggling against their oppressions. Christina described who gets involved in community work and the attraction of working with one's own community:

I am an activist. I am active in women's issues, racism, poverty. They are all interconnected anyway. I see more and more both first- and second-generation Chinese-Canadian women wanting to get involved. In the Chinese-Canadian National Council, women are playing an important role, and without them the work would not get done. Most of these women are the more educated ones and those who have been here for a significant number of years. You don't see a new immigrant coming and saying, 'I want to get involved,' because it takes them a certain amount of time to settle down and get adapted. Then they realize how bad the system is, and then they want to do something about it.

I feel comfortable [doing volunteer work] with the Chinese-Canadian National Council. When I am with other groups, I do not feel as comfortable because of the conflict [between the groups] or because they do not understand our [Chinese] point of view. Sometimes it is hard to get your opinion across even with other visible-minority women. When we talk about racism, sometimes there is a tendency to focus on your own experience, such as that of blacks, Chinese, or Vietnamese. I feel [that these discussions] should be more inclusive of other people's [experiences]. But that does not happen. Such discussions silence other people.

I had volunteered at the downtown University of Toronto Legal Clinic from 1986 to 1989. I wanted to maintain an active role in the community, so I started working with the East Toronto Legal Clinic and then I went to Parkdale Legal Clinic. Six months after I started to work with Parkdale, the director of the Chinese and South East Asian Clinic resigned. So I came here. The attraction to work here is to maintain my volunteer work and incorporate it [into] my professional work so I don't have to compromise my principles.

The needs of non–English-speaking women for 'culturally sensitive services' are sometimes identified in the course of volunteer activities. Christina described the process which led to the establishment of the Chinese and South East Asian Legal Clinic:

[In the early 1980s] the Law School of the University of Toronto had a satellite clinic at one of the Chinese-serving community agencies in Toronto. Every Tuesday students were going there to give advice to Chinese-speaking clients, and it was then recognized that there was a great need for linguistically appropriate legal services for them. So several community agencies got together to make an application to the Ontario Legal Aid Plan to set up this clinic. The application was turned down, but it was appealed. It was at the appeal level that they got the funding in 1987, when Ian Scott was the attorney general. So that's how it came about. The need was identified by the community, and they decided to include several South East Asian communities as well.

I was not involved in the preliminary planning for the clinic. My sister was working for [a government agency], and she said to me that the clinic was looking for Chinese lawyers or law students to sit on the steering committee but there were not many around. I was still in my first year of law school, but I said OK and that's how I started sitting on the steering committee. There were other Chinese women on the committee but there was only one other Chinese woman lawyer. The rest were all male lawyers.

Christina described the clinic's services and its clients:

We serve people from the Vietnamese, Chinese, Cambodian, and Laotian communities. The clinic provides legal services and sometimes legal representation for low-income people and the working poor. Women who come to this clinic have very low income and very little English skills. A lot of them are single mothers. Some are refugee claimants. Sometimes we may get a call from domestic workers, but they usually go to Intercede. We help women apply for legal aid and welfare. We also serve victims of wife abuse. We give them legal advice and provide referral to counsellors.

A lot of women who come to us are sponsored immigrants, so we deal with their immigration problems if there are any. A typical story is of a wife who is sponsored, but her sponsorship application is not completed. She gets beaten up, and the husband threatens to withdraw his sponsorship if she leaves him or calls the police. In that situation, it is hard to intervene because she may not be allowed to stay. There is a risk that she may be sent back. Anyway, we advise her that she can leave if she wants, and if there is a sponsorship breakdown we can try to do a humanitarian, compassionate application that will allow her to stay in Canada.

Sometimes the women may be refugee claimants, and for some reason their application got separated [from that of their husband's]. The husband gets refugee status first. [He then has to apply for her as his sponsored dependant.] Sometimes [the woman may have come to Canada] as a fiancée. They have to marry within ninety days, but they didn't marry, because the abuse started or because they don't know if they should marry. Sometimes the women come in as visitors. The sponsored immigrants have very little protection. They can easily be sent back. Sometimes there are children involved, and [that] makes the woman very reluctant to do anything [lay charges or seek separation].

A lot of times we set up appointments, but the women do not come back. We are reluctant to call them at home because we may get the husband. Now with the new telephones you can [recall] the numbers. We are trying to set up a system to block our number. We wait for the woman to call us back. Sometimes they don't, but that is not the majority of the cases.

The Chinese and South East Asian Legal Clinic helps women sort out difficulties with their immigrant status. The applications to immigrate of most sponsored women are processed while they are outside Canada, and they enter Canada as permanent residents (i.e., landed immigrants). When abuse occurs, the legal status of the sponsored immigrant is not in jeopardy, and the man cannot have his spouse deported. Nonetheless, an abusive man may still persuade his wife not to call the police or lay charges by threatening to have her deported or to withdraw his sponsorship of her or of her relatives, even though the law protects the abused woman. She may not be aware of her legal rights – hence the importance of clinics like the Chinese and South East Asian Legal Clinic.

Women who come to Canada as fiancées (or as students or visitors) without landed immigrant status are in a much more difficult position. Immigration regulations (1985) require that an application for immigration be processed while the individual is outside Canada, but it grants some exemptions on 'humanitarian and compassionate grounds.'[1] For example, it may allow a wife to apply for immigration from within Canada if she can prove that her marriage is genuine and was not merely entered into to gain landed immigrant status. If the woman is admissible on medical and security grounds, she can obtain landed immigrant status as a family class member (i.e., sponsored dependent spouse) (Stairs and Pope 1990, 214). However, she has to receive an Order in Council, and that may take a year or two. If abuse occurs while the Order in Council is still being processed and the woman leaves her spouse, a new set of rules comes into operation. Now the spouse of the abused woman can withdraw his sponsorship, and she can be deported. Nevertheless, a woman can seek to stay in Canada and apply for immigration on 'humanitarian and compassionate' grounds.

Immigration officers have to follow departmental guidelines in determining eligibility for landed immigrant status on 'humanitarian and compassionate' grounds. The guidelines concern the nature of the abuse, the process of application, and the economic prospects of the woman's establishing herself in Canada. The guidelines advise immigration officers not to consider abuse alone as sufficient grounds for granting permanent landed status to a woman; rather, they should consider whether it may not be a better option for a woman to 'return home to the safety and security of [her] famil[y].' Officers are advised to determine whether the applicant has suffered physical or mental cruelty in the relationship. (Threats of withdrawing sponsorship by the sponsor constitute abuse.) Other factors for consideration are the presence of Canadian-born children, the availability of help in the country of origin, and the degree of economic and educational disruption (as opposed to mere inconvenience) to the family if they were to return (Pope 1991, 40–1).

In examining the application for landed immigrant status, officers have to ensure that the abused wife showed 'good faith' in voluntarily reporting to immigration officers the breakdown of her relationship with the sponsor. However, the very nature of abuse makes it difficult for abused women to comply with this requirement. Abuse usually follows a pattern in which an incident of abuse is followed by what is commonly referred to as a 'honeymoon phase' and then more abuse. Since the woman does not know whether one incident is isolated or will be repeated, she may be reluctant to report the abuse to immigration authorities for fear of jeopardizing her application altogether (Stairs and Pope 1990, 216–20).

A primary concern of immigration policy with respect to sponsored abused women is that they do not become public charges, dependent on social assistance. Therefore, officers are required to assess a woman's potential to 'establish herself successfully in Canada.' The economic criteria include the woman's education, job training, and work experience. Officers may take into consideration help that is available to an abused woman from her relatives and the 'composition of sponsorable family members here and abroad.' Felicite Stairs and Lori Pope regard these requirements as 'systemically discriminatory':

> Many women who come here do not obtain work permits, even though they may be eligible, often because their husband has not wanted them to work, or because they felt it unnecessary, as they intended to stay at home to care for their children. When the marriage breaks down and they attempt to obtain a work permit they are often denied. Thus they cannot show their ability to establish themselves. (Stairs and Pope 1990, 217)

Although it is possible for lawyers of abused women to submit supporting documents to immigration officers about a woman's work history in her country of origin, working-class women who use publicly funded, community-based clinics (e.g., Parkdale Legal

Clinic) often have no experience of paid work or have been 'ghet-toized in low-paying, low-skill jobs.' The community-based clinic encourages these women to take upgrading courses or to join 'sole-support mothers' programs through social assistance at the earliest opportunity. Although childcare responsibilities may make it difficult to take these initiatives, applications by women who fail to do so may be rejected. Similarly, if a woman has not attended English-language classes, regardless of her personal difficulties or the availability of such classes, her application is perceived nega-tively by officers (Stairs and Pope 1990, 214–21).

Feminists have argued that the patriarchal values of police offic-ers make them reluctant to charge violent male spouses. Advocacy on behalf of the victims led to changes in 1982 which make it man-datory for the police to lay a charge when they 'witness an offence, for example, an assault,' or 'where there are reasonable and proba-ble grounds' to believe that an offence has occurred (Barbara Schlifer Commemorative Clinic 1991, 39). Since abused women are sometimes fearful of retaliation by their spouses and reluctant to lay charges, the changed policy was intended to shift the onus from the victim and place it on the police officers. However, the Ontario Association of Interval and Transition Houses argues that the police still 'ask far too often that the victim make the decision about whether charges will be laid' (1989b).

According to the Ontario Association of Interval and Transition Houses, abused women have a 50 per cent chance of securing 'appropriate police intervention and support' (1989b). There are officers who give abused women a referral to a local shelter or to a community-based organization, but in 1986 charges were not laid in 59.4 per cent of the cases of wife abuse, and in 1987 they were not laid in 53.4 per cent of the cases of wife abuse (Ontario Associ-ation of Interval and Transition Houses 1989b). A 1989 survey revealed that although women wanted to lay charges in 56 per cent of the cases, the police charged only 40 per cent of the perpetra-tors. Women were evidently discouraged from laying charges by being told by the police of 'the consequences of such an arrest, the often prolonged period of time before the case might come before a judge, and the difficulties the woman might experience in obtaining any support' (Ontario Association of Interval and Transition Houses 1989a).

Sexism and racism in the police force aggravate the difficulties of an abused woman who cannot speak English. Handbooks which explain the rights of assaulted women do not take into account the difficulties of non–English-speaking, working-class immigrant women may have in interacting with the police. Abused women often feel insecure, as their confidence has been eroded by years of abuse; they cannot easily follow the handbook recommendations. They are advised to ask to speak to the police alone; and if police are reluctant to lay charges, they should ask for an explanation. If that does not result in the police laying charges, the woman should ask for the 'sergeant's name and phone number and call the sergeant'. Abused women also have the added recourse of laying a complaint against the police officers with the Police Complaints Commission (Barbara Schlifer Commemorative Clinic 1991, 39–40).

Christina described the difficulties that non–English-speaking women may encounter with police officers:

Police don't always lay charges even though they are required by law to lay charges in cases of domestic violence. There could be several reasons. For example, sometimes the police are reluctant to lay charges because they can't communicate with a woman who does not speak English and they won't bother to find an interpreter. Sometimes the police will not lay charges because there is no physical evidence – that is, the injuries are not visible. In one case, the woman was hit on the head, so all the injuries were internal. The police came, she was crying, she did not speak very much English. The police talked to the husband, who looked [like a] very respectable businessman, and he said that she was upset because he told her that he wanted to divorce her. So the police just took his word for it and did not lay any charges. Later, the woman went to see a doctor and found out that one of her eardrums was completely damaged and she had lost complete hearing in one ear and 30 per cent in the other ear. There were [other] internal bruises. But because there was no visible physical evidence, the police did not lay any charges. Afterwards we had to call the police and tell them to lay charges.

For Chinese women, racism of the police is a big issue. A lot of Chinese women are reluctant to call the police. Some obviously poor women are discriminated [against] by the police. If the women are refugees, they do not know how it will affect their application status.

The Chinese-Canadian National Council has been most effective on the policing issue. It was effective because racism of the police is easy for people to understand. We raised awareness and we made people realize that they don't have to take abuse [from the police]. Now people are more willing to come out and talk about their experiences; they are coming forward to voice their concerns and to make complaints.

Christina described the efforts of community-based agencies to make services more accessible to non–English-speaking women:

Calling 911 is not a problem anymore. There is interpretation. It started two years ago. Myself and Olivia Chow [formerly a Toronto school trustee and now a city counsellor] went to the police service board to make a representation on how 911 is inaccessible for people who do not speak English. If you call 911 and do not speak English, you cannot talk to the police. We asked the board to study the issue. They sent somebody to Vancouver because Vancouver has a volunteer program [to provide interpretation].

The campaign [to introduce interpretation services] was headed by the Chinese inter-agency network, but we connected with other social service agencies and got the support of the Portuguese and other [ethnic] groups. We came up with evidence [for the police board] to show the need [for such a service]. For example, so many people are waiting to get into English classes – they obviously don't have the language skills. The police eventually installed the 911 interpretation services. But after it started, there were problems. For example, if you call and say, 'I speak Chinese,' they won't call an interpreter because they say you are speaking in English. Now the system can transfer the person to the appropriate language.

Third Interview

The South Asian Women's Group was started by some South Asian women students and staff at the University of Toronto in the late 1970s. Originally they met as an informal group to raise women's consciousness about their oppression, but when the needs of non–English-speaking South Asian women, particularly victims of wife abuse, were brought to their attention, they organized themselves formally and obtained their first funds in the early 1980s. At the time of the interview, the South Asian Women's Group had a large office and several full-time staff members, and its range of services had expanded further to meet the changing needs of the community. By 1996, however, it had lost its funding because of government cut-backs and internal conflicts. The Centre has moved to smaller quarters and currently delivers services primarily through volunteer workers.

Rafath (a pseudonym) is a Muslim counsellor at the South Asian Women's Group. She is divorced and is the mother of one daughter. Her parents live in Toronto. In an interview on 3 March 1994, she described the ethnic identity of the women who come to the group and the kinds of services they require. She began by describing her career path:

I started as a volunteer with a community group. Then I went to school full-time for two years as a mature student and studied social work, gerontology, and specialized in community development. I did my placement at Baycrest and at Don Mills Foundation, where I worked with the seniors in the Ismaili community. After I graduated, I joined the South Asian Centre as a volunteer coordinator and then became its outreach coordinator.

The two major groups of women who come to us are from Tamil- and Punjabi-speaking communities. The Tamil community is very large in Toronto, and they network among themselves very well. If a new Tamil family comes to the city, they immediately get to know about us. Then it is just a matter of time before they access our services. Gujarati women also come to us. The [Indo-Caribbean] community can speak English, and their needs are being met by Caribbean community groups, but we can also serve them. We have a board member who is from the Caribbean community. Another group of women who come to us are the refugees, primarily from Sri Lanka. They are from their mid-twenties to mid-sixties.

A community group, women's shelter, or mainstream social service agency may refer a client to another organization that can better meet her needs as an ethnic or racialized woman, particularly if she does not speak English:

A lot of women have come to us via the police, or the shelters, or through word of mouth. Women find out about us from people in the area. The women also come to the centre through referrals. For example, a psychiatric nurse may call us in the case of a suicidal woman. In one case, a young woman was being forced into an arranged marriage. The father was preparing to take her to India. But the girl was devastated and wanted to commit suicide rather than go through with the wedding. Because the girl was young and still in school, [the case] came to the attention of the school authorities, and they alerted the social workers and that's how she came to us.

   In another case, the father called – and this is a typical kind of situation – and said his daughters were having real difficulties in settling down and he wanted them to get some help. They were new in the country and had to make lots of adjustments and [were experiencing] a lot of pressure. The father was abusive towards his daughters, but he failed to report that. But we expect that. The men will seldom reveal their own abuse.

Community groups argue that ethnic and racialized women are alienated by the formal and bureaucratic atmosphere of some social service agencies, complex and confusing administrative forms, and lack of flexible hours (Doyle and Visano 1987). Their familiarity with the cultures of abused women makes them better able to respond to their needs. Rafath described some of the factors that make South Asian women feel comfortable in coming to the community group:

There is no formal protocol. We encourage people to make appointments and we see them as soon as we can. But if they come, we do not turn anyone back, because it is [also] a drop-in centre.

   We have a warm, friendly, and non-threatening environment. We work hard to make it [feel] safe to the women. Of course, women come to us because of the language, but there is also a sense of comfort [in coming to us]. Our familiarity with their culture makes them feel comfortable.

We have empathy for their circumstances because we know where they are coming from.

[One counsellor] always takes note of what people have to offer, and whenever the opportunity comes up she will plug them in. Women don't just feel that they are coming to get something. They can also give, and that is what makes them feel comfortable.

Victims of abuse find it difficult to reveal their situation to outsiders. The process of finding help is especially complicated for women who are new immigrants to Canada, do not speak the English language, and are dependent on their spouses for economic support:

A lot of women [are first] brought in by their spouses because they are so dependent on them for transportation. The women come to us for language training and then realize the other services that are available to them. They see the posters about wife abuse in our office and realize what other services we offer.

They let us know about their situation by enquiring about the work we do. If we sense something, we might just talk about wife abuse in a general way and voice our opinion about it and then watch for their reaction. They may open up and tell us what is on their mind. If the man is sitting beside the woman, forget about it! She won't say anything. Or a woman [may first] say, 'I am here to fill out a form, but what else do you do?' Or they will say, 'I have a friend who is in a situation [of abuse]. What kind of help is available to such a woman?' They ask, 'Is it safe for a woman who wants to leave [her abusive spouse]?' It is never up front, like 'Oh, I am being abused. Help me.' It is very, very subtle.

Usually the women are very embarrassed. They always think it is their fault, because that is what they have been made to understand. They are very, very reluctant to talk about it. A lot of it is conveyed through body language, the downcast and watching eyes. She may whisper to a counsellor, 'I have a problem. Can I call you some other time?' Sometimes the spouse is sitting right across the room, because men don't like to leave their women alone with us, and he is watching her. If he is sitting across the room, out of earshot, she may say something, but it is difficult.

We take our cue from the client. We try not to overwhelm her with information or be too anxious [for her]. We have to be careful. A lot of women cannot take pamphlets, etc., home with them. I find that it is very difficult for women who have children to get away from the abuse even though they know they have a right to a safe environment.

It takes a lot of courage for a woman to come [to our centre]. [When she first comes in] we take her to the kitchen and we make her some tea or coffee. This is in line with our culture, and it breaks the ice. We then take the woman in the counselling room to ensure confidentiality, and the worker and the client will stay there as long as it is [necessary].

Volunteer ethnic, social, and religious groups provide emotional and psychological support to new immigrants and facilitate their adaptation and settlement in Canada. These groups become a buffer between a new immigrant who feels lost and alienated and the unfamiliar and sometimes unwelcoming new society. However, a woman who reports wife abuse may be sanctioned by her community. Rafath described the difficulties that a victim of wife abuse may experience within the Muslim community in Toronto:

Here is a woman coming into a foreign place, does not speak the language, does not have the skills to make it on her own (especially soon after arriving here), usually has dependants, and is herself dependent on the husband who beats her. She has lost her extended family and has nothing but the community. In the community, other women are also being abused, so they are saying to her, 'Why are you such a princess that you have to be treated differently? Your [situation] is not unique. We all get abused. We take it and we live with it.' It is very difficult to break [from the community]. A woman who reports abuse may be totally isolated from the community. The community is absolutely not sympathetic to a woman for opening up her situation to public scrutiny.

[Abuse occurred] back home as well, but there were ways of dealing with it. The women took care of each other. If a man went to extremes, it could be dealt with. In any case, back home was a familiar territory, with familiar language and familiar people. Being in a foreign place is an added burden.

In a way, it is worse when [abused women] are in Canada, because they have the knowledge that they can do something about their situation, yet they can't. There is the possibility that they can live on their own. They have the means [i.e., they can get social assistance], but family ties and ties with the community are holding them back.

South Asian abused women, like Korean-Canadian women and black women, are reluctant to report their abuse to the police:[2]

The women are afraid to report abuse to the police, who are usually white men. Some of them feel that their men will be [ill-treated] by the police because they happen to be of a different colour, and they do not want to put their men through it. They have also heard stories about mistreatment by the police from people who have been [in Canada] a long time. The other thing is that if a man has abused his wife, he will plead with her not to report, and he will tell her all kinds of stories about the police. [The woman is afraid] that when the man gets out of prison, she is going to get beaten again for having put that shame on him. The woman may not trust the police partly because of experiences in their own country. Also, if a woman reports [her abuse to the police], she may be chastised by the community. So it is very, very difficult for a woman to report.

Some South Asian community groups that provide services to victims of wife abuse allow men to become members of their boards of directors. Although counsellors generally agree that men who perpetrate violence against women should get professional help to change their behaviour, they do not feel comfortable providing it themselves:

Sometimes even men have become involved with the Centre. South Asian men are coming together to address the issue [of violence against women]. There is no denial of the problem, and they are trying to formulate [a response]. There is a South Asian group called South Asian Men against Violence against Women. These are men in their late twenties to about forties. It is open to all men. I think men have a lot to gain [from groups like these], but they don't [all] see it that way.

The South Asian Women's Group differs in many ways from the

Riverdale Immigrant Women's Centre and the South Asian Family Support Services, the two other South Asian groups that I studied in Toronto. To satisfy government requirements, the South Asian Women's Group has a volunteer board of directors. However, despite this hierarchical structure, it tries to act as a collective by making decisions through a consensus of its staff and board. The board of the South Asian Women's Group is dominated by young, second-generation women. These women are more militant in expressing their ethnic identity. For example, following the South Asian custom, visitors are asked to remove their shoes at the entrance of their office. In a workshop organized by them, they displayed South Asian crafts and burned incense. Their programs are more innovative (e.g., writing workshops), and they provide entertainment to their clients (e.g., taking them on a day-long excursion to Ottawa).

Rafath described how the generational conflict experienced by young South Asian girls mobilized the group into organizing a youth group for them and how they tried to be supportive of lesbian South Asian women:

The media [sometimes publishes stories] about the cultural clash in South Asian families [between first-generation immigrant parents and their Canadian-born children]. These articles misrepresent the community. They portray our community as very oppressive and very narrow-minded. They portray our kids as being very monitored. In one story, they talked about a girl who was beaten because she did not have good grades. It might be true of some families, but it is not true of all South Asians. These reports also discussed [various kinds of abuse]. But they were very biased.

Afterwards a number of young South Asian women called and said that they would like to help these young South Asian teenagers. So I brought it up at the board meeting and said we had to do something about helping these young women. We realized that a space was needed for young people, and we started a youth group. I believe we are the only group [among South Asian community groups] that is focusing on the young women. Time and time we hear from these young women: 'I wish I had known about you ten years ago, when I was in my teens and I needed a place to come to.' They say, 'I could not reconcile my differences with my parents. I needed a safe space to hang out.'

The youth group is very different [from some of our other support groups]. At first we organized a movie night for the group. After the movie, we had a discussion about it, but then other issues started coming out. As women got comfortable, they started talking about ethnic identity, racism, and [physical] safety. As we progressed, the women saw that people did not shy away from issues. Then the sexuality stuff started to come out.

We had one workshop on street-proofing and women's safety. Another [workshop] was a consciousness-raising session. In both these workshops, sexuality was discussed. Women's self-consciousness was raised. For example, a woman may know she is attracted to another woman and was keeping it under wraps. They may even go out with other men, but they knew they were attracted to other women. When they talked about it, they realized they were not alone; there were other women in the same situation. Then they realized that as a group of non-white women they could get together and have a network. We [the South Asian Women's Group] also began to realize that there is a community of lesbians which is not only out there but is within our midst.

It is difficult for South Asian women to come out as lesbians. In a way, there is the choice between coming out as a lesbian or giving up the community. It is very difficult to have both. You can't openly be gay or lesbian and be accepted within the community. I feel very comfortable with the few people that I have known who are gay or lesbian, but when I talked about it in my community, sometimes people would physically move away as if I am contagious. I get so angry.

In the South Asian Muslim community, a lot of women cannot express themselves, or they feel they cannot. The girl may want to express herself, but her father may [respond to her behaviour by] punishing her mother or her siblings. It is very hard for a young woman to accept that responsibility; that is what keeps them in the oppressive milieus. The father does not think he is doing anything wrong; he is protecting his family according to his values and his morality.

A young woman organized a fundraiser. Sixty people came and there was great diversity within the group; they were Hindus, Punjabis, and Christians. I am very excited about young people feeling confident about coming to our centre.

Fourth Interview

Shanaz (a pseudonym) has worked as a wife abuse counsellor at
the South Asian Family Support Services for several years. She has
a B.A. in child psychology and sociology, and has worked in a number of Asian countries. She attributes her success as a counsellor to
having gone through the pain of divorce and separation in her
own life. In these excerpts from an interview on 26 February 1994,
she describes her work with women who have been abused by their
spouses.

An immigrant woman may experience abuse for the first time in
Canada, if she has been recently married, or it may start in the
country of origin and continue in Canada. Women who come
from South Asia or other Third World countries may believe that
difficulties should be resolved privately, without seeking the help
of outsiders, which could bring shame to the family and involve a
'loss of face.' Shanaz described how immigration may exacerbate
the situation of victims of wife abuse:

Most of the women who come to SAFSS will not admit to being exposed
to violence back home. At first, they say that everything was fine back
home, but when they came to Canada everything changed. But once they
start coming on a regular basis for counselling to this organization and
they start trusting me, they open up more. Then I find out, no, it is not
Canada that has brought out the worst in these men; they were even bat-
terers at home.

   The pain was there. But the support system was there [as well]. Organizations like the [South Asian Family Support Services] do not exist in
Muslim countries [or in most of South Asia]. Counselling means going to
the grandfather, or grandmother, or aunt, or to a member of their
extended family and getting advice. They say, we will go to our elders and
sort out the problems or our disagreements. [Consequently], the women
did not feel so isolated. They don't have the support system here [in Can-
ada] – so when they come here to me they don't necessarily look upon
me as a counsellor. They look upon me as their older sister. The women
call me didi (older sister). Women from Pakistan call me Baji or Aunty. I
don't mind that.

An abused woman may be unaware of her rights. This is particularly true if she is also a non–English-speaking immigrant. Then she cannot understand public service announcements about wife abuse that are broadcast on television or appear in other media. Recently, some multicultural television stations have started to broadcast information in several different languages. However, even though such announcements inform a woman that wife abuse is a crime in Canada, they do not address her other concerns – for example, whether she will be deported if her spouse withdraws his sponsorship. Sometimes an abusive spouse deliberately misinforms his wife. A wife may be hesitant to report abuse if her husband has told her that he will withdraw his sponsorship of her relatives, or she may fear that her children will be removed from her care if she reports the abuse.

Community-based groups endeavour to reach women from their own ethnic communities. The most effective way for the South Asian Family Support Services to reach South Asian victims of wife abuse is through word-of-mouth recommendations. SAFSS also tries to reach victims of abuse by putting up posters in public places and by making its services known to service providers in the neighbourhood. In 1990, when SAFSS first started, it had a case load of only 7 women, but in 1994 the active cases were approximately 250 women.

Although victims of wife abuse are usually referred to SAFSS by South Asian (and other) physicians, social service agencies, the police, hospitals, and shelters for women in the borough, victims may also contact the agency themselves. The first contact is most frequently just an enquiry about the services offered by the agency. A woman may pretend to be calling for a friend and ask about her immigration status or about the social services available to victims of wife abuse. Only after several visits, and only when she begins to feel confidence and trust in the personnel, will she reveal her own situation. Shanaz described some of the barriers that abused women encounter in getting help:

The man has beaten up the woman and left her. A woman doesn't know how to call the police because of the language barrier. [She thinks], who is *she* to call the police anyways? She [may] have gone crying to a neighbour, and the neighbour may say, 'I know someone who might help,' and that someone will know someone else. Sometimes it takes the women two or three days before they will get to our organization. When women [eventually] phone us, they are [frequently] hysterical on the phone. They are in no condition to catch a bus and come to the office. Or they have little kids. I [have] to go there.

I cannot call women during my [regular] working hours. The men are [often] at home if they are unemployed or doing shift work. The new phones have become a curse. The numbers are displayed, or, if the number does not appear because the organization has blocked them, what comes on the screen is a 'private caller' or 'caller unknown.' The husband is angry. Who is this private or unknown caller? [He may suspect that some] organization has called his wife and they have blocked their number. She is in trouble. So I am teaching the women, when you call me, after that dial any number at random, or call his sister or mother or someone, so that my number is not the last number on the phone. It is a [lesson in] survival; it is not counselling.

Sometimes social service agencies call SAFSS on behalf of their clients, but the contact may be lost, and the woman may return to an abusive home:

Social workers from the crisis centre or from the hospital may call and say, 'We have a case here of an abused woman. She is very nervous; she hasn't got over the trauma. Can you provide some services that she needs?' I will say, 'Sure, give me her name and number.' Then they will say, 'No, I will get back to you with her name and other details.' After a couple of days, they may call again and say, 'The victim was not very comfortable with my giving her name and number to you, but she asked me to give your name and number to her, because she doesn't know what time her husband will be home or her in-laws will be home. She will call you from a public phone.' Quite understandable. But 99 per cent of them do not call, and it is quite frustrating. It is so important to give immediate service when the client first contacts the organization. It may be our hundredth call for the day, but it is the client's first call. We discuss this all the time in the organization. Women are being abused, [they need our services], but we can't reach them. The hospital has lost touch [with them].

Shanaz described the family structures of the women who come to SAFSS:

For South Asian women, the in-laws are a contributing factor to the abuse. A typical example is something like this. A young couple immigrate. Both work very hard. [Let's say] he works as a machine operator and she in a garment factory. They are enjoying two incomes. They rough it out and live in basement apartments. Very soon they have managed to save money for a down payment for some house. But then the woman may get pregnant and cannot work. Their income drops, plus they have the added burden of a newly acquired property. They start thinking what to do now. They say, 'OK, we will call our parents to babysit for us.'

The grandparents get frustrated by the language barrier, [social] isolation, and [the rigorous] climate. They are used to having neighbours dropping in on them informally. They miss their social activities. They start making demands – they want a break from babysitting; [they want] to go to the mall. Frustration grows in the family. The parents cannot direct this frustration and anger at the son. They will direct it to the daughter-in-law. They may complain that she is rude, or that she does not [show her] appreciation for their work. The man has been conditioned to believe his parents. The wife becomes the outsider, and eventually such a situation may escalate into abuse. [In some cases, it also leads to elder abuse.]

A South Asian woman may become a virtual prisoner in her home because she is constantly under the vigilance of her spouse and his family. Even when she decides to seek help, she will still have great difficulty in communicating with service providers since she is constantly watched by the spouse and his family. Such a woman is most likely to come to the agency through a hospital or because neighbours become alarmed at sounds of struggle and alert the police.

Women who live in nuclear families may, during a crisis, call a community-based group such as SAFSS, and the counsellors' familiarity with South Asian cultural norms and their ability to communicate with the women in some (though not all) of the South Asian languages facilitate a quick response to her situation. Counsellors define a situation as a crisis when a woman is unable to cope or when her safety or that of her children is threatened. After speaking with the woman, the counsellor determines whether a house call is necessary; if so, she visits her, either alone or, if there is a threat of danger, accompanied by the police. In crisis intervention, the first thing to do is to provide safety for the woman by taking her to a doctor or to a shelter. In the following, Shanaz described the process of leaving the marital home:

Sometimes, when I prepare [a woman] to leave the family home, I will tell her, 'Get all your clothes, passport, and bank books ready.' I'll ask her, 'What time does your husband go to work?' If the man is unemployed, I have to know [whether there is a time] that he regularly goes out. The woman will brush all that aside and will be concerned about her jewellery. I tell [her], 'Forget the jewellery and think about your *life*.' They have no money and nowhere to go. The cultural conditioning of South Asian women is that the jewellery will provide some security. This [sometimes causes] cultural misunderstanding between the clients and the welfare workers, who cannot understand this obsession with jewellery.

In a crisis situation there are lot of things involved. A man has beaten his wife and gone off. She and I have no way of knowing if he has gone [to cool off] or he has gone for good. We don't know what his decision is.

In crisis intervention, if there is evidence of physical abuse, I will call the police. I will also take her to a doctor, and the doctor will write a report. That report will also be used as evidence [during legal proceedings].

I have to call the superintendent of the building, and let him know that I am moving this woman to a shelter, because if the woman leaves without informing the superintendent, she may, if they have signed a lease for a year, be asked to pay three or four months' rent. Sometimes even before the court hearing, I will go [back to the apartment] with the woman and the police, and pick up the clothing, etc. But it takes a long time before we can move the furniture. [Anyway] she has to have a place to put the furniture.

Women who have been sponsored to immigrate by their husbands are legally his dependants and are normally not allowed to
go on welfare. However, victims of violence can leave abusive families and obtain social services if they can provide proof of violence:

We have to prove that a woman is a victim of abuse [for her to qualify] for
welfare. It is easy [to prove abuse] when the police have been called and
the charges have been laid. [And] it is easy when there is evidence of
physical abuse.

I work closely with welfare workers. Welfare exists to help women. It is
the [service providers'] responsibility to screen people, but that does not
mean they can humiliate women. But a lot of them are getting away with
it. The way they talk to my clients who are non–English-speaking women!
[They say], 'Come here. Go, go, go!' Can they do that to a white person?
The workers need to be educated how to deal with clients from different
cultural groups.

Shanaz described her approach to counselling women who
come to the organization and how she gets her clients to talk about
themselves:

I cannot remain emotionally detached from my clients. I greet the
women at the door of my office and sit beside them (rather than behind
my desk). I cry with my clients. I share my own life stories with them. I tell
them what I went through during my separation and divorce. I [do this to
let them know] I can relate with them. I understand what they are going
through. When the women are telling me their stories, I am nodding to
tell them that I can hear them, I feel what they are feeling, I have gone
through it myself.

I start off by saying, 'Why don't I tell you of the services we are providing here and see where you fit in here?' I will not talk about wife abuse
initially. I will go round and round the topic. I will say, 'We have a lot of
immigrants coming here who are not aware of the existing laws in [Can-
ada]. We help them with immigration matters, we recommend lawyers to
them, we escort them to courts for interpreting and for giving them
moral support.' I will say, 'We have English-language classes here.' Then I
will say, 'Have you heard that in Canada there is such a thing called the

Children's Aid Society?' And then I will say, 'If you see your neighbour raising his hand to his wife, it is your duty to report to the police.' I bring up the issue very indirectly, because she will completely deny it the moment I ask her. She will say, 'Me? No way!'

A victim of wife abuse who comes to the agency is told about the choices available to her. The counsellors give her information about the process: she would have to meet with lawyers and crown attorneys and appear in court for hearings; there may be an investigation by the police. A woman who does not speak English is assured of the agency's support through the process, particularly in providing linguistic and cultural interpretation; and she is informed of programs like the Crown Attorney's Witness Protection Program. Nevertheless, deciding what to do can be difficult:

Social work theory says, you [explain] the choices a women has and she decides. We are dealing with women who have never decided anything [significant] in their lives. It was the mother, or father, the brother, the husband, etc. [who made the big decisions]. Suddenly there is no decision-maker in their lives. The woman says, 'I can't decide. You tell me what to do. I am in this situation because I can't decide.' Unorthodoxly I end up deciding for these women. I am not going to decide for them that they should go back to an abusive situation. I will not make a decision for them when safety issues are involved. But I may get involved in other issues.

Once a woman has decided to lay charges against her spouse, SAFSS provides support to the woman in meeting with lawyers and attending court hearings. I observed one woman at a sentencing hearing. She had been supported throughout the process of laying charges against her spouse by SAFSS and the Witness Protection Program. On the day of the sentencing, after waiting in the offices of the Witness Protection Program (located away from the busy activity of the Provincial Court), she entered the courtroom accompanied by a counsellor from SAFSS, a language interpreter assigned by the court, a case worker from the Witness Protection Program, a cultural interpreter assigned by the Witness Protection

Program, the director of the Witness Protection Program, a detective who had worked on the case, her attorney, and her father. (Her spouse was accompanied by his attorney and a court-appointed language interpreter.)

I escort women who do not speak English [to the courts] mainly for emotional support. But even a woman who can speak English may still not be familiar with the court system. The women are nervous, they have never been to court, and they are [going to] face a man who has beaten the life out of them. The room is full of strangers because the criminal court is open to the public. The man may bring his relatives [in an attempt] to intimidate her. So I am there mainly for emotional support. But as I am getting more and more familiar with the judicial system, I sometimes go to the crown attorneys and say they have got the information wrong. A cultural interpreter [may be there], but she is not a counsellor. She is there just to interpret. She does not know the client's background. Some crown attorneys are not sensitive to the physical and mental state of the client – they cannot tell when the woman is starting to break down. [When I see that], I can go and complain to [the director of the Witness Protection Program]. When [the attorneys] are trying to prove the woman was abused, [evidence of] physical, sexual, and psychological abuse comes out. The defence lawyer will force a South Asian woman to discuss sexual abuse, knowing that it is one thing that she would not like to talk about. He will do that just to intimidate the woman. But we can't tell the defence lawyer to treat the woman with kid gloves. That is the reality.

I think the judges also have some stereotypes of these women. Some judges are prejudiced. My clients need a very sensitive judge.

In the following, Shanaz recommended counselling for men as well:

It's not enough to counsel women. South Asian women do not want the marriage to end. They want the violence to stop. Not all [the women end up going to the] shelters or living in Ontario housing. After the counselling, they go back home to the same abusive environment. When she comes to me, I am saying to her, 'You have rights, you have options, you do not have to tolerate [abuse], you don't have to stay in an abusive environment.' She goes back home armed with all this information. We are talking about South Asian men or Middle Eastern men who think an assertive woman is aggressive. [The abuse may have] initially started because the man complained that the woman talked back to him and [did something] she would not have dared to do in India or Pakistan. The man comes to me and says, 'What are you doing? Instead of patching things up you have sent back an assertive woman.' Sometimes in such situations the violence [increases].

We [SAFSS] must open our doors to men. The man can sometimes come to our organization with [his spouse]. But there are a lot of safety issues involved, and some legalities. If there is a restraining order, or if the man has been charged, they cannot come to our organization together. They must come separately. But when there are no charges, and they come in voluntarily, they can come together.

Our Indian and Pakistani doctors have become very active and they [sometimes] send abusive men here. But I am not going to throw questions at him right away. I won't ask him if he is beating his wife or if he has been abusive towards his children. The whole idea is to make him comfortable [and then discuss his behaviour].

We have to change the men. Maybe I am using the wrong word. Some of the men cannot change.

Case Study: The Dilemma of Providing Culturally Sensitive Services to South Asian Women

Community-based groups have argued that their services are necessary because working-class, non–English-speaking, immigrant women are alienated by the Eurocentric norms of mainstream social service agencies and experience discrimination from some of the service providers in these agencies. The community-based groups, in contrast, offer linguistically appropriate and culturally sensitive services. However, no community-based South Asian group can provide services in all South Asian languages. A group's ability to provide services in any particular language (e.g., Tamil, Punjabi, Gujarati, or Marathi) depends on its having personnel who speak that language. As the personnel changes, so does the ability of the group to offer services in particular languages.

In defending their claim to be more culturally sensitive than the personnel of mainstream agencies, my respondents argued that they had an overall understanding of South Asia and could transcend regional differences between the different cultures. As South Asian immigrant women, they have all experienced feelings of dislocation and faced similar difficulties in adapting to Canada. Similar experiences of race, class, and gender discrimination create empathy between South Asian women of different classes. Middle-class service providers can understand the reluctance of working-class, non–English-speaking women to confide in white service providers in mainstream social service agencies. The women feel more relaxed and comfortable in discussing their situation with women who look like them.

The counsellor and the client may have different political ideologies. For example, a counsellor may be a feminist committed to removing an abused woman from a violent home; but the abused woman herself may not favour such a solution. The counsellor may believe that patriarchal domination is the source of the woman's problem, but the victim may be more concerned with how things went wrong for her personally and refuse to question patriarchal norms. A woman who comes to SAFSS may not wish to charge her husband but only want someone to mediate in order to prevent the more extreme acts of violence which threaten her or her children's safety.

Counsellors are aware that racism in the larger society, particularly racism among employers, makes the process of reorganizing a South Asian woman's life extremely complicated. She may also encounter biases in sections of the South Asian community as an abused woman or, if she leaves the man, as a divorced woman. Counselling focuses on finding practical solutions to her problems, rather than attempting to raise her consciousness or engaging in political discussion.

South Asian family structures in Canada pose additional problems for women trying to escape abuse. South Asian households frequently include relatives of the male spouse, usually his parents and unmarried siblings. Sometimes two brothers may set up a 'joint family,' with the elder male acting as the head of the household. Males may initiate violence against their spouses, but their mothers and sisters may condone or even encourage it.

Power in South Asian families is held by the eldest male, but women also have a sphere of influence, which includes, for example, maintenance of the home, care of the children, and decisions regarding matrimonial alliances. Among the women in the family there are further hierarchies according to the age and status of the individual: mother, wife of the older male sibling, married daughter, or unmarried daughter. There is competition between the women and between them and the older males in the family. Another source of conflict in South Asian families is the rivalry between a man's wife and his mother and between the man's wife and his sisters.

Abuse in South Asian families stems not only from the desire of the male to control and dominate his spouse but also from the desire of the other women to reinforce their own authority within the home. A mother-in-law may assert her authority over a young bride by threatening her with violence from the males. Other female family members may participate in oppressing a young wife who is assigned low status as an outsider. Patriarchal norms internalized by women make it hard for them to challenge hierarchies of gender, age, and status. They may accept the violence in their homes, abhorring only its more extreme manifestations. Some mothers-in-law argue that it is part of the life-cycle: an abused young woman will one day be a mother-in-law and will have the responsibility of ensuring the subordination of other women of the family, even if that involves violence.

An abused South Asian woman who openly challenges patriarchal norms jeopardizes the support that may be available to her from her natal family. Culturally, a South Asian woman has the right to be supported by her father and brothers, and they are responsible for caring for her and her children in times of crisis; but the natal family may turn a blind eye to the violence inflicted on sisters and daughters if they are unable to provide for them. As immigrants, they do not experience the social disapprobation that they would encounter in their communities of origin in South Asia for shirking their responsibilities. The woman sees the violence as an aberration on the part of her spouse. Identifying patriarchal norms as part of the explanation of her problems would threaten the positions of her own male relatives.

Community-based groups such as SAFSS, in their published reports, and in their discussions in workshops and conferences, seldom question the patriarchal norms that may form part of the mental and psychological framework of the friends and family of an abused woman and make them hesitant or unwilling to intervene. Such groups have argued that immigrant women lack the support of friends and relatives that they would receive in their countries of origin. However, an examination of violence against women suggests that support may be lacking even there.

In India, abuse of a woman often begins with some recrimination about the inadequacy of her dowry (jewellery, household goods, and other gifts) or of the subsequent gifts she receives from her parents. Sometimes the harassment becomes particularly severe if her parents refuse to satisfy the demands made by the spouse or his family for additional gifts. Though the dowry is usually given voluntarily, some families may negotiate its size. This practice has become more widespread in the last twenty years, and failure to meet the 'requests' of the spouse's family leads sometimes to the harassment of the wife and may result in a 'dowry death' or 'kitchen death.' The term 'kitchen death' refers to the death of a young woman that occurs in suspicious circumstances and in which the husband or his family are the prime suspects. South Asians commonly use a kerosene stove for cooking. An unhappy man, or his family, whose requests for additional dowry have been turned down, may pour kerosene on the woman and burn her. Such a death can be passed off as an accident, but more stringent regulations in investigating kitchen deaths are now being sought by the women's movement in India (Kishwar and Vanita 1991; Datar 1993).

The dowry is a symbol of women's low status in South Asia. The practice of giving the dowry is not prescribed by religion but by custom. The content and value of the dowry vary in different regions, castes, classes, and groups. Some South Asians continue the practice of giving and receiving dowries as immigrants in Africa, Britain, and Canada (Bhachu 1985). The dowry's content and value are dependent on the resources that are available to a family or on what a young woman has accumulated through her own earnings.[3] Since some South Asians consider giving and receiving a dowry as a public assertion of 'izzat' (i.e., respect) and as reflecting their standing and prestige in the community, it has become burdensome for the parents of the woman's family. Complaints about the dowry can thus arise regardless of its size or value.

My respondents usually considered comments about the inadequacy or lack of a dowry as constituting emotional and psychological abuse aimed at ensuring the new wife's compliance with the authority structure of her matrimonial home. (Parents of daughters seek to provide a substantial dowry to their daughter to bolster her position in her new home.) However, it is not clear what counsellors should say or do in order to deal with such situations in a 'culturally sensitive' way.[4] Counsellors and administrators in community-based groups are not a homogeneous group subscribing to a common set of beliefs or values. They have different views about feminism and about the desirability of maintaining their own cultural practices and norms in Canadian society. Many South Asian counsellors have received a dowry, and they would argue that it symbolizes the family's care and affection for their daughter. Some would equate the dowry with the Western practice of giving gifts to brides. Few of these women would consider complaints about the dowry to be an adequate reason for breaking up a marriage or charging the spouse and his family with abuse.

Some South Asians are strongly committed to their own cultural values and wish to arrange marriages of their offspring. They disapprove of cross-cultural and interracial dating by their children. The dowry is an integral part of an arranged marriage. However, since dowries are a symbol of women's low status, giving or receiving a dowry perpetuates women's oppression.

During my research, I did not come across any evidence to indicate that counsellors are seeking to undermine the dowry. They took a more pragmatic approach. When abuse involved harassment over a dowry, counsellors usually did not challenge the institution of the dowry itself but only argued that the harassment was excessive or that it was inappropriate behaviour, especially in Canada. They framed the situation in the language of crime and punishment. They did not engage in political analysis of the tradition of the dowry or seek to raise the women's consciousness about gender inequities.

Sensitivity to a patriarchal culture might encourage advising a woman to accept her dependence on male relatives. In practice, of course, community-based groups do not give that sort of advice. It is difficult for them, nevertheless, to explain how to decide which aspects of which cultures to support, and difficult for them even to discuss the issue. Identifying the ways in which a culture's norms and values accord privilege to males poses risks for stigmatized minority groups. Members of these groups may fear that discussing them will only reinforce stereotypes held by the dominant society and be construed as another sign of the backwardness or inferiority of their culture (Thobani, quoted in Razack 1994). Uma Narayan notes that, in fact, both cultures privilege males:

> As an Indian feminist living in the United States, I often find myself torn between the desire to communicate with honesty the miseries and oppressions that I think my culture confers on its women and the fear that the communication is going to reinforce, however unconsciously, Western prejudices about the 'superiority' of Western culture. I have often felt compelled to interrupt my communication, say on the problems of the Indian system of arranged marriages, to remind my Western friends that the experience of women under their system of 'romantic love' seems no more enviable. (Narayan 1990, 250)

Middle-class South Asian women have done valuable work in encouraging service providers in mainstream agencies to become culturally sensitive to their South Asian clients, and they have also provided services under their own auspices. However, they have not clearly articulated what they mean by 'cultural sensitivity,' or developed policies to deal with cases in which patriarchal cultural practices conflict with feminist goals such as freeing women from dependence on males or empowering them to become autonomous decision-makers. Sometimes they seem to reduce issues of culture to relatively minor variations in 'customs,' such as differences of food or dress. Often, too, they portray culture as timeless and constant, unaffected by, for example, colonization, industrialization, or urbanization. Their unwillingness to attack male domination in the old culture or racism in the new is further manifested in the restriction of their work to providing social services for individuals. Their work is a limited response to systemic racism and patriarchy, and it rarely encourages women to question the system.

Conclusion

The tensions between providing services and promoting political goals arise when community-based women's groups become dependent on governments for resources. Service providers, conscious of how their actions will be interpreted by funding agencies, moderate their critiques of patriarchal, racist society. Providing good-quality services to a large number of women makes them credible to government agencies and ensures continuation of resources, but it diverts them from the feminist goals of destabilizing patriarchal norms and values.

The services provided by community-based agencies are valuable. The process of obtaining services may raise a woman's political consciousness. It can help her to avoid blaming herself, to realize some of her own hitherto unexplored abilities, and to feel empowered. Nonetheless, these are not the central aims of the service providers, and any social changes that might be brought about through them can occur only indirectly and slowly.

Services are important, but unless they are embedded in a larger political vision of change and transformation, they correct only some of the worst abuses produced by the social system, and like other social-work practices intended to deal with 'exceptional

cases,' they tend to maintain the status quo of race and gender inequalities. Community-based agencies must foster greater consciousness of the causes of women's oppression and encourage
women to become more political in their interpretations of their
abuse if they want to be true to their feminist goals of eliminating
violence against women.

SEVEN

Counsellors and Women in Shelters

Women who have been abused by their spouses may be ambivalent about leaving their homes. Gender roles that give priority to being a wife and mother, and cultural norms that make it difficult for women to acknowledge abuse, trap abused women in oppressive homes (Greaves, Heapy, and Wylie 1988). Immigrant women often lack supportive family in Canada, are unable to speak English fluently, and have little or no 'Canadian' work experience. A non–English-speaking woman's lack of knowledge about the existence of shelters keeps her living with the abuse until it escalates and threatens her or her children's lives. However, life within the shelter is also difficult for a woman who does not speak the English language and is unfamiliar with the norms of Canadian society.

Shelters for abused women have tried to implement, to some extent, feminist ideals of cooperative living, sisterhood, and non-hierarchical environments. Nevertheless, over the years, their dependence on government funding has made them more like many other institutions for the homeless. Now shelters emphasize services to abused women rather than political action to transform gender relations. The staff at the shelters are not necessarily linked to the women's movement but have chosen a career of social work and opted to work with abused women. Abused women who come to the shelters are looking for safe refuge from the violence against them but are not necessarily interested in challenging gender relations, although they may begin to understand abuse as a systemic problem of gender relations rather than a matter of personal fail-ings or temperament. Women's consciousness is raised in a way that may incrementally lead to social change.

The literature on shelters has emphasized the trauma experienced by the women and their need for safe housing (Beaudry 1985; MacLeod 1987), but there is little published material that explains the process by which a woman enters a shelter or describes her everyday life there. In this chapter, excerpts of two interviews present the perspective of the workers on the organizational structures of the shelters, the racism that sometimes emerges in them, and the services the shelters provide for abused women living in them.

History and Everyday Working Life of the Shelters

Before the 1970s, emergency housing for abused women was not provided by social service agencies. The need for housing was sometimes met by religious and philanthropic organizations or by shelters for women. When the plight of abused women became a subject of public discussion, feminists argued that women would remain trapped in violent homes unless they could go to a safe place for a short period of time during an emergency or a crisis. In the 1970s, women who worked in drop-in centres attempted to find a few days' accommodation for abused women in 'safe houses' (private homes which provided refuge). The first shelters for abused women opened in 1973 in Vancouver (Transition House) and in Toronto (Interval House) (Gilman 1988, 10–11; Walker 1990, 22).

Feminists advocate shelters for abused women, but the shelters require financial support from provincial and federal governments. Shelters in Canada are funded primarily under two programs. The Canada Assistance Plan of the federal government (Department of Health and Welfare) shares 50 per cent of costs incurred to provide social assistance and welfare to those in need. The plan's program for 'homes for special care' has provided some funds to shelters. Capital costs for shelters can be obtained under the social housing assistance program of the Canada Mortgage and

Housing Corporation (Gilman 1988, 15–16), but shelters must lobby politicians and government personnel over a period of time before their applications for these funds are successful (North York Women's Shelter 1994). The operating costs allocated to shelters fluctuate depending on the political priorities of the government which is in power.[1]

The establishment of the North York Women's Shelter demonstrates the need for service providers to collaborate with government agencies. In 1980 a steering committee was formed that was composed of front-line workers, social service agencies, and 'community people' who wanted to establish emergency housing for women and children in North York. It made a presentation to the Family Life Education Subcommittee of the North York Inter-Agency Council, which was examining support services for assaulted women. In the winter of 1981, the steering committee organized four public meetings to mobilize support for setting up the shelter, find interested women to serve on its board of directors, and define its goals. In December 1981, the City of North York adopted a motion in support of the shelter and allocated a sum of $10,000 to get it started. It took another three years to locate a property, construct a building, and obtain a mortgage from the Canada Mortgage and Housing Corporation. The shelter opened on 10 September 1984. In 1996 the shelter had ten bedrooms, which housed approximately thirty women and children (North York Women's Shelter, fact sheet, n.d.).

Although most shelters are largely funded by government agencies, they also obtain funding from private organizations like the United Way or raise funds directly from the public. The Emily Stowe Shelter, in Scarborough, Ontario, receives funds from the Municipality of Metro Toronto Hostel Services, City of Scarborough, and three provincial ministries, the Ministry of Housing, the Ministry of Citizenship, and the Ministry of Community and Social Services. It has also received donations from the United Way (Emily Stowe Shelter 1990–3).[2] The annual operating budget for the North York Women's Shelter is $1.3 million, which is obtained from federal, provincial, and municipal governments. A small part of its budget comes from the United Way or through private fund-raising activity (North York Women's Shelter, fact sheet, history). Occasionally, some private corporations give donations or sponsor fund-raising campaigns. For example, a private land developer offered to organize a campaign at one of its shopping malls to raise money to renovate and expand the premises to better meet the needs of women and children living in the shelter (North York Women's Shelter, board meeting, 19 Feb. 1996).

The rapid establishment of a large number of shelters attests to successful lobbying by feminist groups to provide abused women with emergency housing. In 1979 there were 71 shelters in Canada, but by 1987 there were 230. Of these shelters, 44 per cent were only for battered women and their children, and 37 per cent were primarily for battered women and their children but also 'accepted women experiencing other types of crises' such as 'drug and alcohol dependency, mental health problems, and pregnancy or family problems.' The other shelters provided for women with a variety of needs. Even though the number of spaces in shelters has increased substantially in the last decade, the number of women who need a safe haven in shelters far exceeds the number who can be accommodated in them (MacLeod 1987, 47).[3] Statistics Canada reports that between April 1994 and May 1995, eighty-five thousand women and children spent time at shelters and other housing for victims of family violence (Gadd 1995, A8). However, support for shelters and women's organizations has declined since 1995, and it is unclear to what extent gains made in previous times can be sustained.

A woman who is living at a shelter cannot claim welfare since she is being provided with housing and food; she is entitled, though, to a 'personal needs allowance,' which in 1996 was $25 each for herself and her children.[4] The allowance is being questioned in the fiscally conservative 1990s, and shelter workers fear that it may be eliminated altogether. Shelters are meant to provide emergency housing for up to six weeks for abused women and their children, and funding for them depends on their occupancy rates. The maximum stay for which the shelter can receive funding for any one woman is six weeks. In practice, however, most women end up staying for much longer periods since affordable public housing is difficult to locate in a city like Toronto. The slow rate of turnover means that while some women have safe refuge, other women cannot locate emergency housing during a crisis (interview, 15 April 1996).

In order to ensure the safety of the residents of a shelter, its location is rarely advertised. Only after initial contact has been made with shelter staff is the location revealed to the abused woman. The contact may be made through a telephone call or through a community-based group, the police, or a hospital. The process of locating a shelter is especially difficult for a woman who does not speak English, and she is likely to need the help of a third party.

The Emily Stowe Shelter is a large house on a residential street in Toronto and there is little on its exterior to distinguish it from other homes on the street. When I visited the shelter, however, I found that inside it had an impersonal atmosphere and was quite unlike a home. The office located next to the entrance had an elaborate safety-alarm system for the protection of residents and staff. There were several desks crowded into the room, and a 'weekly chore chart' was taped on the wall. On the other side of the entrance was a small room with a chesterfield, but it had a cold and uninviting appearance.

The basement was divided into several rooms – a recreational area with a television, offices for one-to-one counselling, storerooms, and laundry rooms. The kitchen was clean, and on the morning I visited, a paid cook was making a meal. A woman with a small child sat at the kitchen table looking out the window, which had one-way glass panes. From time to time, women were summoned by the public intercom system to the phone or to the office. I was not allowed to see the bedrooms that the women share with their children. There was a small playground for the children, but I found the atmosphere depressing, and it seemed to me that only women in dire need and with no other alternatives would want to use the shelter.[5]

In the following excerpt from an interview, a worker at the shelter describes how women first make contact and come to the shelter and how the workers try to ease them into the everyday routine of the shelter. Pat (a pseudonym) is a black woman who emigrated from Trinidad to Canada in 1968. She divorced her husband a few years later and was left with four children under six years of age. In addition to raising her children on her own and doing paid work, Pat attended university as a mature student. When I saw her recently at a workshop at the Emily Stowe Shelter, she reminded me that she had taken a course of mine at York University and received an *A*. That grade, she told me, convinced her that she was smart enough to get an education, and she completed a B.A. in 1986. Two of her children have graduated from university, and the other two are now attending university. Pat became a relief worker at the Emily Stowe Shelter for Women in 1985, and she has been a full-time worker there since 1986. I interviewed her on 4 June 1993 at her home:

A woman may call on her own for space, or come through the police or through an agency. If she doesn't speak English, an agency or a friend can call on her behalf.

Usually we do a telephone interview, where we determine whether the woman is abused or not. If she can speak English, then we speak directly with her because you want to be sure that she wants to come. If she cannot speak English, then we would get the history from the agency or the police or the friend, and we sort of go back and forth and ask her if she wants to come to the shelter. If she says yes, then we will take her – if we have space.

When a woman who doesn't speak English comes to the shelter, we get an interpreter. We try not to use her children. We would use the children if, let's say, it's the weekend and we couldn't get an interpreter and we have to show her the house, how to use the stove, or show her the exit. That's the only time you would use the kids, because otherwise the roles [of parents and child] are reversed. Even if you use the child for a short time, you could see the roles reversing – the way the child [begins to] speak to the mother. The mom doesn't want to say what has happened to her in front of that child, either. We also try not to use neighbours and friends. If the woman comes with her friend, sometimes it's difficult, but we'll ask the woman if she wants her friend to go. Some friends and some family want to stay, but it doesn't really work out, because you don't always want to say everything in front of friends, so we do try to get an interpreter.

[As soon as a woman] comes to the shelter, we do an 'intake' to get her history. The intake lasts two to four hours. Sometimes when the woman comes in, she is like a wet spaghetti – she cries and cries. You are a professional person and you try not to cry. But what she is telling you is really painful and [sometimes] you can't do the intake. She tells you what has been happening to her. But some of the things she tells you, you may not put in the file because the file and the [daily] log of the shelter can be subpoenaed. So you have to be very careful what you write down. We advise her, if the husband beat her up and the police didn't charge him, to lay charges. We don't force the woman to take our advice; she can do it if she wants. We suggest that she get custody of her children, because under the Ontario law the children belong to both husband and wife. If the husband takes the children away from her, the police are not going to get them back, [because the husband] could accuse them of kidnapping. The only time the police will get that baby back is if it is being nursed by the mother. It's very important the woman leaves with the children.

Sometimes the woman is brought to the shelter in the clothes she is wearing, no shoes, no nothing. If she had to run from the house, run from that man, and run to the police station, she doesn't have anything, the kids don't have anything. Sometimes she comes with a little garbage bag with some stuff. [If we have a chance to talk to the woman on the phone before she comes to the shelter], we suggest that she gets all her legal papers and things like her health card. In the case of immigrant women, the man has the passport; he has all the legal papers locked up in his little suitcase.

[Sometimes the women] don't even know anything about their legal rights. There was this woman from Africa and she was here for three years. The man kept telling her, if she called the police he's going to send her back home. When that woman came to the shelter and I told that woman that he couldn't send her back home, that woman cried and cried. It was so pitiful, because for all these years he beat her so much but she didn't say anything, because she was afraid he was going to send her back. So women have to know they will not be penalized for leaving [their spouses and sponsors].

It's very difficult for the outreach to reach the women. Let's say you have a workshop on a Saturday in the plaza, [where a] woman could go and walk inside and get information. She can't go in there. If there could be some sort of a drop-in – but the man is going to say, what do you mean that you're going to a drop-in centre? It's very difficult to meet the woman.

The North York Women's Shelter is on a busy street. It is housed in a new building, but its architecture blends in with the other houses in the neighbourhood. Its physical arrangement inside is much like that of the Emily Stowe Shelter. Since I am a member of its board, I go to the shelter regularly but mostly during the dinner hour. The atmosphere of the dining-room is like that of a cafeteria. The women talk amongst themselves and the children play with one another, but there is usually a subdued atmosphere in the room. There is a sitting-room with a television near the dining-room, but I have seldom seen anyone sitting there. A notice on its door reminds residents that the bedtime for children is 9 o'clock.

A worker at the North York Women's Shelter described the difficulties of assessing a woman's situation to determine if she needs to stay at the shelter. Carol (a pseudonym) came to Canada from Jamaica when she was five years old. She has a bachelor's degree in social work from York University. She did her practicum (student placement) at the Parkdale Legal Clinic and while she was there attended monthly meetings of the Parkdale Community Health Centre. During this time, she became interested in the problem of violence against women and after graduation sought employment working with abused women. In 1989 she was hired by the North York Women's Shelter as a temporary worker and became a full-time staff member shortly after that. She has worked there since that time.

Carol describes herself as a feminist but says that 'whether you are a feminist or not is irrelevant to the work of the shelter.' She is a Canadian citizen but regards herself as an African Caribbean since 'Canadians don't accept [her] as one of them' and describe her as 'a visible minority.' Carol is married to a white Canadian and has two children. I interviewed her on 15 April 1996 in an office in the basement of the North York Women's Shelter:

When we get a phone call from a woman asking for space, we have to assess [her] situation and find out if she meets our mandate. Our mandate [states] that a woman has to be leaving an abusive relationship with somebody that she has been intimately involved with. So when we get a phone call from a woman who says that she is being abused by her father, well, that is certainly not our priority, or that she is being evicted for not paying her rent, we are not going to take her. We give priority to women who are physically abused because their lives are in danger [although] we consider emotional and psychological abuse.

When a woman calls and says, 'I am abused,' we ask, 'Can you tell me about your situation?' We have to assess [whether] it is abuse or is it a breakdown of a relationship. We are looking for key words: 'Did he hit you?' It makes our assessment easier if the woman can give us details, if she says, 'I have a black eye,' or 'The police have been called,' or 'Charges have been laid,' or 'I went to the hospital with broken bones.' Yes, she is physically abused and we take her in. It is when there is emotional and psychological abuse that it is difficult [for us to decide. If the woman says,] 'We are not talking,' yes, that is emotionally and psychologically abusive, [but we ask] has there been a pattern. Or if the woman says, 'I have not been allowed to go out for a month,' we [recognize] that she is socially isolated, but we are also going to want to find out what else is going on: is he threatening her, is he calling her names? With physical abuse we don't need to know what else is going on. It is clear-cut.

Once a woman comes here [to the shelter], we let her know that she is safe and with women who support her decision. We also get as much history of the woman as possible or as much as she wants to give. After she has been here for two days, we do what we call a forty-eight-hour assessment. In that assessment, we want to get a sense from the woman how she views herself, her partner, what are some of the concerns she has about the children, and her short- and long-term goals. [We also find out] what is her understanding or sense of why she was abused. Is she ambivalent about what has happened? What are her self-esteem issues?

It has never ever happened, at this shelter, that somebody has called and identified that they are in a lesbian relationship and are being abused. The woman doesn't know if it is a homophobic shelter or staff, and doesn't feel safe [in disclosing her situation]. We have had some instances where we suspect that the abuser is another female, but the abused woman has not disclosed that information. When a woman does come to a shelter, she talks about her partner. But 'partner' is a generic term, so you can't really tell. A person may talk about her room-mate who was abusive without identifying whether it was a male or female, but we may suspect. But when the woman feels safe, she may disclose that her partner was another woman, but that happens very very rarely. Mostly it is male abuse.

In 1993 the North York Women's Shelter had 125 residents from 29 different countries, speaking 23 different languages. Although nearly half of these women spoke English and an eighth spoke Spanish, many of the other languages were spoken by only one or two women (North York Women's Shelter 1994). One-quarter of the women who stayed at the Emily Stowe Shelter in 1992 did not speak English or French. The staff at the shelter were familiar with four or five languages, and they used the services of Scarborough Cultural Interpreters to provide counselling in fifteen different languages to the residents (Emily Stowe Shelter 1992, 9).

Women of all ages are abused, but a large proportion of women who came to the Emily Stowe Shelter in 1992 were between the ages of twenty and fifty (Emily Stowe Shelter 1992). At the North York Women's Shelter, I have seen primarily young women under the age of thirty, most of whom have children ranging from infants to seven years.[6] The decision to leave the home and go to a shelter usually follows 'social, psychological, economic, or physical violence,' but over 90 per cent of the women go to a shelter after incidents of physical abuse (Emily Stowe Shelter 1991–3). Pat compared the two shelters:

At Emily Stowe you find women from every walk of life [and] every age group. We have had several women who were sixty or sixty-five years old, and they have been with their spouse thirty, forty, fifty years. We have young girls, sixteen years old, as long as they have a child. If they are sixteen years and single, we will not take them, because there are other agencies that they can go to. We have had preacher's and pastor's wives. We have had people from all religions. We have had more or less the low end of the group, but that is not to say that the people at the higher levels are not beaten. The people at the higher levels would probably have enough money to go to a hotel or go on a vacation. We've had some lawyers', doctors', firemen's, policemen's wives. Let's say a policeman's wife is in a shelter. What does he do? Gets some other police to call for her. It's very difficult for wives [of policemen or firemen] to be [at the shelter] because they know where the shelters are.

I must say the Emily Stowe Shelter has worked hard. In some other shelters they'll say, 'Okay, I can't keep this woman here because she speaks Polish (or she speaks something else), and we don't have the staff.' We wouldn't do that. We would get an interpreter to deal with the woman no matter where she comes from or what language she speaks.

At the shelter, we take anybody who comes. We don't care about her legal status. We have lots of women who are illegal immigrants from Hong Kong, Vietnam, South America, Yugoslavia – they could be coming from anywhere. [A woman becomes an illegal immigrant because] the man says, 'Come over and visit and then I will apply.' When she comes to visit, the man does not sponsor her, or withdraws the sponsorship. The woman then doesn't go back to immigration to have her visa extended [but continues] to live with him, sometimes four years, or eight years. He is supporting her. Then she has a child; the child is a Canadian citizen. But she is still illegal, and this man [begins] to ill-treat her. If you are illegal, would you call the police?

The woman can call the police and they will not, then and there, check her status. But she doesn't know if the man is going to say that she is illegal in front of the police. All she knows is that 'I am illegal, I am being beaten, what shall I do?' When things get too bad, and she can't take it anymore, she comes to the shelter. Or she may end up at the hospital, and the police may bring her to the shelter from there. Sometimes neighbours call the police because they hear all this screaming. But after one month, two months at the shelter, whatever it is, what does she do? She has nowhere to go. She cannot work, she is not entitled to welfare. So where does the woman go? See how the women are trapped? It's tough.

Organizational Structure of the Shelters

The mission statements of shelters frequently include feminist explanations of abuse and express feminist commitment to empowering women. For example, the Emily Stowe Shelter says that '[woman abuse] is perpetuated by a patriarchal system that devalues women and children and condones the use of violence to control them.' Similar sentiments are expressed by the Ontario Association of Interval and Transition Houses, which states that 'woman battering ... reflect[s] patriarchal attitudes and the economic structure of society' (1991b, 10). The North York Women's Shelter notes that organizations like it 'challenge mainstream structures that disempower women and children and are permissive to violence against them.' Educating the public on the extent of violence against women and children would 'initiate positive change in society' (North York Women's Shelter, leaflet, background information).

Feminists have argued that hierarchical institutions of society oppress and disempower people and make it difficult for them to take control of their own lives. 'If violence has its roots in hierarchy, as the theory of patriarchy suggests, then nonhierarchical, empowering forms of organization are an integral part of the struggle against domestic violence' (McGregor and Hopkins 1991, 23). Accordingly, all shelters should be collectives, but only some of them are so organized in practice. The Emily Stowe Shelter describes itself as a 'feminist organization' that 'is administered on a collective basis; that is, all collective members equally participate in decision making and share the tasks necessary to keep the shelter operational' (Emily Stowe Shelter 1992, 2). Interval House describes itself as a 'feminist collective' striving 'to work in such a way that no one person has power and control over others.' It seeks to share 'the decision making and responsibilities of working for and with abused women and their children to provide individual safety and support and to work on the societal level to help end violence against women' (Interval House n.d.).

Most shelters, however, have conventional hierarchical structures (MacLeod 1987, 53). Teresa Janz surveyed fifteen shelters in Ontario and Manitoba and categorized them as either hierarchies or collectives by determining how staff were recruited, where authority was located, and how tasks were differentiated. She found that only three of the shelters were collectives, while the others had hierarchical structures. (Shelters with hierarchical structures did engage in consultation with their staff before making decisions.) Janz found that in ten of the fifteen shelters 'staff are recruited on the basis of formal criteria and skills,' and staff assignments of jobs and duties were clearly differentiated. Tasks were shared on a rotating basis in two shelters (Janz 1993, 237).

The predominance of hierarchical structures may be traced in part to government funding. Government agencies frequently require that a board of directors take responsibility for an organization and that clear lines of accountability be established. These requirements sometimes transform the relationship between paid and volunteer staff from rough equality to stratification, with distinctions between paid staff, volunteer staff, and volunteer board members (Ng 1988; Agnew 1996). Sometimes new staff are hired or new members join the board of directors, and they change the structure of the organization. Sometimes there is a mix of collective and hierarchical structures. For example, the North York Women's Shelter describes itself as a collective, but the collective includes only the full-time paid staff. The collective reports to the volunteer board of directors that oversees the management of the shelter, and the board in turn is accountable to government agencies for the disbursement of funds.

Shelters are meant to be places where women live together cooperatively and share in the tasks of maintaining the 'home' (Pizzy 1974). In practice, however, shelters have to enforce rules and regulations about what kinds of behaviour are acceptable (these cover things like smoking and alcohol consumption, curfew at night, and visitors) (Loseke 1992).[7] In the dining-room of the North York Women's Shelter, rules and regulations are clearly posted on the bulletin board. Notices refer to the duties of the residents for the week, specifying how some chores are to be handled, bedtimes for children, and weekly checks of bedrooms by the staff for cleanliness. When shelters have sufficient funds, they may hire a paid cook and cleaning staff; otherwise, residents have to take turns to do the cooking and cleaning. Residents are responsible for taking care of their own children.

In the following, Pat describes the structure of Emily Stowe Shelter and how it is funded:

Emily Stowe is a collective – we all get together to run the house. There [are] about fifteen women working there, and each person has a responsibility. We have a meeting every Tuesday, and we decide what area we want to work on and feel comfortable in. So, you pick that area and then you could be in it for a year or two years. If you want to give it up, then someone else will take it. One person would do the hiring or relief staffing; then one person will do the administration, [like] writing for grants; [another] person will do house management, like doing big repairs or ordering food; and then somebody does public action, and she goes to speak in the community and things like that. So that's how it's done.

Emily Stowe is a short-term shelter. We are paid for the nights the woman sleeps there. [The funders] pay us for thirty people. After a certain amount of time, [they] want to know why is the woman still there. They won't pay us for that. Sometimes we allow the woman to stay six months. Last year, we had someone who stayed eight months – so she could have her baby there. It was also Christmas time.

Carol finds working at a collective 'really tough.' In the following, she describes some of the challenges that members have to resolve to make the collective work:

The philosophy we abide by at the shelter is a feminist one, but if you were to ask each of us our definition of feminism you will get a different answer. We recognize that there is an unequal distribution of power between men and women. However, acknowledging that there is unequal distribution of power between women, [particularly] within a collective structure, can create tensions. We are not supposed to behave like that [exercising power over others]. We [are supposed to] look at equity issues and feminist principles. But all kinds of tensions come up.

When you are first hired, you feel [that working in] a collective is great because people have the same beliefs. But when it comes to the actual running of the shelter and the committee work, policy[-making] differences start to surface. It can take a long time to arrive at decisions because we are aiming at consensus. But there are differences of personality, politics, class, and all these differences have to be ironed out. [Difficulties arise] around people having resentments over a decision that was made, or the behaviour of a staff person, and they have not been able to communicate [with others] to resolve the issue. A lot of times these feelings have to do with racism. Or there are accountability issues: some woman didn't come for her shift and was able to get away with it, and this person came late and doesn't get away with it. People watch and they just keep it to themselves. It, however, plays out in decisions that you make and in how you communicate and behave in a meeting.

Most of our problems in the collective have arisen when there are differences of treatment of residents by staff. You find there are differences between how a white Canadian woman may be treated compared to an immigrant woman or a woman who doesn't speak English. For example, one staff may feel that a resident who has broken a house rule should be asked to leave, yet they decide not to ask that woman to leave. A white woman [staff] may ask an immigrant woman to leave but not another white woman. But sometimes a woman of colour has broken a rule, and a woman-of-colour staff person may feel more understanding. She may think, ' I know this woman is going to be facing discrimination in trying to find a place,' so that may cloud her judgment. But white staff may raise the question why is this woman still here? And you may not feel safe enough to say all the reasons behind that decision.

Resolving issues through consensus doesn't always work. We have procedures for grievances in our personnel policy and we have a 'communication model.' When there is an issue involving an individual we try to resolve it one-to-one. But if it cannot be resolved one-to-one, then it goes to a group and we try to resolve it that way. I am sorry to say, many times we have had to call in a mediator to work with the staff around issues of communication [or to deal with] racism and classism. Some women have not been able to [express] their anger, or have not been able to communicate their thoughts and feelings in a respectful manner. Some women were not feeling safe and did not feel that they could communicate their feelings to the group without outside mediators. Resentments might simmer for a long period of time. When the mediator is there, everybody will speak and the mediator will encourage us to resolve issues, but after a while we go right back to the old way of behaving and communicating. Unfortunately, some people have left the shelter feeling very angry because they felt that their voice had not been heard or that the shelter had been discriminatory towards them.

Generally speaking, it is really tough working in a collective. We've talked about going to a hierarchical system. The advantage would be, instead of eleven of us having to work out all of our differences and having to make decisions around tough issues, it would be the executive director's responsibility. Not that the issues will be any different, but it would be just that the executive director would have the final word, as opposed to the collective.

Racism in the Shelters

The shelter is home to women of different cultures, political beliefs, and socio-economic status, all of whom have recently endured an emotional and physical crisis. When the class and racial divisions of the larger society reappear in shelters for abused women, they create tension and conflict between residents and between staff and residents (Loseke 1992). Most residents are working-class women, but the staff are typically middle-class. Women of all ethnic and racial backgrounds live at shelters, but it has been difficult to ensure a non-racist environment within them. My respondents complained that they felt they had to choose between abuse by their spouses and racial abuse by other residents at the shelters (Chinese Family Life Services 1989; Kohli 1993; Rafiq 1991). Racism in shelters makes life more stressful for abused women from Asia, Africa, and the Caribbean and undermines their resolve to escape the abuse of their male partners.

Some shelters have devised strategies for dealing with racist incidents. They may ask disruptive women to leave. The staff of Shirley Samaroo House treated incidents of racism as opportunities for raising the consciousness of the offending woman and to make her aware of her own behaviour (interview, 6 Oct 1992). Along with its 'House Rules,' the North York Women's Shelter issues an 'important warning' that a resident who demonstrates 'racist behaviour' would be asked to leave the shelter immediately (House Rules, North York Women's Shelter, n.d.).[8] Although shelters have formally articulated their commitment to antiracist hiring practices and to providing services to women from all ethnic and racial groups, allegations are frequently made that there is a low number of racialized counsellors, staff, and board members in some shelters and social service organizations (Agnew 1996).[9]

The ideal of women living cooperatively and harmoniously frequently breaks down in practice and there are disputes and conflicts between the residents; for example, over chores. Shelters, after some initial problems, now allocate funds to buy the customary food of women from Asia, Africa, and the Caribbean, but other residents may complain about the flavour of the food or its method of preparation (interview, 6 October 1992). When food preparation leads to disagreements or hard feelings, staff are called upon to mediate and resolve the conflict (interviews, 28 June 1993, 6 Oct. 1992).

Some problems have simple solutions (e.g., calling in interpreters to communicate with non–English-speaking women); but non–English-speaking women may feel socially isolated and culturally alienated by the Eurocentric norms of a shelter. Some non–English-speaking women are unable to discuss their trauma with staff or other residents or to receive support from them. A Korean counsellor at the Korean-Canadian Women's Association said:

> When Korean women go to a shelter, they are so grateful that there is a place where they can stay and get food that they start doing all kinds of housework. They clean the bathroom and wash the dishes [even when it is not their turn]. Other women may start taking advantage of this and pushing their shifts onto [such a Korean woman]. [Eventually] the Korean woman gets frustrated [but feels] that if she doesn't do it then the other women will get angry. The Korean woman usually does not have enough confidence to confront the other women. (Interview, 28 June 1993)

Conflicts and disputes necessitate imposing more rules and regulations, further undermining feminist goals and making the shelter more like other mainstream agencies or places for the homeless.

The Shirley Samaroo House was established specifically for immigrant women. Its mission statement declared that it 'recognize[d] the oppression of women based on gender, race and class.' It addressed 'the special needs of immigrant women because of the difficulties in confronting the barriers imposed by race, class position, language and the pressure to assimilate into mainstream society' (Shirley Samaroo House 1988, 4). Similarly, the Emily Stowe shelter's mission statement states that it 'strives to ensure that race, ethnic origin, language, religion, or sexual orientation do not serve as barriers to access or full participation within the agency' (Emily Stowe Shelter 1992, 2). However, the highly publicized conflict between black staff members and middle-class, white feminist board members at the shelter called Nellie's reveals that even within collectives conflicts over power, authority, and jobs can easily acquire racist overtones (Dewar 1993).

Pat described some of the racial conflicts that occur in the shelter:

When we do an intake, we tell the woman: no racial slurs, no physical fights, no name-calling. We try to have the women respect each other. We are a centre for assaulted women. We have a no-hitting rule – you can't hit your child, nobody. (Sometimes a mother would give a whack or two to her child. We look the other way, because sometimes the children need it.) We have a rule: if two women get into a fight, they both have to leave.

This is what happens. Some women will refer to others as 'the black woman,' 'the Indian woman.' We pull them up immediately. 'What is the woman's name?' we ask. They answer, 'I don't know. It is a funny name.' We say, 'You do not call people by their race. That means you are not seeing the person, you are only seeing the race. This woman that you are calling Chinese, she could be from Vietnam, Korea, Malaysia, Cambodia.' The shelter is a small place; they have to know everyone's name.

We have a weekly women's meeting, to raise whatever concerns the residents may have. Sometimes, and this may sound stereotypical, white women at the shelter are ethnocentric; they feel things should be done in a certain way. But we try to have every woman keep her culture. [Someone may complain that another] cooks curry every day. The staff will say, 'She is allowed to cook whatever kind of food she likes. You go somewhere else.' When I eat my plantain and my yams, I feel good. I encourage the women to cook the food they like, although we have a cook who [prepares meals for] the women.

One thing I must say – the staff is not racist towards the women of different cultures who come to the shelter. Isn't that amazing? If one woman says one [racist] thing about another woman, that woman is brought into the office and spoken to. I've never seen the staff condone any racism towards the women, and I've never seen them treat any of the women – maybe with preference, which everybody does sometimes – but I have never seen the staff treat any woman in a racist way. [Non-white] women are treated equally and fairly; they're probably treated a little better.

At the Emily Stowe Shelter, all members of the collective participate in new hiring in some way, and they try to make it a fair and open process. Pat argues that the candidate 'must fit in' because, otherwise, 'it's not going to work' and it would just be 'a battle for the next few months.' In the following, Pat describes the hiring practices that the shelter has adopted to ensure that staff reflect the ethnic and racial composition of women who come to the shelter:

When I went to work [at the Emily Stowe Shelter] there was one woman [on staff] from India and one from Jamaica and myself. So that means their collective did not reflect the people who were coming there. Nowadays we have tried to deliberately hire people to reflect [the racial and cultural identities of the women who come to the shelter]. We hired one woman from Vietnam and an Indian woman; we have a Chinese- and a Spanish-speaking woman. We have two black workers doing childcare, which we never had before.

If a woman comes from India, or no matter where she comes from, if she doesn't see a worker representing her at the shelter and looking like her, she feels, 'Something is wrong with me.' Even if you don't speak the language, the point is just seeing a face that represents you helps, and that's what we have tried to do over the years.

The last time we were hiring a childcare worker, I was really upset. I think I'm still upset with the collective right now. We had two black childcare workers [who worked on relief], and they used all sorts of excuses not to hire them and I realized it was racism. I said, 'Wait a minute, this woman has a degree in psychology. She has a childcare diploma. She has worked here for six months and you don't hire her. Why? What's the reason?' I said they can't bring somebody from outside, you have to hire [the internal candidates first]. So we finally get to hire two black childcare workers.

You know what I'm saying to myself – you have three, four white-Canadian women – why can't we hire a woman who will bring different skills and perspective to the shelter? White women talk about discrimination and sexism for women, but when it comes to a non-white woman getting a position, the white woman cannot support that woman. It showed me [they just pay] lip service. When it comes to the crunch, why don't I get [a position]? How come a white woman could get it? This is why I don't go to any woman's group. I feel, white people start racism and it's up to them to change it.

When I started here, eight years ago, except for one black and then me as a relief, all the other people were white. Then it started changing. We started pushing for it. But there was resistance to the change, but now it's okay – especially since the United Way, who supports us, are happy with our staff composition. When we do our report to the United Way, we say our staff composition complements [the women who use the shelter], we have all these languages – so they like us. [The collective is] not against hiring another race or another culture anymore, because out in the public it looks good.

Carol is more critical of the systemic racism of shelters:

What draws me towards feminism is working towards eradicating oppression and unequal distribution of power. In the shelter movement, you will have white women in positions of power, making decisions, and not wanting to share that power. But they are feminists and they believe that oppression is wrong. Yet when it comes to their own organization, they want to hang on to that power and they don't want to share it. That is a contradiction.

Originally the shelters were very white-Canadian, [they] may have had one or two token immigrant women that [spoke] a second language other than English. It was not until the late 1980s that immigrant women started being hired in shelters, and even now it is not [often] in full- time [jobs] but as relief workers. [At the North York Women's Shelter,] we have improved our hiring [of women from Asia, Africa, and the Caribbean] to reflect more equity, but it is still slow. We now have quite a diverse group. Of the eleven full-time staff members, five are white-Canadian women, two are of Hispanic background, two are black, two are South Asian woman. Some are working on a bachelor's degree or their master's degree in social work, some have degrees in psychology or [have a nursing background]. Some staff are formerly abused women.

In 1989 when I came to the shelter, staffpeople wouldn't identify racism, and even few women of colour would take the initiative to name it. Sometimes it would be so obvious that the issue we were talking about was racism yet nobody would name it. It was such a hot issue, the minute that somebody mentioned the 'R' word everybody would just be silent. But through mediation, [things] are better now, we do name it. And it is not always women of colour who are speaking up. White women will now say, 'What I am hearing is racism.' We have also implemented an antiracism policy at the shelter, and we have had a number of anti-oppression workshops that are mandatory for all staff. Having those policies in place has helped, but we still have a long way to go.

Our programs have more respect for cultural diversity, but ten years ago we wouldn't have given importance to that. Women [at the shelter] are now encouraged to maintain their cultural identity [through] food [or] celebrations, like Chinese New Year and Ramadan. We [also] try to incorporate some cultural [sensitivity] in our children's programs.

Services at Shelters

Feminists have argued that the support given by traditional agencies to women who have been abused is counterproductive because they focus on treating the wife, keeping the family intact, and being 'fair' to the husband: 'In this way, agencies have missed the primary point of the physical violence and the need to provide safety for the woman and the opportunity for her to choose her future course of action based upon her own needs' (Bentzel and York 1988, 56). Shelter workers seek to provide support to the women but not expert advice or direction. Their resolve not to impose their own view is sternly tested when women return to their abusive spouses, but workers try to support a woman regardless of her choice.

In recruiting staff and volunteers, shelters initially gave priority to women's experiences of abuse and to their political commitment to eradicating women's oppression, arguing that their own experiences of oppression enabled them to understand and empathize with abused women and to help them. The guidelines of the Ontario Association of Interval and Transition Houses say that the 'fundamental qualification for working against violence is recognizing that all women and children, including ourselves, have been hurt and discriminated against. This recognition is more important than formal credentials' (1991b, 33).

Feminist workers at shelters were critical of professionals for having imposed a 'secondary victimization' on women by applying oppressive, androcentric categories and definitions to them. They were wary of professional social workers and psychologists, who seemed to have little political commitment to helping battered women.[10] They argued that social workers tended to see work at the shelters as merely a job where they could acquire necessary experience and expertise to enhance their career paths (MacLeod 1987, 53–4). However, Sara Bentzel and Reginald York found that many professional social workers were able to look beyond traditional theories that identified 'interpersonal dynamics' or 'characterological' faults as the causes of abuse and to consider as well the social and economic independence of the abused woman (Bentzel and York 1988, 56). Nevertheless, sometimes volunteers and paid workers at the shelters adopt the norms and values of social workers, and although feminists allow that this is not 'in itself negative or culpable,' they do argue that 'it is assimilative' (Walker 1990, 213).

The Emily Stowe Shelter provides 'safe refuge, individual and group crisis counselling, children's counselling and recreation, advocacy and support' (Emily Stowe Shelter 1990).[11] While women are at the shelter, they are encouraged to sort through the emotional and physical aftermath of the abuse that they have experienced. They are provided with a variety of services, including referrals, counselling, and being escorted to courts or hospitals (Janz 1993, 215). They are also helped in finding accommodation, applying for welfare, and registering children at schools or daycare. Pat discussed some of the ways in which shelter residents are helped to find housing and to apply for welfare:

A lot of times, women are already in public housing before they come to the shelter. So what they need now is a transfer. So the [housing authorities] would give the woman another place, far away from [the abusive spouse].

If [she comes from] a private house, the woman can try through the courts to get exclusive possession. But then the man knows exactly where to get you. He's not giving you any space. And the man usually feels, 'This woman is trying to take my house.' What I suggest to the woman who is bent on getting exclusive possession is that she tell the judge exclusive possession for a few years – like until the kids grow up, until they are finished school. In that way the man doesn't feel threatened, like she's taking the house from him, and he goes and tries to kill her. If she says [that] in five years the kids will be out of school and then they'll sell the house, the man is not as angry.

If they qualify for Metro Housing, we look for housing for them. They have to just fill out a form. We have two women from Metro Housing who work with the shelter and they are very good. We have to advise the residents, 'Tell her everything, so that she can find a good place for you to go.' Or Metro Housing calls us and sets up an interview. If the woman needs an interpreter, we get [one] for her. After the interview, [we do the follow-up work] and call Metro Housing and ask when is the house coming. I have heard other places say that when it is non-white people, the workers may assign them an apartment but not a house. I have never seen it happen at the shelter. They are on top of the list and they get whatever comes up.

Some of the women feel good about the housing, others don't. There is a stigma attached to Metro Housing. They are going into poverty. They are going onto welfare. (That is not a lot of money.) Those women who were well established, it is a lot of steps down. Other women are so grateful that they have a little house and some money.

Even if the women have left the shelter, the staff would go with them to the court, especially if the man is going to be there. Supposing the woman speaks a different language, while you are [in the courts] the spouse would be cursing her in another language, telling her off. So we

have to be there all the time to make sure he doesn't come near her.
Who knows? He may have a knife. Sometimes we have to ask the police
to keep the man in the room until we get into the subway or into a car
because we don't want this man to follow us. Some men respect the law,
some don't.

Carol described the process of applying for public housing and
welfare in this way:

After a woman has been here for a week, we will interview the woman
again and ask what her action plan is about housing. The staff will [help]
the woman complete an application and provide a verification letter
[which states] that the woman has been abused. Metro Housing regulations are that a woman has lived with the man for at least one year, there
has been physical abuse, and she should be planning to permanently separate from her partner. They want some sort of documentation from the
police, a woman's doctor, or a social service agency that is aware of the
abuse. In some instances, [Metro Housing] may consider psychological
and emotional abuse. They also want to know if the woman has children
and if she has custody of the children. They want to make sure [when]
this woman is going to be given housing and it will be a fresh start. It used
to take three months, but because of cutbacks it is now taking women
four to six months to get subsidized housing.

[Workers] at Metro Housing were complaining that African women
are really vague about some personal details. The interviewer would ask,
do you know the man's date of birth [or enquire about her own date of
birth] and the woman would pause. Last week I was doing an intake from
a woman from Ghana, and I asked for her date of birth. She paused and
then she explained that she was sponsored by a family and although she is
twenty-four years old they had lied on the passport and said she was
twenty-eight because they felt if she was younger she would have a more
difficult time getting immigration. Now when she is asked [about her
date of birth] she has to think, 'Do I put the date that is legally on my
passport? But I know that is not the correct one.' Workers from Metro
Housing [doubted that the woman was in] an established relationship
with a man [but] does not know his date of birth or his salary. [There-
fore] a lot of times they were being denied priority housing. But cultur-

ally it may be considered a bold question [and a challenge to] a man's authority for a woman to enquire about his wages or date of birth. So we have had to coach women and prepare them in advance by [letting them know that they] will be asked about date of birth [of their spouses], salary, or other relevant information.

Sometimes there is bias [in allocating housing]. Immigrant women complain that they are [placed] in buildings [dominated by people from one] cultural or ethnic background. Or run-down buildings, or buildings with bad reputations of drugs. I have observed that white-Canadian women have been placed in nicer areas and buildings. [For example,] the units in private apartment buildings which belong to Metro Housing would be given to English-speaking Canadian women or to a middle-class woman who applies for subsidized housing from a shelter. Not to say that immigrant women and women of colour never ever get those, but the ratio is much, much smaller.

[Women also have difficulty in locating housing in the open market.] Women with children find that it takes longer to find housing. If women have an accent, or if her colour is not white, it may take her ten or fifteen tries to get a place, while somebody else, who is white and speaks English, doesn't face that discrimination, and by the fifth application they may get [a house].

We also have a welfare worker who comes to the shelter once a week. We have not run into problems with welfare staff because it is all quite straightforward. The only benefit that women are entitled to, while they are at the shelter, is prescription drugs and emergency dental visits. [They are also entitled to] first month's rent and start-up allowance [when they locate housing]. Discretion is exercised [by welfare workers] in giving women start-up allowance. Some workers may give that and some won't. Where the legislation [gives] discretion to the individual worker, we run into problems.[12]

In the following, Pat describes counselling at the shelters:

We don't have support groups where everyone talks about their own problems. This may lead to a breach of confidentiality. We don't talk about one woman to another. When the woman comes in and tells us about herself, this information is confidential. We tell her, 'You don't

have to discuss your problems with the other women.' If two women are
in the office [at the same time], we ask one to leave.

Once a week we do a residents' meeting where they raise their concerns about the shelter and what is going on there. In addition, every
Thursday we have a relaxed group, and the women talk about everything
– anger, housing, and life after the shelter. We give information to them;
sometimes it may mean bringing in a lawyer or a guest speaker.

Since we are there twenty-four hours of the day, we talk to the women
one-to-one. Most of the counselling happens at night. The woman usually
comes in to talk to you. Sometimes we have to go and get the woman and
say, 'Let's have a talk.' You have to develop trust. Some women develop
trust more with some workers than others. We talk about whatever she
wants to talk about. Sometimes these sessions last till 2 or 3 o'clock at
night – if the worker can do it. The information that the woman gives us
will be passed on to another worker, but not to the other residents.

All staff are trained, [including] relief staff and volunteers, not to
advise the woman. We tell the woman what her options are, but she
makes the final decision, no matter what. All the workers are trained to
support the woman – when a woman is going back to the home, it is very
important to make the woman feel good about herself, and let her know
she can come back if it doesn't work. We don't separate from the woman
even after she leaves the shelter. All the women know they are welcome to
come back to the shelter to just talk, have a cup of coffee, or whatever.

Carol explained why some women feel compelled to return to
their abusive spouses and how the staff try to help them make plans:

Immigrant women, [unlike] Canadian-born women, don't know the system, don't know what services are available, or what are their rights. If
you are a newly arrived immigrant woman, you don't know how to go
about getting welfare, housing, a job, or even how to open a bank
account, or do grocery shopping. These problems are more intensified if
you don't speak the language.

Immigrant women often go back [to their abusive spouses] because of
cultural pressure. [Some] immigrant women who come to the shelter lit-
erally lose all their family and community support. That is hard. I have
had some women from Asian communities say that they are feeling sui-

cidal because the family wouldn't talk with them. [For example,] a Tamil woman's husband was applying for immigration for the extended family to come to Canada, but he stopped that [when the woman left him]. So the family was putting pressure on the woman to go back to the man. When the woman has unmarried sisters, there will be a lot of pressure [from her family] to go back. It is really, really sad because sometimes the family knows there is abuse, but to save face in the community they will not support the abused women and are worried what impact [this disclosure] will have on the unmarried sisters and mother. They are afraid that their family will become ostracized. Sometimes women experience so much emotional and psychological stress that they physically collapse. Women who are able to survive emotionally and psychologically are the ones that have the support of the family. [For example,] a South Asian woman whose family supports her may not care about what the community says and she is not likely to go back. [Sometimes when] a woman has been isolated, she is so terrified of being on her own that she will go back to the spouse. But there is no clear-cut answer.

When a woman decides to return to her spouse after staying here for three or four months, we are not angry, just disappointed and sad, especially when we know that she is going back to an abusive situation. We develop a simple and basic safety plan for the woman [when she leaves the shelter]. We encourage women to regularly chat with a friend or a family member and to let their neighbours know that they are back and ask them to call the police if they hear anything [noise]. Or sometimes we have had a woman call the shelter on a daily basis just to say that 'I am ok,' and if we don't hear from her then we know something is wrong. A safety plan [may be just] putting away a little bit of money for a taxi [in an emergency], or leaving [a few pieces of] clothing at [a family member's] or friend's house.

[We tell the women] not to share the information with the man about where she was [i.e., at the shelter], or its address. Many times we just ask them to make up something up like she was staying with a friend. We tell [a woman] that if a man was to know where she had stayed [i.e., at the shelter], she wouldn't be able to come back [because she would] put [herself] and everyone else at the shelter at risk. Through our individual counselling sessions, we help the women to rebuild their self-esteem and to demand better for themselves and their children.

Carol discussed the practical and emotional work of supporting a woman:

Our job at the shelter is to get the women to feel positive about themselves. Women who can get to the point [of recognizing] that abuse is wrong, or [who can say] that 'I have the right to live free of violence, I am a worthy human being, I like myself, I deserve better,' have a really really good chance of getting out of the abusive relationship. But if a woman is feeling helpless, if she is feeling that she is no good, no one else is going to want her, she is stupid, or she is ugly, then her dependency will be higher on the man. Women who have gotten to the stage where they actually like themselves will not go back.

Some women will come into the office and they will want us to do everything for them. We are not helping them if we do that. We encourage the women to do things for themselves – for example, make calls to their children's school, doctor, or their lawyer. We sit beside them and we will even write out the questions for them. We are trying to prepare them [for the time] when they will leave the shelter. Then they are going to have to take the initiative and do those things and become more independent.

We don't let the woman sit here watching television all day and not working. We encourage the women [at the shelter] to get into the ESL programs. Or to go out to work and get involved in schools or community programs. Some women work or go to school while they are living in shelters. Women with children also work and we help them get daycare. We try to emphasize that just because they are in a shelter it doesn't mean that they have to give up their activities, but they do and some [even] give up contact with relatives and friends. They have had to because of safety factors.

Women who come to the shelter are fearful of the violence of their spouse or another male. Although the courts and the police can offer some protection to shelter residents and workers, nevertheless they are vulnerable to violent retaliatory actions from irate males. Carol described the psychological and emotional impact on the staff of working at the shelters:

We are dealing with volatile situations, but [despite that] we don't really [consciously] think how risky our work is every single day. For example, when I come in the morning, I don't think that some man may be lurking around the corner with a gun, but at nighttime we will think more like that. Even if a man shows up at the door looking for his partner, we are calm and cool about it and say [through the intercom], ' She is not here. We can't give you any information. Please get off the property or we will call the police.' Sometimes we forget how unsafe [we really are], and how dangerous it is, but it is a coping mechanism so that we can come in and do our shift. Psychologically we are affected.

In 1989 [when I first started working here] I used to take it personally if a woman decided to go back. [I interpreted it to mean that] somehow I had failed as a worker, I hadn't given her enough support, and my counselling wasn't effective. I have learnt over the years that, no, it is the woman's decision [to go] back to being abused. I am not responsible. When my shift ends, the work ends. Somebody else can take over from where I have left off.

Pat described the danger faced by the staff in this way:

We [the staff] work in a lot of danger. We have about a hundred women who come to the shelter a year – that is one hundred irate husbands who feel that we are holding their wives captive, who feel, 'If only I could get in there, I could talk to her.' They come to the door and we say to them, 'If you don't leave, we will call the police,' and we do. Because of the danger, we don't trivialize the job we do. Like the police, we act as if we are brave, but we are not.

The shelter is safe as long as the access to the shelter is locked. We have a rule: no man on the property. No men can even park their cars on the property. Let's say, if you are coming to the shelter, you don't know who is that man on the property. We have bars on the door – you noticed when you were at the shelter? We live in real danger. We don't have any guns. Any husband could come and kill us anytime he wants. Nothing would stop them.

I see myself as doing time. Because if I am working there thirty-five hours a week under lock and key, I am doing time. I stand the chance of being murdered anytime. But like the assaulted woman who feels that she must sleep even if her husband is going to murder her – it is just the same with us. I must work. I like what I am doing. But we are taking chances.

Services are valuable for helping abused women cope with the violence in their lives, but the emphasis on services leaves little time for advocacy and thus detracts from the political goals of feminism (Schechter 1982). Many of the staff work at the shelters because of their commitment to feminism, but in their everyday working lives they find that they have little time for political work. Staff at shelters and community-based groups complain of being overworked and having to spend much time on administrative work (e.g., writing applications for funds) in addition to helping women sort out their day-to-day problems. After the initial founding of the shelters, collective action and advocacy receive much less emphasis than services (Pennell 1987; MacLeod 1987, 51). Shelter workers who face a 'chronic struggle for financial survival, the overwhelming feeling of inadequacy in meeting the needs of battered women, and the desire to preserve staff cohesion' feel compelled to postpone 'philosophical' issues to a later date (Pennell 1987, 113). One shelter worker explains:

> At one time it was politics, an ideology of empowerment and feminism, that held us together and kept us going. Now we focus more on the service, the quality of the service and how well it meets the needs of the women. We haven't given up our feminist ideals, but we feel we have to provide a really professional service to gain the trust and support of battered women and of the community. (MacLeod 1987, 51)

Service and advocacy are not mutually exclusive activities. When women meet each other in a shelter, they have the opportunity of sharing their personal experiences of abuse and hearing of similar experiences of other women. Their consciousness can be raised about the causes of their abuse (i.e., not their personal shortcomings, but systemic gender relations), and they can shed self-blame, overcome their feelings of isolation, and feel empowered.

Shelters allow women some time to overcome their immediate

crisis, but life after the shelter 'is a long, long road.' They must find a safe home, establish themselves in a new neighbourhood, overcome social biases, enrol in classes to acquire job-related skills, and find jobs. There is some second-stage housing available to women who have left the shelter, but most continue to require support and services from counsellors (Scyner and McGregor 1988). They need the help of counsellors to guide them through 'the maze of income support programs, legal and judicial proceedings,' and so on (Dhillon and Walter 1993, 2).

Pat described some of the difficulties that a woman encounters after she leaves the shelter:

The only thing that the woman really gets in the shelter is a bit of strength, because she sees that it is not her fault [that she was abused] and she is not alone. They are safe and their husbands are not beating them. I think there is relief that the abuse is over, but there is no joy. Normally you would want things to work, so [being single] is second best.

They are safe in the shelter. But [after they leave], the women have to struggle for many, many years. In many cases, the problem begins when the woman leaves the shelter, because the man has access to the kids and he starts bugging you again. He begins to harass the woman. He gets stuff about the woman from the children.

You are not starting on a happy note. You are scared. You don't know how you are going to raise these kids. You might be moving into a house with nothing, not even a bed. I find that older women who are sixty or so feel good. They say, 'Good, I don't want that man anymore. I am going to a seniors' home. I am going to relax.' They have found happiness. For the young woman, it is not happiness. They still have to raise a child. You are worried, you have to get the [children] to behave. The men sometimes have gotten the children to beat the [mothers], or tell them horrendous things to tell the mother. How do they raise a male child? She is scared – 'How do I feed them? What if I can't feed them?' Some women don't even have a sister or brother here. You don't have a choice: you have to keep going

In 1995 and again in 1996 the Ontario government reduced funding to women's organizations and cancelled many programs.

The Social Planning Council of Metropolitan Toronto conducted a survey of community agencies and found that 43 per cent of all 'supportive housing programs' were 'at risk of cancellation.' Other programs which were either likely to be cancelled or which were under review included 51 per cent of all programs for women, 49 per cent of all programs for ethno-cultural groups, and 43 per cent of all programs for refugees and immigrants (*Toronto Star*, 2 May 1996, A1).

Carol discussed the impact of these cuts on the shelter and on the women:

The big scare for the shelter was when we didn't know how much we were going to be cut, and if there were going to be lay-offs. The morale was low. But in October [1995] the government announced a 5 per-cent cut, so we had to take that, but we didn't have to lay off staff [and were able to keep] some part-time staff on. [However,] we have had to cut back on getting people from the outside like a psychologist or an art therapist.[13]

The impact has been more on the users of the service. Women are at the shelter for a longer period. They are experiencing more tensions, they are more upset, and it plays out in their behaviour and communication. We have had an increased number of women calling and saying that their welfare cheque has been cut and the man has taken out his frustration on the family. We have had increased demand from ex-residents who want to access our food bank because their welfare cheque has been reduced. Their morale is down, and they don't know if they will get a job or even welfare.

Conclusion

Shelters provide a refuge to women escaping abuse. Although shelters for abused women began as a grass-roots movement by activist feminists, their political goals have become subordinated to the need to provide services to abused women. The need for funds to establish shelters and to operate them has made shelters dependent on governments and private institutions. Consequently, shelters have become integrated into a network of services provided by governments to women (Findlay 1988).[14] Arguments for additional shelters emphasize the need for housing and equitable access to social services by abused women. They rarely talk about changing unequal gender relations and transforming society (Dhillon and Walter 1993).

Feminist principles hold out the hope to women from Asia, Africa, and the Caribbean of overcoming their oppression. Nonetheless, everyday life at the shelters can itself present obstacles that make the realization of their hopes more difficult. On the one hand, feminist explanations of abuse have gained widespread acceptance in society and have mobilized government agencies to allocate resources for supporting victims of abuse; but, on the other hand, the racism of the larger society has been reproduced within shelters, presenting additional challenges to women from Asia, Africa, and the Caribbean who choose to leave abusive homes. Such contradictions point to the difficulties of practising feminist solidarity in everyday life.

A goal of many feminist struggles is to empower women. The existence of shelters gives abused women some choices and alternatives, however limited and circumscribed. They do not have to suffer in silence or blame themselves for their misfortune, but can identify patriarchal gender relations as the problem. Women who work at the shelters may not fully implement feminist ideals of non-hierarchical and egalitarian relationships, but they are doing valuable practical work to help women cope with the violence in their lives. Women who come to the shelters have the immediate goal of sorting out the practical details of their lives, but living with other women who have had similar experiences of abuse has the potential of raising their consciousness about gender, race, and class oppression.

Conclusion

Feminism includes a wide range of perspectives. Women like Christina Sommers (1994), Katie Roiphe (1993), Camille Paglia (1994), and Donna Laframboise (1996), who refer to themselves as 'equity feminists' or 'dissident feminists,' want to distance themselves from 'gender feminists' or 'mainstream feminists' like Catherine MacKinnon, Marilyn French, Gloria Steinem, and Naomi Wolf. They feel that mainstream feminism has become rigid and doctrinaire – 'a bourgeois prison' (Paglia 1994, ix) that stifles debate.

Calls to reassess and re-evaluate the goals and directions of the feminist movement have also come from prominent spokeswomen in the mainstream. Naomi Wolf, for example, notes that while a large percentage of women support the goals of the movement – equality and justice for women – they are reluctant to call themselves 'feminists' or to identify closely with some of its political struggles. They perceive feminism as 'proscriptive' and 'ideologically overloaded' (1993, 62). The socialist feminist bell hooks argues that feminism has become academic and confined to women's-studies classrooms (1988). The language of some feminist writing has become extremely convoluted and nearly inaccessible to most readers. MacKinnon complains that many feminist debates are purely intellectual, utterly divorced from the realities of working-class women (1991).

Critics of mainstream feminists have also challenged their accounts of violence against women. The critics acknowledge that women experience violence and that perpetrators should be dealt with severely, but they argue that commitment to the thesis that 'battery is caused by patriarchy' has led feminists to exaggerate the incidence of violence or to examine it in partial and biased ways. To Sommers it seems that the feminists' 'primary concern is to persuade the public that the so-called normal man is a morally defective human being who gets off on hurting women' (Sommers 1994, 199). Laframboise says:

> Feminists who are convinced that women are the only aggrieved sex, under siege from all directions, and who consider men violent brutes, suffer from a view of the world so skewed that no matter what outrageous claim is made, if it 'proves' female victimization they're prepared to believe it. Although feminists carefully dissect 'male' data, treating it with both suspicion and scepticism, evidence that originates from feminist sources is automatically presumed to be true. (Laframboise 1996, 114–15)

Laframboise has even expressed misgivings about the increased attention being given to racial issues by mainstream feminists, claiming that this has alienated white middle-class women, who have left the movement in droves. She asserts that Sunera Thobani, the South Asian president of the National Action Committee on the Status of Women, did not merely want to expand the 'feminist agenda' to include points of view that had been historically absent but believed that the 'leadership of feminist organizations should be decided on the basis of criteria that included skin colour' (1996, 153).

However, few of the respondents in this study – victims of wife abuse, counsellors, and social workers – were familiar with these feminists or their critics. They knew about the Canadian Panel on Violence against Women, as it had invited community-based groups to its meetings and solicited their views, but few had read its report on violence. Their concern was with real, live victims – women who want to stop the violence in their homes.

The need-assessment studies, reports on wife abuse, and manuals on counselling victims of abuse written by community-based groups do not include discussions of theories of oppression, or bias in interpretation, or the exercise of power through language. They are written primarily from an experiential perspective, showing how race, class, and gender oppressions intersect in the lives of working-class abused women from Asia, Africa, and the Caribbean in Canada. These studies do repeat some common feminist assertions; for example, that wife abuse is an exercise of power, not the aberrant act of a male driven by momentary passion, excessive alcohol consumption, or stress. Nevertheless, their focus is on the everyday lives of women – how they experience abuse, the difficulties they encounter in leaving abusive families, and the problems they face in accessing social services.

To overcome some of these problems, middle-class women from Asia, Africa, and the Caribbean mobilized groups of volunteers in the late 1970s and 1980s and formed organizations by obtaining resources from government agencies to provide services to women in their ethnic and racial communities. They argued that racism in mainstream social service agencies alienated women and made them reluctant to seek help. Community-based groups initiated programs and workshops to educate their own communities on wife abuse. They printed posters and pamphlets in various languages which addressed the shame and sense of isolation and alienation experienced by abused women. Counsellors listened sympathetically to the experiences of abused women, gave them information, and discussed the choices that were available to them. They helped women apply for social assistance and public housing, and accompanied them to lawyers' offices and courts. In these ways, abused women from Asia, Africa, and the Caribbean were empowered to take control over their own lives and to rid themselves of the oppression of abuse.

Working-class and even middle-class respondents in this study rarely engaged in abstract theoretical discussions about violence against women or about race and gender oppression, preferring instead to 'take action' and 'do something concrete.' The present study thus reveals a gap between academic, intellectual feminism and the feminism that is practised in the day-to-day life of community-based groups. Many of the services provided by the groups were initiated within a feminist paradigm, but the groups have become more pragmatic and moved closer to conventional values and norms.

A woman who obtains services from a community-based organization is unlikely to want to overthrow conventional gender roles; she is seeking help to stop the violence against her. She and the counsellor do not debate ideology but devise practical strategies for her individual life situation.

A counsellor in a community-based organization relies on her own experiences and her knowledge of the culture of her ethnic or racial group to guide her in her work. Handbooks on counselling abused women emphasize gender oppression, but even a feminist counsellor has to balance her desire to overthrow gender oppression with her client's need to survive in a racist and classist society. Militant assertions of gender oppression risk driving a woman back to an abusive home and jeopardizing the support that she might receive from her extended family in Canada, or from her ethnic or racial community. The counsellor gives priority to the woman's need to survive in a racist and classist society, rather than to ideology or politics. Counselling may raise the consciousness of a woman and invite her to reflect on the inequities of traditional gender roles, but that is a bonus.

The work of middle-class women in community-based groups poses a challenge to feminist theorizing about the relationship between women's organizations and the state. Feminist theoreticians have argued that the dependence of women's organizations on the state has replaced the feminist agenda of social change with service to individual women (Walker 1990; Barnsley 1985). However, community-based groups have not passively and unquestioningly accepted whatever resources are allocated to them. They have resisted the rules and regulations that state agencies want to impose upon them and the criteria that the agencies set for eligibility for services. The Ontario Council of Agencies Serving Immigrants argued before the Social Assistance Review Committee for a more even distribution of resources between mainstream social service agencies and community-based organizations, and it argued for more antiracist programs and more culturally sensitive programs.

Although feminist theory condemns the exercise of power by 'professionals' relying on 'androcentric' knowledge, perceptions of expertise and knowledge differ between white middle-class women and women from Asia, Africa, and the Caribbean. Women from Asia, Africa, and the Caribbean value their training and education, even though it displays some gender biases. They want to be regarded as professionals with more than just the 'authority of experience.'

Sometimes power is exercised by white counsellors when they help women from Asia, Africa, and the Caribbean, but it is also exercised by counsellors who are of the same ethnic or racial background as their clients but of a different class. Yet the counsellors I interviewed generally did not acknowledge the asymmetry of the relationship between themselves and their clients. Manuals and handbooks advise counsellors to show respect for the different cultures of women who come to them, but they do not discuss racism, and counsellors' hesitancy in examining their own assumptions about the race and class of the abused woman or their own class and racial identity tends to perpetuate the status quo of race, class, and gender inequality.

The work of community-based groups confirms feminist assertions of the significance of social context in discussing any aspect of women's lives and experiences. When the problem of wife abuse was first identified, social services for women were infused with feminist ideals, but over time the idealism has faded. Organizational structures have changed, either because new staffs and boards of directors had different ideological commitments from those of the founders or because state regulations led them to implement rules and regulations which undermined the collective nature of the organizations and made them more akin to government agencies. Flexibility and pragmatism have created hybrid structures which diverge substantially from feminist ideals of the 1980s.

In the early 1980s, many workers came to community-based organizations and shelters for women out of an interest in feminist struggles (e.g., for abortion rights), but now they come looking for a job rather than desiring to participate in the politics of social change. The organizations have only very tenuous links with feminist political struggles. Few, if any, of these organizations are members of the National Action Committee on the Status of Women. They are members of the Ontario Council of Agencies Serving Immigrants. Since the staffs at community-based organizations interact with various levels of state bureaucracy (welfare offices, children's aid societies, and housing departments), they tend to adopt elements of the culture of these agencies.

The organizations do retain some feminist ideals. The social services offered through the community-based organizations and shelters focus on the woman and prioritize her welfare rather than that of the family unit. They give importance to the woman's experience of abuse, and they do not blame her for the abuse, but assign responsibility to patriarchal norms and institutions. As well, they consult with formerly abused women, some of whom participate in designing services and programs. Pragmatism, however, has led them to cooperate with the patriarchal state, and their emphasis is on services to individual women rather than the struggle for wider social change. The dream of cooperation and harmony among women supporting one another through the trauma of abuse has not been achieved, but at least abused women no longer have to suffer in silence in their homes.

The community-based groups have not only experienced change within themselves. The political and economic environment around them has also changed considerably since I began writing this book two years ago. At the present time, the women's movement is being severely challenged from the political right, which is calling for a return to 'family values.' In the 1990s, the government in Ontario has responded to the cry against 'reverse discrimination' by overturning progressive legislation (e.g., pay equity and employment equity) and cancelling many programs that provide services to women, ethno-cultural groups, and refugees. My hope, as I finish writing the book, is that the documentation and arguments presented in it can be used by community-based groups to convince government agencies of the need for more, not fewer, social services for abused women.

Notes

Introduction

1 The centre was located in a large spacious room and equipped with photo-copying machines. By the early 1990s, it had collected a number of books and reports on immigrant women, and it maintained files of newspaper clippings on topics such as domestic workers. A librarian was available to help research-ers locate material. When the centre was closed in 1995, its collection was transferred to the Department of Labour, where it is unavailable to research-ers, having been packed in boxes and stored in the basement. In fact, the department tried to find an interested institution to which to give the collec-tion. It contacted the Nellie Langford Library for Women's Studies at York University, but the library did not have the resources to enable it to even examine the material, and it therefore declined the opportunity to obtain any of it.

2 For example, the resources collected by Education Wife Assault include three or four shelves of books commercially available in libraries, its own publica-tions, and a few reports and studies prepared by other community-based groups. There has never been much money available for obtaining material, but what it has acquired has been catalogued. Access to these resources has always been restricted, but staff cutbacks in early 1996 make access even more difficult.

Chapter 1   Immigrant Communities in Canada

1 There is a great deal of literature on various aspects of racism, race relations, and the prevalence of racism in the workplace. For an overview see Henry 1986. One of the earlier studies of racism in employment was Head 1975. Two

of the better-known studies of racism and employment are Henry and Ginzberg 1984 and Billingsley 1985. For a Marxist interpretation of racism and employment, see Satzewich 1991 and Bolaria and Li 1988. At the government level, racism in employment was documented in a report to the Canadian House of Commons in 1984 and in Abella 1984.

2 There is an extensive literature on the discrimination that women experience in the labour force. See, for example, Armstrong and Armstrong 1977; Pierson and Cohen 1995; Parr 1995; Sangster 1995; Duffy and Pupo 1992; Royal Commission on the Status of Women 1970; and Phillips and Phillips 1983.

3 See, for example, Arnopoulos 1979; Giles and Preston 1991; Gannage 1986; Seward 1990; Cohen 1991; Daenzer 1993; Bakan and Stasiulis 1995; Arat-Koc 1990; Silvera 1983; Women Working with Immigrant Women 1988; Adamson 1991; and Boyd 1991.

4 For an exhaustive documentation of the problems of evaluating educational qualifications and professional training, see Cumming 1989.

5 For example, see Giles 1987; Go 1987; Eberts 1987; Boyd 1990; Paredes 1987; and Ontario Council of Agencies Serving Immigrants 1992.

6 For a race, class, and gender analysis of this literature, see Agnew 1996.

7 Ann Paquet-Deehy, Maryse Rinfret-Raynor, and Ginette Larouche did research in Quebec for *Training Social Workers in a Feminist Approach to Conjugal Violence: Summary of the Action Research* (1992). They did not include any discussion on how to counsel ethnic and racialized women.

8 Some service providers have tried to develop a consensus on how to serve non–English-speaking, working-class immigrant women. *Setting the Precedent: Process as Change in Meeting the Needs of Immigrant and Refugee Women Surviving Abuse and Sexual Violence*, produced by the advisory committee of Education Sexual Assault (1992), is a verbatim transcription of some workshops, but the report is poorly organized and confusing. Service providers and activists have produced handbooks that have some useful articles; for example, Rafiq 1991.

Chapter 2 Wife Abuse

1 In Linda MacLeod and Maria Shin's study of non–English- and non–French-speaking women, interviewees were asked to define abuse, and they gave these responses: 'Making women earn money to pay the bills'; 'giving no financial support'; 'using the women as cheap labour'; 'treating his wife like a slave'; 'taking her rights and freedom away'; 'imprisoning the woman'; 'loss of independence'; 'making degrading remarks'; 'being ignored by husbands'; 'having an affair outside marriage, or going with prostitutes'; 'arguing all the time'; 'using dirty language'; 'I was always shaking from fear'; 'I was prevented

from fulfilling my goals'; 'not being able to meet the needs of my children'; 'feeling helpless'; 'sexual abuse'; 'I think of physical torture' (MacLeod and Shin 1993, 28).

2 MacLeod uses the following argument to arrive at her figures. In 1985 she studied 110 transition houses across Canada and found that of 20,291 women accommodated, 15,730 were 'admitted explicitly because they were physically, psychologically, or sexually abused by their husbands or partners.' She then notes that 'extrapolating from these figures, it is likely if we had similar statistics for all 230 shelters which existed at the time of writing about 42,000 women were accommodated in crisis shelters across Canada, almost 33,000 explicitly because they were battered by their husbands or partners.' Most of these shelters were forced to turn away at least one woman for every one who stayed with them (although some were forced to turn away more). 'Therefore, from these calculations in 1985, a total of almost 85,000 women stayed in crisis shelters or requested such shelter. At least 65,000 of these were women who requested shelter explicitly because they were battered by their partners or ex-partners.'

MacLeod describes a study in London, Ontario, which estimated that 89 per cent of the battered women who sought help in their community in 1985 did not seek or require emergency shelter, but instead needed non-residential services such as 'referral, counselling, information and/or accompaniment to court.' MacLeod says that 'applying this estimate to the totals means that almost 600,000 battered women across Canada may have sought some sort of outside help, and of these 532,000 may have sought help but did not require emergency shelter' (MacLeod 1987, 6–7).

3 For a detailed account of how, at the turn of the century, Japanese women coped with a racist society by adhering strictly to traditional Meiji ideology, see Kobayashi 1994.

4 For a discussion of the significance of exploring feelings and sentiments in interviews, see Anderson et al. 1990.

Chapter 3   Settlement Services and Community-based Organizations

1 For a discussion of the gender biases in discourses on multiculturalism, see Martin 1991 and Gabriel 1996.

2 For an analysis of the subject of 'contracting out' social services, see Agnew 1996, 167–172.

3 A black shelter worker also noted the recurrent difficulty of women who do not know the date of birth of their spouses when they apply for welfare and housing (interview, 15 April 1996). In countries where home births are a

norm, attention may not be paid to recording the date of birth or to registering the birth of a child. An example is provided by my own situation. I have no
birth certificate, and when I first applied for a passport in India, I obtained a
notarized letter from a justice of the peace to attest to my date of birth. But my
father's memory of my date of birth, which is recorded on my passport, differs
from that of other members of my family.

Culturally, in a traditional South Asian family, it would be inappropriate for
a wife to enquire about the date of birth of her spouse or even about his salary,
or any other personal detail. Since men often hold important family documents in their possession, a woman may never have had the opportunity to
examine his passport.

4 One woman described her encounter with social services in this way:

I am now moving out from living with [my] partner for the second time. I
left about a year and a half ago and went to social services for help. My husband started counselling and after some months I went back. Social services now is treating me like I am going to rip them off. It is because, I
believe, that they didn't like the fact that I went back. They don't understand why women have to do that. So they are making it difficult by stalling,
threatening, and cross-examining why I need money to start over. They
insist that they make cheques out directly to my new landlord. My landlord
didn't know I was going to be on mother's allowance until I could find
work. Now I'm going to have to deal with his prejudices. I also had to get a
letter from him stating the cost of the rent. Do you know how humiliating
that is, to ask a landlord for a letter because your worker doesn't trust you?
Finally, with advocacy from the shelter and a counsellor, social services
made the cheque out to me. (Ontario Association of Interval and Transition Houses 1991a, 28).

Another woman said:

There's not enough housing and there's too long a waiting list. I find myself
so overwhelmed with all the different things I have to do around housing
and I'm already trying to deal with my emotional state. They first tell you
that you need an application, so you fill out an application. If you're [living
at] ... a shelter, you start your papers there [begin the application process
from there]. Now if you're in a shelter, the reasons are usually very obvious.
And once you go for your interview, you have to go through everything, why
you were in the shelter, why your application started there, and everything.
And after your initial interview, they say they'll be in touch with you and the
first time they're in touch with you, they send you a letter saying we need
this, this and this, we need more information. Now you just went for your
interview and you just gave them half the information in your purse. And

now they want more? (Ontario Association of Interval and Transition Houses 1991a, 26).

5 The South Asian Family Support Services was started by Aruna Papp, a survivor of wife abuse. She found that women in the South Asian community were unaware of services available to them or had been alienated by discriminatory treatment by service providers in government agencies. Papp's disclosure of her own situation and her advocacy on behalf of other abused South Asian women enabled her to obtain a small grant in 1988 from the federal government (Secretary of State). She documented the occurrence of abuse among South Asian women and the lack of services available to them in her *Report on Abused South Asian Women in Scarborough* (1990). Although the sample on which she based her report was narrow (the informants were women utilizing services that she provided) and her assessment that there was an 'epidemic' of wife abuse was debatable, she did identify a need to help South Asian victims of wife abuse.

Government agencies gave her additional funds, enabling her to open an office in Scarborough Centenary Hospital, a location which ensured anonymity for the women seeking help and provided access to medical practitioners who were dealing with victims of wife abuse. The organization was incorporated in 1990. Its constitution declared that its primary focus was 'to reduce the incidence of domestic violence,' but it also included three other goals: to provide services that were culturally sensitive to the needs of South Asian women; to educate other service providers to their needs; and to promote 'life skills which facilitate settlement and adjustment' (South Asian Family Support Services, constitution, n.d., 1).

6 For a detailed analysis of how power struggles between the board and staff can bring the work of the organization to a standstill, see Agnew 1996, 154–9.

7 Although Education Wife Assault lost its entire funding from government agencies, it successfully found alternative funding from a private source (the Trillium Foundation), and a continuing grant from the United Way has enabled it to survive, albeit with reduced staff and programs.

8 For example, the South Asian Family Support Services has received funds from the Department of Employment and Immigration, the Ministry of Multiculturalism and Citizenship, the Ministry of Community and Social Services, the Ministry of Health, and the Ontario Women's Directorate.

9 See, for example, the articles in the volume on feminist perspectives on the Canadian state in *Resources for Feminist Research* 17, no. 3, (Sept. 1988). See also Brodie 1996 and Gordon 1990.

10 There are many coalitions of agencies at the local and provincial levels. In Metro Toronto 'there is the Access Action Council, the Black Action Defence

Committee, the Coalition of Agencies Serving South Asians (CASSA), the Coalition of Visible Minority Women, the Hispanic Council of Metropolitan Toronto, the Multicultural Coalition for Access to Family Services, the Toronto Refugee Affairs Council (TRAC) and the Urban Alliance on Race Relations. On the provincial level the ethno-racial communities express their concerns through the Alliance for Employment Equity, the Ontario Immigrant and Visible Minority Women's Organization (OIVMWO), the Ontario Immigrant Settlement Workers' Association, and the Ontario Racial Minorities Organizing Committee for Training (ORMOCT). On a Canada-wide basis there is the Canadian Council for Refugees (CCR), the Congress of Black Women, and the National Organization of Immigrant and Visible Minority Women of Canada (NOIVMWC)' (OCASI 1993, 12–13).

Chapter 4   Social Services and Advocacy by Community-based Groups

1 For a discussion of different uses of 'community,' see the articles in Ng, Walker, and Muller 1990; and Godway and Finn 1994.
2 For a discussion on the impact of racism on women, see Essed 1991; Li 1990; and Centre for Contemporary Cultural Studies 1982.
3 Some of the better-known studies of the racism of employers are Henry and Ginzberg 1984; Billingsley 1985; Satzewich 1991; and Bolaria and Li 1988.
4 See also Radford 1989; Agard 1987; Doyle and Visano 1987; and Henry et al. 1995.
5 For a critique of this argument, see Agnew 1996, chapter 9, which points out that an analysis of violence against women in India would not support the claims of service providers that relatives can protect women from the violence of their spouses.
6 Musisi and Muktar describe one incident (1992, 163):

In Africa it is taboo for women to talk about certain parts of the body in public. An African immigrant woman whose spouse burned her vagina with cigarette butts was ashamed to tell her male lawyer, shelter workers and the police that she had been assaulted in her most 'sacred' part. To her, the abuse was an attack on her personal identity as a woman. She said it would be like telling these men, 'Look here, I do not have a vagina any more.'

The Canadian Panel on Violence against Women argues that 'Canadian mainstream ways of dealing with wife abuse may be ineffective and culturally offensive' (1993, 89–90):

An example is the case of a policeman asking a Somali woman to show him the physical marks on her body as proof of the beating her husband allegedly inflicted on her. Such a request revealed a total disrespect for her reli-

gious beliefs, and her inability to comply with the police officer's request
because of those beliefs places her under continued threat of abuse.

7 The fear of reporting abuse to the police is also documented in Henry et al.
1995, 162: 'Linguistic, cultural, and racial barriers make it difficult for [non–
English-speaking immigrant women] to seek help from social workers, police,
counsellors, doctors, and religious leaders. In an Ontario study, 62.2 percent
of the battered immigrant women interviewed cited the fear that they would
lose "everything – house, children, reputation – everything I worked for" as an
important reason for not calling the police. And 42.2 percent of the women
cited the fear that a husband or partner would be brutalized or victimized by
the police as a reason for not calling the police (ARA Consultants, 1985).'

8 The complaint of racism in shelters is corroborated by the highly publicized
dispute between staff and board members of Nellie's, a shelter for abused
women in Toronto. For a detailed account, see Henry et al. 1995, 162–5; and
Dewar 1993.

Chapter 5   Counsellors and Their Work

1 Government agencies which provide funds to community-based organizations
require them to adopt hierarchical structures to ensure accountability (Ng
1988; Agnew 1996).

2 A similar manual was also prepared by Alma Estable for the Ontario Women's
Directorate, but I could not trace it.

3 Problems also emerge when the counsellor is a woman from Asia, Africa, or
the Caribbean and the client is a white woman. Many of my respondents in
shelters for women said that white women resented having to seek help from
them and avoided engaging in one-to-one counselling with them, preferring
to wait until a white counsellor came on duty, although one Southeast Asian
counsellor said that abused women often felt too distraught to look down
upon anyone.

Chapter 6   Interviews with Counsellors

1 The immigration regulations of 1990 stated that 'humanitarian and compassionate grounds exist when unusual, undeserved or disproportionate hardship would be caused to a person seeking consideration. A humanitarian and
compassionate review is a case-by-case response whereby officers are expected
to consider carefully all aspects of a situation, use their best judgement and
make an informed recommendation' (Stairs and Pope 1990, 211).

2 The solution of having more police officers from different ethnic and racial

groups would not necessarily resolve the difficulties experienced by abused women. For example, a Hindu woman from India may have some reservations about obtaining help from a Sikh police officer in Canada given the political hostilities between Hindus and Sikhs in India since the late 1980s.

3 In practical terms, it means that a woman has used her salary to purchase jewellery, clothing, or household goods for her own use. At the time of the wedding, however, it is presented as a dowry that she has received from her parents.

4 Canadian multicultural policy holds that when cultural norms and values do not violate any Canadian law, it is up to ethnic groups and communities to decide whether to maintain or discard them. In the case of genital mutilation, practised by some immigrant groups from Somalia and Ethiopia, the issue has been addressed by introducing legislation which makes it illegal for doctors to perform that operation in Canada.

Chapter 7   Counsellors and Women in Shelters

1 For example, the Conservative government in Ontario cancelled second-stage housing funds and reduced transfer payments to municipalities, which pay the shelters' per diem costs (Gadd 1995, A8).

2 An atypical profile of funding for shelters is that of Nellie's, a shelter for 'transient women, battered women, women released from hospitals, from jails, women evicted legally or illegally, women in search of affordable housing.' A brochure describes the sources of its funding. 'Original seed money came from YWCA and a grant from the United Church of Canada. The Atkinson Foundation provided a capital grant and the United Community Fund offered an emergency grant for one year. In January 1978, a capital campaign was launched to purchase and renovate the house. The campaign, including a generous contribution from the Rotary Club of Toronto, was successful, a loan secured from Canada Mortgage and Housing, and a complete renovation was undertaken.'

3 An informal survey conducted by MacLeod in 1988 revealed that there were 208 transition houses, 33 safe homes / safe environments, 14 satellite houses, 30 multi-purpose emergency shelters, and 23 second-stage housing units (MacLeod 1989b, 38).

4 Sometimes shelters have enough resources to supply some toiletries (e.g., toothpaste and soap) to the residents, enabling them to spend their allowance on other needs (e.g., bus tokens, clothing, and shoes).

5 In contrast, during an evening's visit to the North York Women's Shelter, there was a buzz of activity in the dining-room as women supervised dinner for

their children and themselves. After dinner, the shelter celebrated the birth-days of three children that had occurred during that week. Each child received a present and a birthday cake. The staff tried to encourage a happy and light atmosphere. Music was played, and some women danced very briefly.

6 During one of my visits to the North York Women's Shelter, a staff member and I happened to meet at the laundry-room on our way to a board meeting. A woman in her sixties summoned us inside and proudly showed us how she had tidied and rearranged the room. But then suddenly she started sobbing. She said tearfully that she was really grateful to the shelter and wanted to do something in return, but was 'too stupid' to do anything. The staff member put a reassuring arm around her and reminded her of the work she had just accomplished and also how she frequently helped the other women by playing with their children. The woman acted like a grandmother to the children and pampered some of them by giving them candy, which she bought with her own money. Just as suddenly as she had started crying, she stopped, and we went on to our meeting.

7 The following is an example of a 'weekly chore chart' of the Emily Stowe Shelter:

	– Vacuum all carpeted stairs and mop all uncarpeted stairs.
	– Vacuum all hallways 1st, 2nd, and 3rd floors.
	– Vacuum all offices, vacuum and tidy up the living-room. – Vacuum all chairs and chesterfields in the living-room.
	– Mop all first-floor non-carpeted hallways.
	– Clean and mop laundry-room, clean washers, dryers. Wash off built-up detergent on the machines. Wipe freezers. Empty garbage, put out in the bin.
	– Wash bathroom on second and third floors – DAILY – Empty garbage, put garbage in the bin (on street) – Wash floor – chore must be done between 4:00 p.m. and 10:00 p.m.
	– Wash bathrooms on first floor DAILY, 4:00 p.m.–10:00 p.m. – Empty garbage, put garbage in bin (on street).

	– Clean and mop basement hall, and between the stairs.
	– Clean rec room, remove all toys and food, wipe marks off the wall. Vacuum all chesterfields and chairs.
	– FLOAT – Help put away the food. – FLOAT – Help put away the food.

A second 'chore chart' identified tasks related to cooking:

These chores are not completed until everything is done, especially emptying the dishwasher and cleaning up counter tops, floors, and garbage.

BREAKFAST – must be done by 10:00 a.m. – Wash dishes, put them away – Clean counters and table tops – Empty garbage, put in bin on the street – Sweep the floor			
LUNCH – must be done by 2:00 p.m. – Wash dishes, put them away – Clean sink and counters – Dishwasher must be empty			
SUPPER – must be done by 7:00 p.m. – Wash dishes, put them away – Clean sink and counters – Dishwasher must be empty			
Pots – must be done by 8:00 p.m. – Wash all pots and pans – Wipe stove and microwave – Put away leftovers in small containers – Put away all pots and pans			
Kitchen sweep – must be done by 7:30 p.m. – Clean table tops and chairs – Sweep floors			

– Empty garbage, put in bin on the street – Sweep the floor			
LATE NIGHT – not before 10:00 p.m. – Wash all dishes and pots and pans – Clean tables and counters – Empty garbage, put in bin on the street – Sweep and wash the floor			
SUPPER ON THE WEEKEND FLOAT			

8 The North York Women's Shelter formally adopted an antiracism policy in September 1992. The policy states:

The North York Women's Shelter affirms as a source of enrichment and strength the diversity of its residents, staff and community, in terms of race, culture, ethnicity, language, religion, creed, gender, age, sexual orientation, physical ability and socio-economic status.

The Shelter recognizes its responsibility to develop positive attitudes, increased knowledge and fair practices with respect to these diversities among residents, staff, directors and community.

To this end, the North York Women's Shelter will establish and implement multicultural/anti-racism policies that ensure:

- Volunteers and staff are reflective of the community they serve
- Services are sensitive to the needs of culturally and racially diverse groups
- Programs seek to eliminate systemic barriers to full participation and promote positive race relations and attitudinal change
- Discriminatory or racist incidents or behavior are not tolerated
- Communications present a positive and balanced portrayal of racial and cultural minorities.

9 For a case study of a racial conflict between staff and board members at Women's Health in Women's Hands, see Agnew 1996.

10 For a discussion of the professionalization of services for victims of rape, see Foley 1994

11 Interval House lists a variety of services (brochure): 'Safety and protection for women and children fleeing family violence. No-cost accommodation, food and emergency clothing for 22 women and children. Telephone distress coun-

selling, 24 hours a day, 7 days a week. Counselling and group discussions to help women sort out tangled marital, legal, health, childcare, employment and housing problems. Referrals to a wide range of community services and government agencies. Referrals to lawyers who accept Legal Aid Certificates and are knowledgeable about the issue of wife assault. Referrals to interpreters and lawyers who speak languages other than English. Help and support for residents who must revisit the marital home to collect belongings or who must encounter a spouse in court. A children's program including counselling, support and referrals for children while they are in crisis. An ex-resident outreach program which includes advocacy, counselling, and support. Court support program which includes information on our legal system and advice on our legal system and advice on the various legal issues a battered woman may have to face.'

12 For a discussion of how discretionary authority is used to deny women some forms of social assistance, see Lawrence 1990.

13 Carol explained that 'an art therapist can draw a woman out and get her to talk about herself by interpreting her artwork. [For example,] she may draw a picture of a little girl, but the therapist may help her to identify through that picture childhood abuse.' Carol argued that such therapy was 'really effective for women who have difficulties talking about their feelings.'

14 For a discussion of a similar trend in shelters in Britain and the United States, see Lupton and Gillespie 1994.

References

Abel, Allen. 1989. Scenes from an arranged marriage. *Toronto Life*, June, 32–5.

Abella, Rosalie Silberman. 1984. *Equality in employment* [Royal Commission Report]. Ottawa: Canadian Government Publishing Centre.

Acker, Joan, Kate Barry, and Johanna Esseveld. 1991. Objectivity and truth: Problems in doing feminist research. In *Beyond methodology: Feminist scholarship as lived research*, ed. M. Fonow and J. Cook, 133–53. Bloomington: Indiana University Press.

Adachi, Ken. 1976. *The enemy that never was*. Toronto: McClelland and Stewart.

Adamson, Nancy, Linda Briskin, and Margaret McPhail. 1988. *Feminists organizing for change: The contemporary women's movement in Canada*. Toronto: Oxford University Press.

Adamson, Shelagh. 1991. *Working paper on immigrant women: Education, training, employment*. Toronto: COSTI-IIAS.

Adleman, Jeanne, and Gloria Enguidanos, eds. 1995. *Racism in the lives of women: Testimony, theory, and guides to antiracist practice*. New York: Harrington Park Press.

Agard, Ralph. 1987. *Access to the social assistance service delivery systems by various ethno-cultural groups*. Toronto: Social Assistance Review.

Agnew, Vijay. 1991. South Asian women in Ontario: The experience of race, class, and gender. In *Women changing academe*, ed. S. Kirby, 13–32. Winnipeg: Sororal.

– 1993a. Canadian feminism and women of color. *Women's International Studies Forum* 16(3): 217–27.

– 1993b. South Asian women and feminism. In *Ethnicity, identity, migration: The South Asian context*, ed. M. Israel and N.K. Wagle, 142–64. Toronto: University of Toronto, Centre for South Asian Studies.

– 1996. *Resisting discrimination: Women from Asia, Africa, and the Caribbean and the women's movement in Canada*. Toronto: University of Toronto Press.

Alcoff, Linda. 1988. Cultural feminism versus poststructuralism: The identity crisis in feminist theory. *Signs* 13(3): 405–36.

Anderson, Alan, and James Frideres. 1981. *Ethnicity in Canada: Theoretical perspectives.* Toronto: Butterworths.

Anderson, Kathryn, Susan Armitage, Dana Jack, and Judith Wittner. 1990. Beginning where we are: Feminist methodology in oral history. In *Feminist research methods: Exemplary readings in the social sciences,* ed. J. Nielsen, 94–112. Boulder: Westview Press.

Anderson, Kay. 1991. *Vancouver's Chinatown: Racial discourse in Canada, 1875–1980.* Montreal: McGill-Queen's University Press.

Arat-Koc, Sedef. 1990. Importing housewives: Non-citizen domestic workers and the crisis of the domestic sphere in Canada. In *Through the kitchen window,* ed. M. Luxton, H. Rosenberg, and S. Arat-Koc, 81–103. Toronto: Garamond.

Armstrong, Pat, and Hugh Armstrong. 1977. *The double ghetto: Canadian women and their segregated work.* Toronto: McClelland and Stewart.

Arnopoulos, Sheila. 1979. *Problems of immigrant women in the Canadian labour force.* Ottawa: Canadian Advisory Council on the Status of Women.

Bakan, Abigail, and Daiva Stasiulis. 1995. Making the match: Domestic placement agencies and the racialization of women's household work. *Signs* 20(2): 303–35.

Balakrishnan, T.R., and K. Selvanathan. 1990. Ethnic residential segregation in Metropolitan Canada. In *Ethnic demography: Canadian immigrant, racial and cultural variations,* ed. S. Halli, F. Trovato, and L. Driedger, 399–414. Ottawa: Carleton University Press.

Bannerji, Himani. 1986. Popular images of South Asian women. *Tiger Lily,* 23–7.

– 1987. Introducing racism: Notes towards an anti-racist feminism. *Resources for Feminist Research* 16(1): 10–12.

– 1991. But who speaks for us? Experience and agency in conventional feminist paradigms. In *Unsettling relations: The university as a site of feminist struggles,* ed. H. Bannerji et al. 67–108. Toronto: Women's Press.

Barbara Schlifer Commemorative Clinic. 1991. *Your rights: An assaulted woman's guide to the law.* Toronto: Ontario Women's Directorate.

Barnsley, Jan. 1985. *Feminist action, institutional reaction: Responses to wife assault.* Vancouver: Women's Research Centre.

Bar On, Bat-Ami. 1993. Marginality and epistemic privilege. In *Feminist epistemologies,* ed. L. Alcoff and E. Potter, 83–100. New York: Routledge.

Barrett, Michele, and Mary McIntosh. 1985. Ethnocentrism and socialist feminist theory. *Feminist Review* 20: 23–47.

Barrett, Michele, and Anne Phillips, eds. 1992. *Destabilizing theory: Contemporary feminist debates.* Stanford: Stanford University Press.

Basavarajappa, K.G., and Ravi Verma. 1990. Occupational composition of immigrant women. In *Ethnic demography: Canadian immigrant, racial and cultural variations*, ed. S. Halli, F. Trovato, and L. Driedger, 297–314. Ottawa: Carleton University Press.

Baureiss, Gunter. 1987. Chinese immigration, Chinese stereotypes, and Chinese labour. *Canadian Ethnic Studies* 19(3): 15–34.

Beaudry, Micheline. 1985. *Battered women*. Montreal: Black Rose.

Benhabib, Seyla. 1995. Feminism and postmodernism. In *Feminist contentions: A philosophical exchange*, ed. S. Benhabib et al., 17–34. New York: Routledge.

Bentzel, Sara, and Reginald York. 1988. Influence of feminism and professional status upon service options for the battered woman. *Community Mental Health Journal* 24(1): 52–64.

Bhachu, Parminder. 1985. *Twice migrants: East African Sikh settlers in Britain*. London: Tavistock.

Bhatti-Sinclair, Kish. 1994. Asian women and violence from male partners. In *Working with violence*, ed. C. Lupton and T. Gillespie, 75–95. Hampshire and London: Macmillan.

Billingsley, Brenda. 1985. *No discrimination here? Toronto employers and the multi-racial workforce*. Toronto: Social Planning Council of Metropolitan Toronto.

Bissoondath, Neil. 1994. *Selling illusions: The cult of multiculturalism in Canada*. Toronto: Penguin.

Black, Naomi. 1988. The Canadian women's movement: The second wave. In *Changing patterns: Women in Canada*, ed. S. Burt, L. Code, and L. Dorney, 80–102. Toronto: McClelland and Stewart.

Bolaria, B. Singh, and Peter S. Li, eds. 1988. *Racial oppression in Canada*. Toronto: Garamond.

Borowski, Allan, and Alan Nash. 1994. Business migration. In *Immigration and refugee policy*, Vol. 1, ed. H. Adelman et al., 227–54. Toronto: University of Toronto Press.

Boyd, Monica. 1989. *Migrant women in Canada: Profiles and policies*. Ottawa: Employment and Immigration Canada.

– 1990. Immigrant women: Language, socio-economic inequalities and policy issues. In *Ethnic demography: Canadian immigrant, racial and cultural variations*, ed. S. Halli, F. Trovato, and L. Driedger, 275–93. Ottawa: Carleton University Press.

– 1991. Gender, visible-minority and immigrant earnings inequality: Reassessing an employment equity premise. Working Paper 91–6. Department of Sociology and Anthropology, Carleton University, Ottawa.

– 1994. Language, economic status and integration. In *Immigration and refugee policy*, Vol. 2, ed. H. Adelman et al., 227–54. Toronto: University of Toronto Press.

Brah, Avtar. 1992. Difference, diversity, and differentiation. In *Race, culture, and difference*, ed. J. Donald and A. Rattansi, 126–48. London: Sage.

Brand, Dionne. 1984. Black women in Toronto: Gender, race, and class. *Fireweed* (Summer/Fall): 26–43.

– 1991. *No burden to carry.* Toronto: Women's Press.

– 1994. 'We weren't allowed to go into factory work until Hitler started the war': The 1920s to the 1940s. In *'We're rooted here and they can't pull us up': Essays in African Canadian women's history*, ed. P. Bristow, 171–92. Toronto: University of Toronto Press.

Briskin, Linda. 1991. Feminist practice: A new approach to evaluating feminist strategy. In *Women and social change: Feminist activism in Canada*, ed. J. Wine and J. Ristock, 24–40. Toronto: James Lorimer.

Bristow, Peggy, ed. 1994a. *'We're rooted here and they can't pull us up': Essays in African Canadian women's history.* Toronto: University of Toronto Press.

– 1994b. 'Whatever you raise in the ground, you can sell it in Chatham': Black women in Buxton and Chatham 1850–65. In *'We're rooted here and they can't pull us up': Essays in African Canadian women's history*, ed. P. Bristow, 69–142. Toronto: University of Toronto Press.

Brodie, Janine. 1994. Shifting the boundaries: Gender and the politics of restructuring. In *The strategic silence: Gender and economic policy*, ed. I. Bakker, 46–60. London: Zed.

– 1996. *Women and Canadian public policy.* Toronto: Harcourt Brace.

Brown, Laura. 1994. *Subversive dialogues: Theory in feminist therapy.* New York: Basic Books.

– 1995. Antiracism as an ethical norm in feminist therapy practice. In *Racism in the lives of women: Testimony, theory, and guides to antiracist practice*, ed. J. Adleman and G. Enguidanos, 137–48. New York: Harrington Park Press.

Brown, Lyn Mikel, and Carol Gilligan. 1992. *Meeting at the crossroads: Women's psychology and girls' development.* Cambridge: Harvard University Press.

Brown, Rosemary, and Cleta Brown. 1996. Comments: Reflections on racism. In *Perspectives on racism and the human service sector: A case for change*, ed. C. James, 47–50. Toronto: University of Toronto Press.

Buchignani, Norman, and Doreen Indra. 1985. *Continuous journey: A social history of South Asians in Canada.* Toronto: McClelland and Stewart.

Burnet, Jean. 1988. *'Coming Canadians': An introduction to a history of Canada's peoples.* Toronto: McClelland and Stewart.

Calliste, Agnes. 1989. Canada's immigration policy and domestics from the Caribbean: The second domestic scheme. In *Race, class, and gender: Bonds and barriers*, ed. Jesse Vorst et al., 133–65. Toronto: Between the Lines.

Campbell, Kathleen. 1993. Cross-cultural expectation about counselling. M.A. thesis, York University, Toronto.

Canada. House of Commons. 1984. *Equality now: Report of the special committee on visible-minorities in Canadian society.* Ottawa: Minister of Supply and Services.

Canadian-African Newcomer Aid Centre of Toronto. 1992. Interventionist strategies: CANACT and wife assault in the 1990s. Unpublished workshop report.

Canadian Panel on Violence against Women. 1993. *Changing the landscape: Ending violence – achieving equality.* Ottawa: Minister of Supply and Services.

Cannon, Margaret. 1989. *China tide: The revealing story of the Hong Kong exodus to Canada.* Toronto: Harper-Collins.

– 1995. *The invisible empire: Racism in Canada.* Toronto: Random House.

Carby, Hazel. 1982. White women listen! Black feminism and the boundaries of sisterhood. In *The empire strikes back: Race and racism in 70s Britain,* ed. Centre for Contemporary Culture Studies, 212–35. London: Hutchinson.

Carty, Linda. 1991. Black women in academia: A statement from the periphery. In *Unsettling relations: The university as a site of feminist struggles,* ed. H. Bannerji et al., 13–44. Toronto: Women's Press.

– ed. 1993. *And still we rise: Feminist political mobilizing in contemporary Canada.* Toronto: Women's Press.

Carty, Linda, and Dionne Brand. 1989. 'Visible-minority' women – a creation of the Canadian state. *Resources for Feminist Research* 17(3): 39–40.

Centre for Contemporary Cultural Studies, ed. 1982. *The empire strikes back: Race and racism in 70s Britain.* London: Hutchinson.

Cervantes, Nena. 1988. *From fright to flight.* Toronto: Network of Filipino-Canadian Women.

Chadney, James G. 1984. *The Sikhs of Vancouver.* New York: AMS.

Chaudhry, Ushi. 1992. Beyond need assessment and problem identification. *Sanvad:Canadian Punjabi Journal* 5(45): 11–12.

Chinese Family Life Services. 1989. *Wife assault: The Chinese Family Life Services experience.* Toronto: Chinese Family Life Services of Metro Toronto.

Chong, Denise. 1994. *The concubine's children.* Toronto: Penguin.

Christensen, Carole. 1995. Cross-cultural awareness development: An aid to the creation of antiracist feminist therapy. In *Racism in the lives of women: Testimony, theory, and guides to antiracist practice,* ed. J. Adleman and G. Enguidanos, 209–28. New York: Harrington Park Press.

Chunn, Dorothy. 1995. Feminism, law, and public policy: 'Politicizing the personal.' In *Canadian families: Diversity, conflict, and change,* ed. N. Mandel and A. Duffy, 177–210. Toronto: Harcourt Brace.

Citizenship Development Branch, Wife Assault Team. 1988. *Working with assaulted immigrant women: Report on skill-development and information-sharing workshop for settlement and shelter workers.* Toronto: Ministry of Citizenship.

Code, Lorraine. 1988. Feminist theory. In *Changing patterns: Women in Canada,* ed.

Sandra Burt, Lorraiane Code, and Lindsay Dorney, 18–50. Toronto: McClelland and Stewart.

– 1991. *What can she know? Feminist theory and the construction of knowledge.* Ithaca, N.Y.: Cornell University Press.

– 1993. Taking subjectivity into account. In *Feminist epistemologies,* ed. L. Alcoff and E. Potter, 15–49. New York: Routledge.

Cohen, Marjorie Griffin. 1994. The implications of economic restructuring for women: The Canadian situation. In *The strategic silence: Gender and economic policy,* ed. I. Bakker, 103–16. London: Zed.

Cohen, Rina. 1991. Women of color in white households: Coping strategies of live-in domestic workers. *Qualitative Sociology* 14(2): 197–215.

Collins, Patricia. 1990. *Black feminist thought: Knowledge, consciousness, and the politics of empowerment.* New York: Routledge.

– 1991. Learning from the outsider within: The sociological significance of black feminist thought. In *Beyond methodology: Feminist scholarship as lived research,* ed. M. Fonow and J. Cook, 35–59. Bloomington: Indiana University Press.

Cook, Judith, and Margaret Fonow. 1990. Knowledge and women's interests: Issues of epistemology and methodology in feminist research. In *Feminist research methods: Exemplary readings in the social sciences,* ed. J. Nielsen, 69–93. Boulder: Westview Press.

Cooper, Afua. 1994. Black women and work in nineteenth-century Canada West: Black woman teacher Mary Bibb. In *'We're rooted here and they can't pull us up': Essays in African Canadian women's history,* ed. P. Bristow, 143–70. Toronto: University of Toronto Press.

COSTI. 1993. *Wife assault / woman abuse: Protocol.* Toronto: COSTI. (Report prepared by Marina Morrow.)

Cross-Cultural Communication Centre. 1988. Press kit.

Cumming, Peter. 1989. *Access: Report of the task force on access to professions and trades in Ontario.* Toronto: Ontario Ministry of Citizenship.

Daenzer, Patricia. 1993. *Regulating class privilege: Immigrant servants in Canada, 1940s–1990s.* Toronto: Canadian Scholars Press.

Danica Women's Project. 1993. *The consequences of sexual violence against women and recommendations for action.* Toronto: Danica Women's Project.

Das Gupta, Tania. 1994. Political economy of gender, race and class: Looking at South Asian immigrant women in Canada. *Canadian Ethnic Studies* 26(1): 59–74.

– 1996. *Racism and paid work.* Toronto: Garamond.

Datar, Chhaya, ed. 1993. *The struggle against violence.* Calcutta: Stree.

Davies, Linda, and Eric Shragge. 1990. *Bureaucracy and community.* Montreal: Black Rose Books.

Davis, Angela Y. 1983. *Women, race, and class.* New York: Vintage.

Day, Lesley. 1992. Women and oppression: Race, class and gender. In *Women, oppression and social work: Issues in anti-discriminatory practice*, ed. M. Langan and L. Day, 12–31. London: Routledge.

DeKeseredy, Walter. 1995. Enhancing the quality of survey data on woman abuse. *Violence against Women: An International and Interdisciplinary Journal* 1(2): 158–73.

DeKeseredy, Walter, and Ronald Hinch. 1991. *Woman abuse: Sociological perspectives*. Toronto: Thompson Educational Publishing.

Desai, Sabra. 1996. Afterword: Common issues, common understandings. In *Perspectives on racism and the human service sector: A case for change*, ed. C. James, 246–52. Toronto: University of Toronto Press.

Dewar, Elaine. 1993. Wrongful dismissal. *Toronto Life*, March, 32–47.

Dhillon, Jasteena, and Lisa Walter. 1993. *Aftercare for abused women: A preliminary study and needs assessment with a model for service in Metro Toronto*. Toronto: Working Group for Follow-Up Services.

Dhruvarajan, Vanaja. 1991. The multiple oppression of women of colour. In *Racism in Canada*, ed. O. McKague, 101–4. Saskatoon: Fifth House Publishers.

Di Stefano, Christine. 1990. Dilemmas of difference: Feminism, modernity, and postmodernism. In *Feminism/postmodernism*, ed. L.J. Nicholson, 63–82. New York: Routledge.

Dobash, Emerson, and Russell Dobash. 1992. *Women, violence, and social change*. London: Routledge.

Dominelli, Lena. 1988. *Anti-racist social work*. Hampshire and London: Macmillan.

Dorais, Louis-Jacques, Lois Foster, and David Stockley. 1994. Multiculturalism and integration. In *Immigration and refugee policy*, Vol. 2, ed. H. Adelman et al., 372–404. Toronto: University of Toronto Press.

Doyle, R., and Levy Visano. 1987. *Access to health and social services for members of diverse cultural and racial groups*. Reports 1 and 2. Toronto: Social Planning Council of Metropolitan Toronto.

D'Souza, Dinesh. 1991. *Illiberal education: The politics of race and sex on campus*. New York: The Free Press.

Duffy, Ann, and Norene Pupo. 1992. *Part-time paradox: Connecting gender, work and family*. Toronto: McClelland and Stewart.

Dutton-Douglas, Mary, and Dorothy Dionne. 1992. Counselling and shelter services for battered women. In *Woman battering: Policy responses*, ed. M. Steinman, 113–30. Northern Kentucky: Anderson.

Eberts, Mary. 1987. Language training policy under the Charter of Rights. In *Report of the colloquium: Equality in language and literacy training*, 23–7. Toronto: n.p.

Education Sexual Assault. 1992. *Setting the precedent: Process as change in meeting the needs of immigrant and refugee women surviving abuse and sexual violence.* Toronto: Education Sexual Assault. (Report prepared by Milagros Paredes.)

Emily Stowe Shelter for Women. 1990–3. *Annual report.* Toronto: Emily Stowe Shelter for Women.

Essed, Philomena. 1991. *Understanding everyday racism: An interdisciplinary theory.* London: Sage.

Estable, Alma. 1986. *Immigrant women in Canada: Current issues.* Ottawa: Canadian Advisory Council on the Status of Women.

Estable, Alma, Meyer Mechthild, Joan Riggs, and Lynn Tyler. 1991. *Interdisciplinary training manual on sexual assault.* Toronto: Ontario Women's Directorate.

Fincher, Ruth, et al. 1994. Gender and migration policy. In *Immigration and refugee policy,* Vol. 1, ed. H. Adelman et al., 149–86. Toronto: University of Toronto Press.

Findlay, Sue. 1988. Feminist struggles with the Canadian state, 1966–88. *Resources for Feminist Research* 17(3): 5–9.

Fleras, Augie, and Jean Leonard Elliott. 1992. *Multiculturalism in Canada.* Scarborough, Ont.: Nelson.

Foley, Marian. 1994. Professionalising the response to rape. In *Working with violence,* ed. C. Lupton and T. Gillespie, 39–54. London: Macmillan.

Fonow, Margaret, and Judith Cook. 1991. *Beyond methodology: Feminist scholarship as lived research.* Bloomington: Indiana University Press.

Frankenberg, Ruth. 1993. *The social construction of whiteness: White women, race matters.* Minneapolis: University of Minnesota Press.

Gabriel, Christina. 1996. One or the other? Race, gender, and the limits of official multiculturalism. In *Women and Canadian public policy,* ed. Janine Brodie, 173–98. Toronto: Harcourt Brace.

Gadd, Jane. 1995. More women, children using shelters. *Globe and Mail* (12 Dec.) .

Gannage, Charlene. 1986. *Double day, double bind.* Toronto: Women's Press.

Geiger, Susan. 1990. What's so feminist about women's oral history? *Journal of Women's History* 2(1): 169–82.

George, Usha. 1992. Ethnocultural agencies. Unpublished manuscript.

Ghosh, Ratna. 1981. Minority within a minority: On being South Asian and female in Canada. In *Women in the family and economy,* ed. G. Kurian and R. Ghosh, 413–26. Westport: Greenwood.

Giles, Winona. 1987. Language rights are women's rights: Discrimination against immigrant women in Canadian language training policies. *Resources for Feminist Research* 17(3): 129–32.

Giles, Winona, and Valerie Preston. 1991. Ethnicity, gender and labour markets in Canada: A case study of immigrant women in Toronto. Paper presented at the annual meeting of the Canadian Association of Anthropology and Sociology, Kingston, Ontario.

Gillespie, Terry. 1994. Under pressure: Rape crisis centre, multi-agency work and strategies for survival. In *Working with violence*, ed. C. Lupton and T. Gillespie, 15–38. London: Macmillan.

Gilligan, Carol. 1982. *In a different voice.* Cambridge: Harvard University Press.

Gilman, Susan Thomas. 1988. A history of the sheltering movement for battered women in Canada. *Canadian Journal of Community Mental Health* 7(2): 9–21.

Go, Amy Teng-Teng. 1987. *Discussion paper on E.S.L. funding for submission to the OCASI Board of Directors.* Toronto: Ontario Council of Agencies Serving Immigrants.

Godin, Joanne. 1994. *More than a crime: A report on the lack of public legal information materials for immigrant women who are subject to wife assault.* Ottawa: Research and Statistics Directorate.

Godway, Eleanor, and Geraldine Finn. 1994. Community:Catachresis:Community. In *Who is this we? Absence of community*, ed. E. Godway and G. Finn, 1–10. Montreal: Black Rose.

Gogia, Nupur. 1994. *To whose benefit? A needs assessment on services available for immigrant and refugee women who have been abused.* Toronto: St Christopher Neighbourhood House.

Gordon, Linda, ed. 1990. *Women, the state, and welfare.* Madison: University of Wisconsin Press.

Grant, Judith. 1993. *Fundamental feminism: Contesting the core concepts of feminist theory.* New York: Routledge.

Greaves, Lorraine, Nelson Heapy, and Alison Wylie. 1988. Advocacy services: Reassessing the profile and needs of battered women. *Canadian Journal of Community Mental Health* 7(2): 39–51.

Greene, Beverly. 1986. When the therapist is white and the patient is black: Considerations for psychotherapy in the feminist heterosexual and lesbian communities. In *The dynamics of feminist therapy*, ed. D. Howard, 41–65. New York: Haworth Press.

– 1994. Diversity and difference: Race and feminist psychotherapy. In *Women in context: Toward a feminist reconstruction of psychotherapy*, ed. Marsha Mirkin, 333–51. New York: Guildford Press.

– 1995. An African-American perspective on racism and anti-semitism within feminist organizations. In *Racism in the lives of women: Testimony, theory, and guides to antiracist practice*, ed. J. Adleman and G. Enguidanos, 303–14. New York: Harrington Park Press.

Guberman, Connie, and Margie Wolfe. 1985. *No safe place: Violence against women and children.* Toronto: Women's Press.

Hallett, Mary, and Marilyn Davis. 1994. *Firing the heather: The life and times of Nellie McClung.* Saskatoon: Fifth House.

Hamilton, Sylvia. 1994. Naming names, naming ourselves: A survey of early black women in Nova Scotia. In 'We're rooted here and they can't pull us up': Essays in African Canadian women's history, ed. P. Bristow, 13–40. Toronto: University of Toronto Press.

Harding, Sandra, ed. 1987. Feminism and methodology. Bloomington: Indiana University Press.

– 1990. Feminism, science, and the anti-enlightenment critiques. In Feminism/postmodernism, ed. L. Nicholson, 83–106. New York: Routledge.

– 1993. Rethinking standpoint epistemology: 'What is strong objectivity?' In Feminist epistemologies, ed. L. Alcoff and E. Potter, 49–82. New York: Routledge.

Harney, Robert. 1988. 'So great a heritage as ours': Immigration and the survival of the Canadian polity. Daedalus 117: 51–97.

Harris, Susan. 1987. Violence against women in Etobicoke. Phase one: The response of service providers. Unpublished manuscript.

Hartsock, Nancy. 1987. The feminist standpoint: Developing the ground for a specifically feminist historical materialism. In Feminism and methodology, ed. S. Harding, 157–80. Bloomington: Indiana University Press.

– 1990. Foucault on power: A theory for women? In Feminism/postmodernism, ed. L. Nicholson, 157–75. New York: Routledge.

Hawkesworth, Mary. 1989. Knowers, knowing, known: Feminist theory and claims of truth. Signs 14(31): 533–57.

Hawkins, Freda. 1988. Canada and immigration: Public policy and public concern. 2nd ed. Kingston and Montreal: McGill-Queen's University Press.

Head, Wilson. 1975. The black presence in the Canadian mosaic: A study of the practice of discrimination against blacks in Metropolitan Toronto. Toronto: Ontario Human Rights Commission.

Henry, Frances. 1986. Race relations research in Canada today: A 'state of the art' review. Ottawa: Canadian Human Rights Commission.

– 1994. The Caribbean diaspora in Toronto: Learning to live with racism. Toronto: University of Toronto Press.

Henry, Frances, and E. Ginzberg. 1984. Who gets the work? A test of racial discrimination in employment. Toronto: Social Planning Council and Urban Alliance on Race Relations.

Henry, Frances, and Carol Tator. 1994. The ideology of racism: 'Democratic racism.' Canadian Ethnic Studies 26(2): 1–14.

Henry, Frances, et al. 1995. The colour of democracy: Racism in Canadian society. Toronto: Harcourt Brace.

Hernandez, Carmencita. 1988. The Coalition of Visible-Minority Women. In Social movements / social change, ed. F. Cunningham et al., 157–68. Toronto: Between the Lines.

Ho, Catherine. 1990. An analysis of domestic violence in Asian American communities: A multicultural approach to counseling. In *Diversity and complexity in feminist therapy*, ed. L. Brown and M. Root, 129–50. New York: Harrington Park Press.

hooks, bell. 1984. *Feminist theory from margin to center.* Boston: South End Press.

– 1988. *Talking back: Thinking feminist, thinking black.* Toronto: Between the Lines.

– 1994. *Teaching to transgress: Education as the practice of freedom.* New York: Routledge.

Iacovetta, Franca. 1995. Remaking their lives: Women immigrants, survivors, and refugees. In *A diversity of women: Ontario 1945–1980*, ed. J. Parr, 135–67. Toronto: University of Toronto Press.

Intercede. 1990. *Report and recommendations on the foreign domestic movement program.* Toronto: Intercede.

– 1991. *The bare essentials: A needs assessment of foreign domestic workers in Ontario.* Toronto: Intercede.

Interval House. n.d. Interval House philosophy. Unpublished manuscript.

Jaggar, Alison. 1983. *Feminist politics and human nature.* Totowa: Rowman and Allanheld.

Jaggar, Alison, and Susan Bordo, eds. 1990. *Gender/body/knowledge: Feminist reconstructions of being and knowing.* New Brunswick, N.J.: Rutgers University Press.

James, Carl, ed. 1996. *Perspectives on racism and the human services sector: A case for change.* Toronto: University of Toronto Press.

James, Carl, and Adrienne Shadd. 1994. *Talking about difference: Encounters in culture, language, and identity.* Toronto: Between the Lines.

Janz, Teresa. 1993. Sheltering battered women. Ph.D diss., York University, Toronto.

Javed, Nayyar. 1995. Salience of loss and marginality: Life themes of 'immigrant women of color' in Canada. In *Racism in the lives of women: Testimony, theory, and guides to antiracist practice*, ed. J. Adleman and G. Enguidanos, 13–22. New York: Harrington Park Press.

Jensen, Joan M. 1988. *Passage from India: Asian Indian immigrants in North America.* New Haven: Yale University Press.

Johnson, Adrian. 1996. Towards an equitable, efficient, and effective human service system. In *Perspectives on racism and the human services sector: A case for change*, ed. C. James, 209–21. Toronto: University of Toronto Press.

Johnson, Laura. 1982. *The seam allowance: Industrial home sewing in Canada.* Toronto: Women's Press.

Johnson, Norman. 1995. Domestic violence: An overview. In *Family violence and the caring professions*, ed. P. Kingston and B. Penhale, 101–26. London: Macmillan.

Johnston, Hugh. 1979. *The voyage of the Komagata Maru: The Sikh challenge to Canada's colour bar.* Delhi: Oxford University Press.

Jones, Ann. 1994. *Next time she'll be dead: Battering and how to stop it.* Boston: Beacon Press.

Kemp, Alice Abel. 1994. *Women's work: Degraded and devalued.* Englewood Cliffs, N.J.: Prentice-Hall.

Khayatt, Didi. 1994. Revealing moments: The voice of one who lives with labels. In *Talking about difference: Encounters in culture, language and identity,* ed. C. James and A. Shadd, 77–90. Toronto: Between the Lines.

Khosla, Prabha. 1983. Profiles of working-class East Indian women. *Fireweed* 16: 43–8.

Kishwar, Madhu, and Ruth Vanita, eds. 1991. *In search of answers: Indian women's voices from Manushi.* Delhi: Horizon India.

Kline, Marlee. 1989. Women's oppression and racism: A critique of the 'feminist standpoint.' In *Race, class and gender: Bonds and barriers,* ed. J. Vorst et al., 37–64. Toronto: Between the Lines.

Knowles, Valerie. 1992. *Strangers at our gates: Canadian immigration and immigration policy, 1540–1990.* Toronto: Dundurn Press.

Kobayashi, Audry. 1994. For the sake of the children: Japanese/Canadian/workers/mothers. In *Women, work, and place,* ed. A. Kobayashi, 45–72. Montreal and Kingston: McGill-Queen's University Press.

Kogawa, Joy. 1981. *Obasan.* Toronto: Lester and Orpen Dennys.

Kohli, Rita. 1991a. Living on edge. *Diva,* March, 16–22.

– 1991b. Understanding the nature of crisis. In *Towards equal access,* ed. F. Rafiq, 81–6. Ottawa: Immigrant and Visible-Minority Women against Abuse.

– 1993. Power or empowerment: Questions of agency in the shelter movement. In *And still we rise: Feminist political mobilizing in contemporary Canada,* ed. L. Carty, 387–425. Toronto: Women's Press.

Korean-Canadian National Magazine. 1991. 1(6).

Korean-Canadian Women's Association. 1986. *Project report, 1985–86.* Toronto: The Association.

– 1988. *Annual report, 1987–88.* Toronto: The Association.

– 1992a. *Hear our words: Korean women speak about violence in their lives: A handbook on woman abuse in the Korean-Canadian community.* Toronto: The Association.

– 1992b. *Voice of Korean Canadians on Racism.* Toronto: The Association.

Laframboise, Donna. 1996. *The princess at the window: A new gender morality.* Toronto: Penguin.

Lanphier, Michael, and Oleh Lukomskyj. 1994. Settlement policy in Australia and Canada. In *Immigration and refugee policy,* Vol. 2, ed. H. Adelman et al., 337–71. Toronto: University of Toronto Press.

Lau, Annie. 1995. Gender, power and relationships: Ethno-cultural and religious issues. In *Gender, power and relationships*, ed. C. Burck and B. Speed, 120–35. London: Routledge.

Lawrence, Kathleen. 1990. Systemic discrimination: Regulation 8 – Family Benefits Act: Policy of reasonable efforts to obtain financial resources. *Journal of Law and Social Policy* 6: 57–76.

Levan, Andrea. 1996. Violence against women. In *Women and Canadian public policy*, ed. J. Brodie, 319–54. Toronto: Harcourt Brace and Company.

Li, Peter. 1988. *The Chinese in Canada*. Toronto: Oxford University Press.

– 1990. *Race and ethnic relations in Canada*. Toronto: Oxford University Press.

Lloyd, Siobhan. 1995. Social work and domestic violence. In *Family violence and the caring professions*, ed. P. Kingston and B. Penhale, 149–80. London: Macmillan.

Longino, Helen. 1993. Subjects, power and knowledge: Description and prescription in feminist philosophies of science. In *Feminist epistemologies*, ed. L. Alcoff and E. Potter, 101–20. New York: Routledge.

Loseke, Donileen. 1992. *The battered woman and shelters: The social construction of wife abuse*. New York: State University of New York Press.

Lupton, Carol, and Terry Gillespie, eds. 1994. *Working with violence*. London: Macmillan.

Luxton, Meg. 1980. *More than a labour of love: Three generations of women's work in the home*. Toronto: Women's Press.

MacKinnon, Catherine. 1989. *Towards a feminist theory of the state*. Cambridge: Harvard University Press.

– 1991. From practice to theory, or what is a white woman anyway? *Yale Journal of Law and Feminism* 4: 13–22.

MacLeod, Linda. 1982. *Wife battering in Canada: A vicious circle*. Ottawa: Canadian Advisory Council on the Status of Women.

– 1987. *Battered but not beaten*. Ottawa: Canadian Advisory Council on the Status of Women.

– 1989a. *Wife battering and the web of hope: Progress, dilemmas, and vision of progress: A discussion paper*. Ottawa: Health and Welfare Canada (National Clearinghouse on Family Violence).

– 1989b. *Preventing wife battering: Towards a new understanding: A think-tank report*. Ottawa: Canadian Advisory Council on the Status of Women.

– 1990. *Counselling for change. Evolutionary trends in counselling services for women who are abused and for their children in Canada*. Ottawa: Health and Welfare Canada (National Clearinghouse on Family Violence).

– 1994. *Understanding and charting our progress toward the prevention of woman abuse. An exploration of the contribution to prevention made by projects on woman abuse funded by the Family Violence Prevention Division, Health Canada.* Ottawa: Family Violence Prevention Division, Health Canada.

MacLeod, Linda, and Maria Shin. 1990. *Isolated, afraid and forgotten: The service delivery needs and realities of immigrant and refugee women who are battered.* Ottawa: Health and Welfare Canada.

– 1993. *Like a wingless bird: A tribute to the survival and courage of women who are abused and who speak neither English nor French.* Ottawa: Department of Canadian Heritage.

Malarek, Victor. 1987. *Haven's Gate: Canada's immigration fiasco.* Toronto: Macmillan of Canada.

Martin, Biddy. 1988. Feminism, criticism, and Foucault. In *Feminism and Foucault,* ed. I. Diamond and L. Quinby, 3–20. Boston: Northeastern University Press.

Martin, Jeannie. 1991. Multiculturalism and feminism. In *Intersexions: Gender/ class/culture/ethnicity,* ed. G. Bottomley, M. de Lepervanche, and J. Martin, 110–31. North Sydney: Allen & Unwin.

McGregor, Heather, and Andrew Hopkins. 1991. *Working for change: The movement against domestic violence.* North Sidney: Allen and Unwin.

Mederios, John. 1991. Starting the dialogue: Report of the conference on access to Ontario Ministry of Community and Social Service Programs. Unpublished manuscript.

Medjuck, Sheva. 1990. Ethnicity and feminism: Two solitudes. *Atlantis* 15(2): 1–10.

Mies, Maria. 1986. *Patriarchy and accumulation on a world scale.* London: Zed.

Miles, Robert. 1989. *Racism.* London: Routledge.

Minh-ha, Trinh T. 1989. *Women, native, other.* Bloomington: Indiana University Press.

Minicucci, Maria. 1995. My former life as a therapist. *Fireweed* 48: 61–4.

Minors, Arnold. 1996. From uni-versity to poly-versity: Organizations in transition to anti-racism. In *Perspectives on racism and the human services sector: A case for change,* ed. C. James, 196–208. Toronto: University of Toronto Press.

Mitter, Swasti. 1986. *Common fate common bond: Women in the global economy.* London: Pluto.

Moussa, Helene. 1994. *Women claiming power together: A handbook to set up and assess support groups for/with immigrant and refugee women.* Toronto: Education Wife Assault.

Multicultural Coalition for Access to Family Services. 1991. *Family services for all: Study of family services for ethnocultural and racial communities in Metropolitan Toronto.* Toronto: Multicultural Coalition for Access to Family Services. (Report prepared by John Mederios.)

Musisi, Nakanyike, and Fakiha Muktar. 1992. *Exploratory research: Wife assault in Metropolitan Toronto's African immigrant and refugee community.* Toronto: Canadian-African Newcomer Aid Centre of Toronto.

Narayan, Uma. 1990. The project of feminist epistemology: Perspectives from a nonwestern feminist. In *Gender/body/knowledge: Feminist reconstructions of being and knowing*, ed. A. Jaggar and S. Bordo, 256–72. New Brunswick, N.J.: Rutgers University Press.

National Action Committee. 1987. *Refugee women and Bill C-55*. Toronto: National Action Committee.

Ng, Roxana. 1988. *The politics of community service*. Toronto: Garamond.

Ng, Roxana, Gillian Walker, and Jacob Muller, eds. 1990. *Community organization and the Canadian state*. Toronto: Garamond.

Nicholson, Linda J., ed. 1990. *Feminism/postmodernism*. New York: Routledge.

Nielsen, Joyce, ed. 1990. *Feminist research methods: Exemplary readings in the social sciences*. Boulder: Westview Press.

North York Women's Shelter. 1994. *Shelter News: A Newsletter of the North York Women's Shelter* (Spring).

– 1995. *Shelter News: A Newsletter of the North York Women's Shelter* (Spring).

Oakley, Ann. 1981. Interviewing women: a contradiction in terms. In *Doing Feminist Research*, ed. B. Roberts, 30–61. London: Routledge.

Ocampo, Martha, and Fely Villasin. 1993. *Mag-usap Tayo ... let's talk: A guide to educating on violence against women in the Filipino-Canadian community*. Toronto: Carlos Bulosan Cultural Workshop.

Ontario Association of Interval and Transition Houses. 1984. *Training manual for the staffs and boards of transition houses*. Toronto: Ontario Association of Interval and Transition Houses.

– 1989a. *Stop violence against women: Background report, annual lobby, November 20, 1989*. Toronto: Ontario Association of Interval and Transition Houses.

– 1989b. *Member survey – police* [leaflet]. Toronto: Ontario Association of Interval and Transition Houses.

– 1991a. *Time for change: Social action report, annual lobby, November 18, 1991*. Toronto: Ontario Association of Interval and Transition Houses.

– 1991b. *Training manual for the board and staff of interval and transition houses*. Toronto: Ontario Association of Interval and Transition Houses.

Ontario Council of Agencies Serving Immigrants (OCASI). 1988. Immigrants and access to community and social services. Brief to the Honourable John Sweeney, Minister of Community and Social Services. Unpublished manuscript.

– 1990. *Focus on immigrant women: A study of immigrant women's needs and programs in the OCASI network*. Toronto: OCASI.

– 1991. Immigrant services database. *Research Bulletin* 2(1): 1–13.

– 1992. *LINC: A community response presented to the Honourable Bernard Valcourt, Minister of Employment and Immigration*. Toronto: OCASI.

– 1993. Immigrant service agencies: A fundamental component of anti-racist social services. Unpublished manuscript.

– 1994. The social security review. Submission to the Standing Committee on Human Resources Development. Unpublished manuscript.

Ontario Immigrant and Visible-Minority Women's Organization. 1991. *A provincial dialogue on family violence.* Toronto: Ontario Immigrant and Visible-Minority Women's Organization. (Report prepared by Monica Riutort.)

Ontario Women's Directorate. 1991. Ontario wife assault prevention initiatives. Unpublished manuscript.

Open letters to Catherine MacKinnon. 1991. *Yale Journal of Law and Feminism* 4: 177–90.

Paglia, Camille. 1994. *Vamps and tramps.* New York: Vintage Books.

Pal, Leslie. 1993. *Interests of state.* Montreal and Kingston: McGill-Queen's University Press.

Papp, Aruna. 1990. *Report on abused South Asian women in Scarborough.* Scarborough, Ont.: South Asian Family Support Services.

– 1995. *The seven of us survived: Wife abuse in the South Asian community.* Toronto: Multicultural Community Development and Training.

Paquet-Deehy, Ann, Maryse Rinfret-Raynor, and Ginette Larouche. 1992. *Training social workers in a feminist approach to conjugal violence: Summary of the action research.* Ottawa: Health and Welfare Canada (National Clearinghouse on Family Violence).

Paredes, Milagros. 1987. Immigrant women and second-language education: A study of unequal access to linguistic resources. *Resources for Feminist Research* 17: 23–7.

Parkdale Committee to End Wife Assault. 1994. Bridging the gaps in services for immigrant and refugee women who have been abused. Forum report. Unpublished manuscript.

Parmar, Pratibha. 1986. Gender, race, and class: Asian women in resistance. In *The empire strikes back: Race and racism in 70s Britain,* ed. Centre for Contemporary Cultural Studies, 236–75. London: Hutchinson.

Parr, Joy. 1995. *A diversity of women: Ontario 1945–1980.* Toronto: University of Toronto Press.

Pateman, Carole. 1987. Feminist critiques of the public/private dichotomy. In *Feminism and equality,* ed. A. Phillips, 103–26. Oxford: Basil Blackwell.

Pennell, Joan. 1987. Ideology at a Canadian shelter for battered women: A reconstruction. *Women's Studies International Forum* 10(2): 113–23.

Phillips, Paul, and Erin Phillips. 1983. *Women and work: Inequality in the Canadian labour market.* Toronto: James Lorimer.

Philp, Margaret. 1995a. Programs for women top list of Ontario's budget cuts. *Globe and Mail* (5 Oct.).

– 1995b. UN to hear about Ontario aid cuts. *Globe and Mail* (21 Nov.)

Pierson, Ruth, et al., eds. 1993. *Strong Voices*. Vol. 1 of *Canadian women's issues: Twenty-five years of women's activism in English Canada*. Toronto: James Lorimer.

Pierson, Ruth, and Marjorie Cohen, eds. 1995. *Bold visions*. Vol. 2 of *Canadian women's issues: Twenty-five years of women's activism in English Canada*. Toronto: James Lorimer.

Pinedo, Rosa Maria, and Ana Maria Santinoli. 1991. Immigrant women and wife assault. In *Towards equal access: A handbook for service providers*, ed. F. Rafiq, 65–80. Ottawa: Immigrant and Visible-Minority Women against Abuse.

Pizzy, Erin. 1974. *Scream quietly or the neighbours will hear*. London: If Books.

Pope, Lori. 1991. Immigration law and wife assault. *Diva: A Quarterly Journal of South Asian Women* Nov., 38–48.

Pressman, Barbara. 1994. Violence against women: Ramifications of gender, class, and race inequality. In *Women in context: Toward a feminist reconstruction of psychotherapy*, ed. Marsha Mirkin, 352–89. New York: Guilford Press.

Radford, Benjamin. 1989. Mainstream and ethno-specific social assistance delivery systems. *Currents* 5(3): 34–6.

Rafiq, Fauzia, ed. 1991. *Towards equal access: A handbook for service providers working with survivors of wife assault*. Ottawa: Immigrant and Visible-Minority Women against Abuse.

Ramazanoglu, Caroline. 1989. *Feminism and the contradictions of oppression*. London: Routledge.

Randall, Melanie. 1989. *The politics of woman abuse: Understanding the issues*. Toronto: Education Wife Assault.

Ratna, Lawrence, and Maria Wheeler. 1995. Race and gender in adult psychiatry. In *Gender, power and relationships*, ed. C. Burck and B. Speed, 136–52. London: Routledge.

Rave, Elizabeth. 1990. White feminist therapists and anti-racism. In *Diversity and complexity in feminist therapy*, ed. L. Brown and M. Root, 313–25. New York: Harrington Park Press.

Razack, Shirene. 1994. What is to be gained by looking white people in the eye? Culture, race, and gender in cases of sexual violence. *Signs: Journal of Women in Culture and Society* 19(4): 894–923.

Richmond, Anthony. 1967. *Post-war immigrants in Canada*. Toronto: University of Toronto Press.

Ristock, Janice. 1991. Feminist collectives: The struggles and contradictions in our quest for a 'uniquely feminist structure.' In *Women and social change: Feminist activism in Canada*, ed. J. Wine and J. Ristock, 41–55. Toronto: James Lorimer.

Riutort, Monica, and Shirley Small. 1985. *Working with assaulted immigrant women*. Toronto: Education Wife Assault.

Roiphe, Katie. 1993. *The morning after: Sex, fear, and feminism*. Boston: Little Brown.

Rowbotham, Sheila, and Swasti Mitter, eds. 1994. *Dignity and daily bread: New forms of economic organising among poor women in the Third World and the First.* London: Routledge.

Roy, Patricia E. 1989a. *A white man's province.* Vancouver: University of British Columbia Press.

– 1989b. British Columbia's fear of Asians 1900–1950. In *A history of British Columbia,* ed. P. Roy, 285–99. Toronto: Copp Clark Pitman.

Royal Commission on the Status of Women. 1970. *Report.* Ottawa: Information Canada.

Samuel, John. 1990. Third World immigrants and multiculturalism. In *Ethnic demography. Canadian immigrant, racial and cultural variations,* ed. S. Halli, F. Trovato, and Leo Driedger, 383–98. Ottawa: Carleton University Press.

Sangster, Joan. 1995. *Earning respect: The lives of working women in small-town Ontario, 1920–1960.* Toronto: University of Toronto Press.

Satzewich, Vic. 1990. The political economy of race and ethnicity. In *Race and ethnic relations in Canada,* ed. P. Li, 251–68. Toronto: Oxford University Press.

– 1991. *Racism and the incorporation of foreign labor.* London: Routledge.

Schechter, Susan. 1982. *Women and male violence: The visions and struggles of the battered-women's movement.* Boston: South End Press.

Scyner, Lawrence, and Nancy McGregor. 1988. Women in second-stage housing: What happens after the crisis. *Canadian Journal of Community Mental Health* 7(2): 129–35.

Sedhev, Hersh. 1991. Settlement agencies. In *Towards equal access: A handbook for service providers,* ed. Fauzia Rafiq, 165–70. Ottawa: Immigrant and Visible-Minority Women against Abuse.

Seward, Shirley. 1990. Immigrant women in the clothing industry. In *Ethnic demography: Canadian immigrant, racial and cultural variations,* ed. S. Halli, F. Trovato, and Leo Driedger, 343–62. Ottawa: Carleton University Press.

Seward, Shirley, and Kathryn McDade. 1988. *Immigrant women in Canada: A policy perspective.* Ottawa: Canadian Advisory Council on the Status of Women.

Shadd, Adrienne. 1994. 'Where are you really from?' Notes of an 'immigrant' from North Buxton, Ontario. In *Talking about difference: Encounters in culture, language and identity* , ed. C. James and A. Shadd, 9–16. Toronto: Between the Lines.

Shirley Samaroo House. 1988. *Annual Report.* Toronto: Shirley Samaroo House.

Shragge, Eric. 1990. Community-based practice: Poltical alternatives or new state forms? In *Bureaucracy and community,* ed. L. Davies and E. Shragge, 137–73. Montreal: Black Rose.

Siegel, Rachel. 1990. Turning the things that divide us into strengths that unite us. In *Diversity and complexity in feminist therapy,* ed. L. Brown and M. Root, 327–36. New York: Harrington Park Press.

Silvera, Makeda. 1983. *Silenced.* Toronto: Williams-Wallace.

Silvera, Makeda, and Nila Gupta, eds. 1989. *The issue is ism: Women of colour speak out.* Toronto: Sister Vision.

Simmons, Alan. 1990. 'New wave' immigrants: Origins and characteristics. In *Ethnic demography: Canadian immigrant, racial and cultural variations,* ed. S. Halli, F. Trovato, and Leo Driedger, 141–60. Ottawa: Carleton University Press.

Sinclair, Deborah. 1985. *Understanding wife assault: A training manual for counsellors and advocates.* Toronto: Ontario Ministry of Community and Social Services.

Smith, Dorothy. 1987. *The everyday world as a problematic: A feminist sociology of knowledge.* Toronto: University of Toronto Press.

– 1990. *The conceptual practices of power: A feminist sociology of knowledge.* Toronto: University of Toronto Press.

Sommers, Christina. 1994. *Who stole feminism? How women have betrayed women.* New York: Simon and Schuster.

South East Asian Services Centre. 1992. *Working with abused wives from Vietnam: A manual for frontline workers.* Toronto: South East Asian Services Centre.

Spelman, Elizabeth. 1988. *Inessential woman: Problems of exclusion in feminist thought.* Boston: Beacon.

Srivastava, Anila, and Michael Ames. 1993. South Asian women's experience of gender, race and class in Canada. In *Ethnicity, identity, migration: The South Asian context,* ed. M. Israel and N.K. Wagle, 123–41. Toronto: University of Toronto, Centre for South Asian Studies.

Stairs, Felicite, and Lori Pope. 1990. No place like home: Assaulted migrant women's claims to refugee status and landings on humanitarian and compassionate grounds. *Journal of Law and Social Policy* 6: 148–225.

Stasiulis, Daiva. 1990. Theorizing connections: Gender, race, ethnicity and class. In *Race and ethnic relations in Canada,* ed. Peter Li, 269–305. Toronto: Oxford University Press.

Statistics Canada. 1994. *Family violence in Canada.* Ottawa: Ministry of Supply and Services.

Strong-Boag, Veronica. 1986. 'Ever a crusader': Nellie McClung, first-wave feminist. In *Rethinking Canada: The promise of women's history,* ed. V. Strong-Boag and A. Fellman, 178–90. Toronto: Copp Clark Pitman.

Sunderji, Kass. 1996. Comments: Racism and the issue of voice. In *Perspectives on racism and the human services sector: A case for change,* ed. C. James, 134–6. Toronto: University of Toronto Press.

Sy, San San, and Sudha Choldin. 1994. *Legal information and wife abuse in immigrant families.* Ottawa: Research and Statistics Directorate.

Tator, Carol. 1996. Anti-racism and the human service delivery system. In *Perspectives on racism and the human services sector: A case for change,* ed. C. James, 152–70. Toronto: University of Toronto Press.

Taylor, K.W. 1991. Racism in Canadian immigration policy. *Canadian Ethnic Studies* 33(1): 1–20.

Tifft, Larry. 1993. *Battering of women: The failure of intervention and the case for prevention.* Boulder: Westview Press.

Toronto Advisory Committee on Cultural Approaches to Violence against Women and Children. 1992. Our ways: Anti-racist and culturally appropriate approaches to combatting women assault. Unpublished manuscript.

Tyagi, Smita. 1993. Violence against immigrant women. A report prepared for the Toronto Advisory Committee on Cultural Approaches to Violence against Women and Children. Unpublished manuscript.

Ujimoto, K. Victor. 1988. Racism, discrimination and internment: Japanese in Canada. In *Racial oppression in Canada*, ed. B. Bolaria and P. Li, 127–60. Toronto: Garamond Press.

– 1990. Studies of ethnic identity and race relations. In *Race and ethnic relations in Canada*, ed. Peter S. Li, 209–230. Toronto: Oxford University Press.

Urban Alliance on Race Relations and Ontario Women's Directorate. N.d. *Employment equity for visible-minority women.* N.p.

Valiante, Waheeda. 1991. Social work practice with South Asian Women: Issues, concerns and problems. In *A reader in South Asian studies*, ed. S. Chandraseker, 95–119. Toronto: South Asian Studies Graduate Students Union, University of Toronto.

Valpy, Michael. 1993. The women persecuted for being women. *Globe and Mail* (11 March).

Valverde, Mariana. 1992. 'When the mother of the race is free': Race, reproduction, and sexuality in first-wave feminism. In *Gender Conflicts*, ed. F. Iacovetta and M. Valverde, 3–26. Toronto: University of Toronto Press.

Vickers, Jill. 1992. The intellectual origins of the contemporary women's movement in Canada and the United States. In *Challenging Times*, ed. C. Backhouse and D. Flaherty, 39–60. Montreal and Kingston: McGill-Queen's University Press.

Wagle, Iqbal. 1993. South Asians in Canada, 1905–1920: A bibliographical essay. In *Ethnicity, identity, migration: The South Asian context*, ed. M. Israel and N.K. Wagle, 196–216. Toronto: University of Toronto, Centre for South Asian Studies.

Walby, Sylvia. 1992. Post-post-modernism? Theorizing social complexity. In *Destabilizing theory: Contemporary feminist debates*, ed. M. Barrett and A. Phillips, 31–52. Stanford: Stanford University Press.

Walker, Gillian. 1990. *Family violence and the women's movement: The conceptual politics of struggle.* Toronto: University of Toronto Press.

Wang, Nancy. 1995. Born Chinese and a woman in America. In *Racism in the lives of women: Testimony, theory and guides to antiracist practice*, ed. J. Adleman and G. Enguidanos, 97–110. New York: Harrington Park Press.

Ward, W. Peter. 1978. *White Canada forever: Popular attitudes and public policy toward Orientals in British Columbia*. Montreal: McGill-Queen's University Press.

Westkott, Marcia. 1990. Feminist criticism of the social sciences. In *Feminist research methods: Exemplary readings in the social sciences*, ed. J. Nielsen, 58–68. Boulder: Westview Press.

Westwood, Sally, and Parminder Bhachu. 1988. *Enterprising women: Ethnicity, economy, and gender relations*. London: Routledge.

Williams, Patricia J. 1991. *The alchemy of race and rights*. Cambridge: Harvard University Press.

Wine, Jeri Dawn, and Janice Ristock, eds. 1991. *Women and social change: Feminist activism in Canada*. Toronto: James Lorimer.

Wolf, Naomi. 1994. *Fire with fire: The new female power and how to use it*. New York: Fawcett Columbine.

Women Working with Immigrant Women. 1988. *Racial-minority women and race relations*. Toronto: Women Working with Immigrant Women.

Women's Book Committee, Chinese Canadian National Council. 1992. *Jin guo: Voices of Chinese-Canadian women*. Toronto: Women's Press.

Women's Support Group Committee. 1990. *Support groups for abused women: A client centred evaluation*. Ottawa: Women's Support Group Committee.

Yalnizyan, Armine. 1993. From the dew line: The experience of Canadian garment workers. In *Women challenging unions: Feminism, democracy, and militancy*, ed. L. Briskin and P. McDermott, 284–303. Toronto: University of Toronto Press.

Yee, Paul. 1988. *Saltwater city: An illustrated history of the Chinese in Vancouver*. Vancouver: Douglas.

Young, Iris. 1990. *Justice and the politics of difference*. Princeton: Princeton University Press.

Index